PLATO'S
ANALYTIC
METHOD

PLATO'S ANALYTIC METHOD

KENNETH M. SAYRE

CHICAGO AND LONDON

University of Chicago Press

Acknowledgment is gratefully made to Humanities Press, Inc., New York, and to Routledge & Kegan Paul, Ltd., London, for permission to quote from F. M. Cornford, *Plato's Theory of Knowledge*.

Library of Congress Catalog Card Number 69–15496

THE UNIVERSITY OF CHICAGO PRESS, CHICAGO 60637
THE UNIVERSITY OF CHICAGO PRESS, LTD., LONDON W.C.1

To Lucille

Contents

Preface

This is a commentary on the *Theaetetus* and the *Sophist*, and on certain methodological passages in the *Meno*, the *Phaedo*, the *Republic* and the *Parmenides*. My concern with the latter is to relate them to the philosophic method described and exemplified in the former dialogues. My concern with the former, in turn, is to analyze their logical structure and, from the vantage point of this analysis, to reconsider various problems of interpretation arising from them in recent years. What Plato thought, I am convinced, is not always what Plato said, especially if what he said is construed independently from its particular conversational context. The dialogues themselves are teaching instruments, with lessons to be learned not only from their content but from their structure as well. And one of the remarkable things about the *Theaetetus* and the *Sophist* is that their structure exhibits a logical form which is considerably more determinate and precise than commentators seem yet to have realized.

If I were not convinced of this, I should not have undertaken to comment on dialogues so admirably treated in Cornford's *Plato's Theory of Knowledge*, and other more recent works. Cornford, who was able to remark that no other writer "has approached Plato's skill in concealing a rigid and intricate structure of reasoning beneath the flowing lines of a conversation . . . ,"[1] nonetheless was disadvantaged by the lack of analytic techniques which have become common stock among philosophers in recent years. When viewed from this analytic perspective, however, the *Theaetetus* displays a logical splendor which, to my mind, surpasses that of its literary

[1] F. M. Cornford, *Plato's Theory of Knowledge* (London: Routledge & Kegan Paul, 1934), p. vi.

quality, and the *Sophist* emerges as the most masterful blend
of form and content in the entire Platonic corpus. For it is
in the *Theaetetus*, I argue below, that Plato deliberately tests
and, in that form, rejects the method of hypothesis adumbrated
in *Phaedo* 100A–101D, and moves tentatively into the procedure of division explicitly noted in the *Phaedrus* and the
Sophist. And it is in the *Sophist* that he discloses his mature
method of philosophic analysis, illustrating in its structure the
very procedures of collection and division which are described
in the heart of the dialogue as the source of the "free man's
knowledge." The *Sophist* thus both exhibits and describes
what was kept beyond our reach at the end of the *Theaetetus*,
the sense in which knowledge can be conceived as true judgment accompanied by an account.

Whereas the two middle chapters are commentary, the first
and the last might be considered discourses on philosophic
method. The main task of chapter I is to provide an interpretation of the expression 'to accord' which permits a coherent reading of the methodological comments between *Phaedo* 100A–
101D. The solution proposed for this problem suggests a much
closer relationship between the method of hypothesis and the
method of geometrical analysis than, I think, has been sus-
pected among commentators on this passage to date. In chapter
IV, finally, I undertake a detailed analysis of the method of collection and division, and show reasons in favor of the conclusion that this method and the method of hypothesis differ
primarily in the terminology of their descriptions, and that
for practical purposes they may be conceived merely as different forms of the same analytic technique.

There are many people to thank for the encouragement, advice, and insight that made this book possible. Foremost among
these is Professor R. Catesby Taliaferro, who first stirred my
conviction that the structure of Plato's reasoning in the *Theaetetus* not only is logically sound but moreover is inspired by
mathematical considerations. I am grateful to Professor Freder-
ick Crosson for frequent discussion on matters of interpretation,

and for his ready ability to distinguish between mere "wind eggs" and viable philosophic conceptions. No one has contributed more profoundly than these men to the philosophic culture at Notre Dame out of which this book has grown.

I am grateful to the seminar students who shared with me one afternoon the startling realization that the method of hypothesis and the method of collection and division both are concerned with the necessary and sufficient conditions which determine a thing to be what it is. This was my first awareness of the existence of what might properly be called "Plato's Analytic Method."

Professors Gregory Vlastos and Reginald Allen have seen the manuscript through more than one draft, and I have benefitted greatly from their criticism and encouragement. Professor Amelie Rorty also has been most helpful. I am deeply appreciative to Princeton University for the visiting fellowship during the tenure of which I was able to communicate directly with these scholars, and to the University of Notre Dame for leave of absence during the year 1966–67.

Professor Francis Lazenby graciously supplied help with a difficult translation early in my work with the manuscript. The encouragement of Professor Vere Chappell was of material assistance in the middle period. And at the final stage the skill of Mrs. Norma Davitt was entirely essential.

Grateful acknowledgment goes finally to Lucille, Gregory, Christopher, and Jeffrey, who bore with understanding the inconvenience of those periods when I was home but my mind elsewhere. It is to the first of these especially, this time, that the book is dedicated.

PLATO'S
ANALYTIC
METHOD

I

The Method of Hypothesis: *Phaedo* 100A– 101D

1 / Reasoning about "Causes"

Plato's first [1] explicit remarks on methodology, falling between *Phaedo* 99C and 101D, are interposed into a discussion of the Forms as "causes" [2] of characteristics in particular things. The

[1] What appears to be a similar method is mentioned at *Meno* 86E–87B, but never discussed in general terms.

[2] 'Cause' may be a misleading translation of αἰτία in this context, particularly to someone not favorably disposed to the notion of "formal cause." 'Reason' perhaps is preferable, as in 'the reason a particular thing is beautiful is the presence in it of absolute beauty'. I propose in the present section that the αἰτία of a characteristic in a particular thing is the necessary and sufficient *condition* of its being so characterized. Thus 'condition' might also be a fitting term. When the more standard term 'cause' is used to translate αἰτία, it will be enclosed in quotation marks as above.

method adumbrated there, however, at first appears irrelevant to Plato's theory of the Forms as "causes," and the problem arises why the two matters are so closely associated in the text. My eventual answer will be that *Phaedo* 99C–101D is a preliminary description of a procedure which in later dialogues is developed into a technique for discovering "causes" of this sort. This answer cannot be fully defended until the final chapter. The ground work, however, is begun in the present section by considering in what sense of the term αἰτία Forms can be conceived as "causes" of characteristics in particular things. The remainder of the first chapter is given to an examination of the hypothetical method described in *Phaedo* 99C–101D, and with certain alterations in *Republic* 509D–511E.

Having impatiently dismissed the theory of Anaxagoras, which would make his muscles and bones the reason for his sitting in jail, Socrates confesses despair of ever finding a teleological explanation of natural events, and offers to demonstrate his own "second best" way (δεύτερος πλοῦς) of inquiry about causation.[3] This alternative approach is to seek the truth of things

---

[3] I take the δεύτερος πλοῦς to be the hypothetical method itself, which leads to explanation by formal "causes." This method surely is called "second best" only ironically in contrast with that of Anaxagoras. But other contrasts may be implicit, particularly with certain aspects of the dialectical method of the upper level of the Divided Line. As we shall see, the relationships described in *Phaedo* 100A and 101D are not entirely inseparable from a background of geometrical methodology, which in *Republic* 510C–511A clearly is considered second best. The suggestion has been raised by Lynn Rose ("The Deuteros Plous in Plato's *Meno*," *The Monist*, 50 no. 3 (July 1966): 464–73) that the second-best way is explanation by formal causes, and not the hypothetical method as such by which such explanations might be achieved. This type of explanation allegedly is second best to explanation by final causes, in the search for which Socrates was disappointed by Anaxagoras. The contention is that the *Republic* shows that the dialectician can base his argument on the idea of the Good; hence, if the "hypothetical method can accommodate both explanation by final cause and explanation by formal causes, it is difficult to see how the hypothetical method can be 'second-best' to explanation by final cause; indeed, it is nonsensical" (p. 469). A similar point is made by Robinson, *Plato's Earlier Dialectic* (Oxford: Clarendon

through verbal formulations,[4] rather than through the senses. The first description of the alternative approach is at 100A:

> it was on this path I set out: on each occasion I assume the proposition [λόγον] which I judge to be the soundest, and I put down as true whatever seems to me to be in agreement [συμφωνεῖν] with this, whether the question is about causes or anything else; what does not seem to be in agreement I put down as false.[5]

This statement, however, appears unintelligible to his prison audience, so Socrates undertakes to provide an illustration.

The illustration begins with Socrates' insisting that he means nothing new, at least to those who have heard him speak of such things as absolute Beauty, Goodness, and Magnitude, the hypothesizing of which is the first step in his theory of "causation" (100B). What is beautiful, he then argues, is made so by participation in absolute Beauty, and any other

---

Press, 1953), p. 143. The reply to this is (1) the method at 100A lacks the nonhypothetical principles of the method described in the context of the Divided Line, and there is nothing in the *Phaedo* to suggest that the former method can accommodate explanation by final cause; (2) it is not clear what it would be like, even in the context of the Divided Line, to base an argument on the idea of the Good, and no example of such an argument is ever given by Plato; (3) the δεύτερος πλοῦς is described by Rose as a way "of inquiry about causation" (p. 465) and "as a way of discovering causes" (p. 468); but surely it is wrong to say that *explanation* by formal cause is either a way of *inquiry* about causation or a way of *discovering* causes.

[4] The term λόγος has received many different translations in this context. Bluck uses 'definition', Tredennick 'theory', Hackforth 'proposition'; Jowett uses 'world of the mind' and 'principle' for the successive occurrences at 99E and 100A, and Robinson uses 'discussion' and 'proposition'. Hackforth sums up the difficulty, in *Plato's Phaedo* (Cambridge: Cambridge University Press, 1955), p. 138, by remarking that the use at 99E suggests *argument* or *train of thought*, while that at 100A suggests the *starting point* of an argument. 'Verbal formulation' seems broad enough to cover both uses. For the sake of standardization, however, I shall henceforth follow Hackforth in using 'proposition' as the translation of λόγος.

[5] All translations of the *Phaedo* are Hackforth's, *loc. cit.*, with the exception of that discussed in note 15 below.

explanation in terms of "a bright colour or a certain shape or something of that kind" (100D) he finds confusing and beyond his understanding. Difference by a head, similarly, is not the cause of one man's superior height over another's, but rather Tallness is the "cause" of his being tall and Shortness the "cause" of the other's being short. Again, not two but Largeness is the "cause" of the excess of ten over eight, and neither division of a single unit nor addition of one unit to another is the "cause" of two, but rather participation in Duality. Eschewing all other explanation, the person following Socrates' method would admit only participation in the appropriate Form as an explanation why an object comes to possess a particular characteristic. The discussion concludes with a set of instructions for responding to the critic who challenges the hypothesis.[6]

> if anyone were to fasten upon the hypothesis itself, you would disregard him, and refuse to answer until you could consider the consequences of it, and see whether they agreed or disagreed with each other [ἀλλήλοις συμφωνεῖ ἢ διαφωνεῖ]. But when the time came for you to establish the hypothesis itself, you would pursue the same method: you would assume some more ultimate hypothesis, the best you could find, and continue until you reached something satisfactory. But you wouldn't muddle matters as contentious people do, by simultaneously discussing premiss and consequences, that is if you wanted to discover a truth. (101D–E)

[6] The immediate reference of τῆς ὑποθέσεως at *Phaedo* 101D surely is to the theory that the presence of Forms in things is the "cause" of particular characteristics, since this is the only intelligible referent of the same expression in the sentence directly above, about holding fast to the "security of your hypothesis" and making "your answers accordingly." The instructions, however, apparently are intended for use in the defense of other hypotheses as well. Like the methodological remarks at 100A, these at 101D apply "whether the question is about causes or anything else."

Let us, for the moment, postpone the formidable problem of relating these two passages on method, and attend to the discussion of "causality" into which they are interpolated.

The remarks about the Forms as "causes" are offered as clarification of Socrates' statement that he begins with the proposition which seems to him strongest, and posits as true whatever agrees and as false whatever does not. The intended clarification, however, appears at first to be as obscure as the preceding statement. Its obscurity lies in its apparent inaccuracy, and in its apparent irrelevance to the statement it is intended to clarify. It appears inaccurate in that it seems to deny that color and shape might ever be among the reasons why a thing is beautiful, and that difference in height by a head might contribute to one man's being taller than another. It appears irrelevant because reference to absolute Forms does not seem to explain what Socrates meant in saying that he takes as true everything that agrees with the hypothesis judged strongest and considers not true whatever does not agree. First among the problems to be faced from these passages, then, will be (1) that of determining a sense of the term 'reason' (or "cause": αἰτία) in which the form Beauty but not the color or shape of a given thing can be considered the reason (or "cause") of its being beautiful, and (2) that of explicating the fashion in which Socrates' remarks about "causality" illustrate his methodological remarks at 100A.

What might Socrates have meant in denying, apparently contrary to the facts of the matter, that the color or the shape of a thing is among the "causes" of its beauty? The answer hangs upon the way the term 'cause' (αἰτία) seems to function in this particular context. Let us turn to an analogy for elucidation.

Now there are common contexts in which it is natural to think of oxygen as the cause of combustion, as when explaining why the elements of a vacuum tube burned out after the tube developed a leak. To speak of the oxygen as a cause in this context is to speak of a necessary condition for combustion. There is another sense, however, in which oxygen obviously is not the cause of combustion, for it is not sufficient in itself to make combustion occur. The cause of combustion in this sense is the entire set of conditions, the combined presence of which is sufficient to bring combustion about. Thus, either the necessary or the sufficient conditions for the occurrence of a thing might be considered among its causes. If a thing or event B is a *necessary* condition, or cause in the former sense, of another thing or event A, then A occurs only if B occurs; but it is not necessarily the case that all occurrences of B are occasions upon which A occurs as well. If, on the other hand, the occurrence of A is a *sufficient* condition for B, or cause in the latter sense, then B occurs whenever A occurs; but it is not necessarily the case that A always occurs with B. In general, whenever the relationship *A only if B* exists between A and B, then B is a necessary, but not necessarily sufficient, condition of A, while A is a sufficient, but perhaps not a necessary, condition of B.

These are not the only senses, of course, in which the venerable term 'cause' can be construed, but they have the advantage of being both flexible and precise. They are flexible in that various other senses of 'cause' can be construed in terms of necessary and sufficient conditionality. Among necessary conditions for being a statue, for example, might be its material ("material cause") and the fact that it has purposefully ("final cause") been worked by a sculptor ("efficient cause"), while among its sufficient conditions are its shape ("formal cause") as a finished product in that particular material. And although flexible, the relations of necessary and sufficient conditionality are precise in that they can be formulated without loss of meaning in logical notation. If A is a sufficient condition for B, then the relationship between A and B can be symbolized in the form 'A only if B', with some appropriate notation for the expression 'only if'. The resulting symbolization by the same token will serve to represent the relationship of B as necessary condition for A. An added and most desirable flexibility in these relationships is that the symbolization might be accomplished in various systems of logical implication. For purposes of the present analysis, I will construe the relation 'only if' as a relation of strict implication.[7]

It is clear from the context that the cause which Socrates is trying to explain is not merely a matter either of necessary or of sufficient conditionality. As we shall see, indeed, the difficulty with the other "causes" which he rejects is that none of them is anything more than one or the other of these two. What Socrates is seeking, rather, is what might be called "*the* cause" of a thing's being what it is. This "cause," of course, must be sufficient to bring about the circumstances attributed to it. If it were not sufficient, then some additional factor would make the difference between the thing's being and not being what it is, and this additional factor in turn would have to be considered part of "*the* cause." This "cause," moreover, must be necessary as well, for if there were several sufficient conditions none of which is always present with the occurrence of the thing, no one of these rather than another could be called "*the* cause" of the thing's being what it is. The "cause" which Socrates proposes to find in the Forms, I submit, is one which is both necessary and sufficient for the occurrence of a given property in a given thing. Presence of the Form X in a thing is sufficient for that thing's being x.[8] But at the same time, *only* presence of the Form X in a thing can make it an instance of X.[9]

---

[7] Formal analysis in this study is based upon the system in C. I. Lewis and C. H. Langford, *Symbolic Logic* (New York: Dover Publications, 1959); in particular, the system S2.

[8] A thing takes its name, or description, from the Forms in which it participates (*Phaedo* 103B). To say that a thing participates in a Form, but is not characterized by a property called after that Form, would be contrary to the Platonic conception of participation. A thing which is not beautiful, for example, necessarily does not participate in Beauty.

[9] There is extensive textual support for this between 100D and 101C: (1) "what makes a thing beautiful is *nothing other* than the presence or communion of that beautiful itself . . ." (100D); (2) "the

Hence, presence of the Form X in a given thing is sufficient and necessary for that thing's being x. Let us designate a "cause" which is both necessary and sufficient the "reason" of a thing's being what it is, and return to the dialogue with these guidelines in mind.

The difficulty with Socrates' claim that neither bright color nor the shape of a thing is among the reasons for its beauty is that the claim at first appears counterfactual. The denial here, however, is not that color and shape have nothing to do with beauty, but rather that neither color nor shape is the reason or "cause" of a thing's being beautiful. And in any one of the senses of 'cause' distinguished above, this denial is correct. The particular color of a beautiful thing is not a necessary condition of its beauty, for the thing might also be beautiful with an entirely different color. The same may be said with regard to shape. Granted in general that a thing must have some color and some shape to be beautiful, no particular color or shape counts among the necessary conditions of its beauty. Neither, on the other hand, is the color or the shape of a thing sufficient in itself for the thing's being beautiful. A piece of marble sculptured into a sphere with a few carefully contrived deformities might be beautiful, but it does not follow from this that a beach ball of exactly the same shape would be of more than indifferent aesthetic worth. Similarly, with regard to color, there may be some objects of any particular color which are beautiful and others which are not. Thus it is not the case that a thing is beautiful merely *if* it has a certain shape or color, nor again *only if* it has such an attribute. Granted (by his audience) Socrates' assumptions about the Forms, however, it *is* the case that a thing is beautiful if and only if it partakes in absolute Beauty. If we understand that "*the* cause" or reason

---

only thing you could say is that anything bigger than another thing is so *solely* because of bigness . . ." (101A); (3) "Would you not loudly protest that the *only* way you know of, by which anything comes to be, is by its participation in the special being in which it does participate . . . ?" (101C) [my emphasis throughout].

with which Socrates is here concerned is both necessary and sufficient for the beauty of a particular thing, then Plato's meaning no longer appears muddled when he makes Socrates say:

> I find it all confusing, save for one fact, which in my simple, naïve and maybe foolish fashion I hug close: namely that what makes a thing beautiful is nothing other than the presence or communion of that beautiful itself. . . . (100D)

"That beautiful itself," of course, is the form Beauty, granted by his audience along with the Good, the Great, and "the rest of them" at 100B.

In like fashion, difference by a head is not sufficient for the relative tallness of one man over another, since the same difference contributes in the same way to the shortness of the other man, and what contributes in the same way to tallness and to shortness alike cannot be a sufficient condition for either. Remarks to the same effect apply to the excess by two of ten over eight. The difficulty with the suggestion that either the division of a single unit or the addition of one unit to another is the "cause" of two, on the other hand, is that either is sufficient but that neither is necessary. The "cause" which Plato here depicts Socrates as seeking, I believe, is one which is both necessary and sufficient for the effects attributed to it. Socrates' claim that only the absolute Forms meet this requirement may be relatively uninteresting outside the Platonic context. But contrary to what at first appeared, this claim cannot rightly be charged with obscurity.

There remains the problem of how Socrates' remarks about the Forms as "causes" might be construed as clarifying his methodological comments at 100A. "On each occasion," Socrates states, "I assume the proposition which I judge to be the soundest, and I put down as true whatever seems to me to be in agreement with this, whether the question is about causes or anything else; what does not seem to be in agreement I put down as false." To clarify his meaning, Socrates proposes "to attempt a formal account" (100B) of the sort of "cause" he has been concerned with, and to take as his starting point the familiar theme about the existence of the absolute Forms. Hypothesizing "the existence of a beautiful that is in and by itself, and a good, and a great, and so on" (100B),[10] Socrates promises moreover to proceed to a proof of the soul's immortality. Thus Socrates proposes to satisfy two aims with his discussion of the Forms as "causes": (1) to provide an account of the sense of 'cause' associated with his "second best way," and (2) to rely upon these "causes" for a proof of the immortality of the soul. Although (2) is more important for the *Phaedo*, (1) is more puzzling from the methodological point of view. The result of his attempt to satisfy (1) is the discussion of the Forms as "causes" which we have just reviewed. But in what sense does this discussion constitute an *account* of the Forms as "causes"? And in what sense does this account constitute an illustration of the method sketchily described at 100A?

The answer to both questions is the same: Socrates accounts for the thesis that the Forms are "causes" by positing as an hypothesis the theory that the Forms exist, and by showing how this thesis alone agrees with what has been posited. Since the theory that the Forms exist is judged by him and by all present as being the soundest, acceptance of the Forms as "causes" on the basis of the agreement of this thesis with the theory of Forms illustrates the method described at 100A. And since this method is recommended as the one to use in trying to discover the "truth of things" (99E), the demonstration of agreement with the theory of Forms constitutes an account of the thesis that Forms as present in particular objects are the "causes" of these objects being what they are.[11]

[10] The term expressing Socrates' attitude toward the existence of the Forms in the present context is ὑποθέμενος.

[11] It is not the Forms themselves which are "causes" of a thing's being what it is, as W. D. Ross seems to suggest in *Plato's Theory*

It must be admitted that the fashion in which the theory of the Forms as "causes" agrees with the hypothesis of the existence of the Forms is not made clear in the context. But what Socrates seems to have in mind, as depicted by Plato, is the following. What is not new is the hypothesizing of the existence of the absolute Forms.[12] Absolute Beauty, the reader presumably should understand with Socrates' immediate audience, not only exists "in and by itself," but also according to its nature is present in some unspecified (100D)

---

of *Ideas* (Oxford: Clarendon Press, 1951), p. 29, but rather the presence of Forms in (or communion with, however the relation is to be expressed [100D]) the thing. The existence of the Forms *simpliciter* is the hypothesis "judged strongest" on the basis of which the theory of "causation" is accountable. The theory of "causation" itself which agrees with the hypothesis is that things are what they are by participation in the Forms.

[12] The term ὑποτίθημι does not necessarily mean "to lay down *tentatively* or provisionally," as 'to hypothesize' often means in English. A more accurate meaning in the present context is "to posit as the beginning of a process of discourse or thought." See Robinson's excellent discussion in chapter 7, *Plato's Dialectic*, in this regard, esp. 94–99. As Robinson points out, what is posited is a "thesis," and hence in some sense a proposition. It cannot be the case, as Hare urges, that hypotheses for Plato are sometimes things (R. M. Hare, "Plato and the Mathematicians," *New Essays on Plato and Aristotle*, ed. R. Bambrough [New York: Humanities Press, 1965], esp. pp. 22–24). Things, in and by themselves, do not have consequences of the sort that Plato is treating in the methodological passages of the *Phaedo* and the *Republic*. What might be posited, rather, is that such and such things *exist* (as in *Phaedo* 100B—see note 10 above), or that such and such things have a certain character (as in *Meno* 87A,B). Hare is particularly concerned about the sense of *Republic* 510C, where Socrates speaks of hypothesizing the odd and even, the various figures, the three kinds of angle, and so forth, and suggests (p. 22) that such things are intended as *examples* of hypotheses. But surely the odd, even, and so forth, are not *themselves* hypotheses. The hypothesis in question rather is that such things exist, with certain characters regarding which the mathematicians do not feel called upon to give any account. A detailed rebuttal of Hare's contention is offered by C. C. W. Taylor in "Plato and the Mathematicians: An Examination of Professor Hare's Views," *Philosophical Quarterly*, 17, no. 68 (1967): 193–203; especially pp. 193–99.

way in all beautiful things, and moreover is present in beautiful things alone. If this is a feature of the relationship between absolute Beauty and individual beautiful things, then it follows that the presence of Beauty in a thing is both necessary and sufficient for its being beautiful. But this is to say, according to the analysis of "cause" above, nothing more nor less than that the presence of absolute Beauty in a particular thing is the "cause" of the latter's being beautiful. No more natural interpretation can be given Socrates' description of that stage in his account which follows the hypothesizing of the absolute Forms:

> It appears to me that if anything else is beautiful besides the beautiful itself the sole reason for its being so is that it participates in that beautiful; and I assert that the same principle applies in all cases. (100C)

I have attempted to show thus far that Socrates' remarks about "causality" and the Forms following the description of method at 100A purport (1) to *establish* his theory of "causation" according to the procedures described in that passage and (2) to *illustrate* the method itself by showing how the theory of Forms as "causes" alone, in contrast with "those other learned causes" (100C) people speak of, agrees with the hypothesis that the Forms exist. Thus it appears wrong to say, with Robinson, that the connection between the hypothetical method and the theory of causation "seems perfectly accidental."[13] In a later chapter,[14] moreover, we shall see reason to believe that the hypothetical method was set up to *discover* the "causes" of things in general—that is, to discover for any given type of thing the necessary and sufficient conditions for its being the type of thing it is. If my analysis is correct, therefore, it would be difficult to imagine a more intimate philosophic connection than that

[13] *Plato's Dialectic*, pp. 143–44.
[14] Chapter IV, section 2.

which exists between these two aspects of Plato's account at *Phaedo* 100A–101D.

2 / 'Agreement' at 100A and Geometrical Analysis

The most puzzling aspect of Socrates' methodological remarks at 100A remains untouched by the discussion above. Literally translated, the passage in question reads:

> In every case I hypothesize [ὑποθέμενος] the formulation [λόγον] which I judge to be strongest, and whatever agrees [συμφωνεῖν] with it I posit as really so [ἀληθῆ ὄντα], and what does not as not so, whether with regard to causes or anything else.[15]

Apart from the question of the relationship between this procedure and the theory of Forms as "causes," there is the basic problem of what is *meant* when Socrates says he posits as really so (or true) whatever agrees with the hypothetical formulation and as not so (or false) whatever does not agree. The difficulty here is logical. If Socrates' procedure with regard to propositions that agree with the hypothesis is

---

[15] Although λόγος is being translated 'proposition', it would seem preferable in the abstract to render it 'thought', 'consideration' or 'formulation' instead. See note 4 in this connection. In the same spirit, ἀληθῆ ὄντα seems better translated as 'really so' or 'real being', or perhaps 'the truth', rather than merely 'true', since the latter suggests a quality of statements or propositions which seems a bit too technical for the context. Socrates has announced just previously (99E), after all, that he is trying to discover the truth about things (σκοπεῖν τῶν ὄντων τὴν ἀλήθειαν), which is not quite the same as trying to formulate true statements. But this difference in shading, however considerable to the ontologist or epistemologist, does not alter the problem of explicating a relation, logical or otherwise, which has the peculiar properties mentioned at 100A. For clarity in formulation, the relation will be treated as one existing between propositions rather than among things, and the qualities of propositions in question will be termed 'true' and 'false'.

justifiable, then 'agrees with' here must carry the sense of 'is implied by'. Yet if his procedure with regard to propositions that do not agree is justifiable, then 'agrees with' must carry the sense of 'is consistent with'. But it would appear that the term cannot carry both meanings at once, since consistency and implication are different logical relationships. And Socrates cannot be said to mean 'is entailed by' in one use of the term and 'is consistent with' in another, since συμφωνεῖν occurs only once in the immediate context in question. It seems to follow that Plato, in making Socrates utter these words, is guilty of a crude logical mistake. Another possible conclusion, that of Robinson, is that Plato "does not say quite all that he means"[16] in the passage, perhaps because an accurate expression of the two meanings involved would not "preserve conversational simplicity."[17] I think it can be shown, to the contrary, that Plato's use of the expression 'to agree with' in this passage is both logically sound and relatively precise, and that Socrates' immediate audience (if not his more distant commentators) could have been relied upon to understand the meaning he intended to convey by the expression.

The apparent difficulty in the description of method at 100A is that two distinct logical relationships are required for its interpretation, but that it contains only one term (συμφωνεῖν) which can be construed as an expression of logical relationship. If 'agrees with' means 'is entailed by' or 'is deducible from', then the instruction to posit as true whatever agrees with the hypothesis is sound; but the instruction to take as false what does not agree with the hypothesis does not make sense logically, since for any hypothesis there are other propositions which are not deducible from it but which nonetheless are true. On the other hand, if 'agrees with' means 'is consistent with', then the latter

[16] *Plato's Dialectic*, p. 128.
[17] *Ibid.*, p. 129.

instruction is sound but the former becomes unacceptable, since for any true hypothesis there are false propositions consistent with it. The appearance of paradox here is heightened by the fact that both interpretations can be supported by common uses of the term συμφωνέω. One basic meaning of the term is "to agree in saying," and there are several ways in which such agreement might be manifested in a relationship between propositions. Two assertions might agree in what they say by both saying exactly the same thing. The formalization of this relationship would be one of logical equivalence. Two assertions, again, might agree in that one says only what the other says, although not all the other says. This suggests the relationship of entailment. And yet again, two assertions might agree merely in that neither disagrees with the other. The relationship here is consistency. The difficulty of interpretation remains unalleviated, however, for it appears impossible to burden a single occurrence of the term συμφωνεῖν with two distinct meanings of this sort.

To facilitate discussion of these various relationships, let us symbolize the assertion that a proposition is necessarily true by prefixing 'L' to the symbol for that proposition. Thus 'Lp' designates the assertion that p is necessarily true. The assertion that p is possibly true will be symbolized similarly by 'Mp'. Negation will be symbolized with the help of 'N', in such a way that the appearance of 'N' in a formula indicates the denial of the least complex assertion-component designated by the expression immediately following as can be meaningfully denied. Thus 'Np' designates the denial of p, and 'NLp' the denial that p is necessarily true. Either 'L' or 'M' is eliminable in favor of the other, since NMNP is equivalent to Lp and NLNp to Mp. Let 'C' symbolize further the relation of conditionality, so that 'Cpq' represents the assertion that p is true only if q is true as well. In this notation, 'LCpq' symbolizes the assertion that p strictly implies q. Conjunction and alternation, finally, are symbolized respectively by 'K' and 'A'. This, of course, is the so-called "Polish notation," one advantage of which is its use only of symbols available in a standard font of type.

In these terms, the difficulty posed by the passage under discussion is that the instruction to posit as true whatever proposition (p) agrees with the hypothesis (h) requires the relationship LChp, the negation NLChp of which does not provide a relationship which would justify taking p as false on the basis of the truth of h; while the instruction to take as false whatever does not agree with h requires the relationship LChNp,[18] the negation of which (equivalent to Mhp) does not provide a relationship which would justify positing p as true on the basis of the truth of h.

At this point, however, we may well be reminded of the hazards of imposing a highly structured propositional logic in the interpretation of a passage in which precision of expression obviously was not one of the author's major concerns.[19] It is natural for us who are imbued with the discipline of propositional logic to think of the negation of a certain relationship between propositions as the negation of the assertion that those propositions stand in that relationship. Thus we have assumed, in the discussion above, that if the agreement of p with h is asserted by LChp, then the failure of p to agree with h is asserted by NLChp. There is no reason why Plato, however, being innocent of a systematically developed logic of propositions, might not have thought of that which does not agree with the hypothesis as *disagreeing* with it—might not have construed the nega-

[18] Inconsistency between h and p is NMhp, which is equivalent both to LChNp and to LCpNh.

[19] The warning is only against reading details into the context which are not there by the author's intention, not against the use of carefully formulated logical relationships in interpretation. More of the latter would further the cause of responsible Platonic scholarship.

tion at 100A7,[20] that is, literally to qualify the verb 'agrees with' itself, and not to qualify the assertion of agreement between hypothesis and proposition. *Not to agree* with h, in this case, could be construed as *disagreeing* with h in such a fashion that if h is true then p is false. Failure of p to agree with h then would be asserted by LChNp. If this expedient of interpretation were adopted, LChp would assert agreement of p with h, and LChNp would assert the lack of agreement of p with h, providing just the relationships needed to make logically good sense out of Socrates' methodological remarks at 100A.[21]

Interpreting the relationship of agreement to carry the sense of entailment, however, presents problems beyond that of how to construe its negation. For one thing, understanding the agreement of p with h to consist in the fact that p says only but not all of what h says is not as *natural* as the interpretation merely that p says nothing contrary to h. The term συμφωνέω, or its equivalent in our language, seems inappropriate as a vehicle for the sense of logical entailment. Second, as Robinson points out, Plato used the terms συμφωνέω and διαφωνέω in other contexts, but never clearly to indicate entailment or its absence. Yet there are several contexts in which they indicate consistency or in-

---

[20] The negative part of the instructions at 100A6–7 is ἃ δ' ἂν μή, ὡς οὐκ ἀληθῆ. Note the use of μή to negate the presence of accord, and of οὐκ to negate the presence of truth.

[21] This is compatible with Hackforth's statement that he takes the passage in question "to mean that any proposition arrived at by what the inquirer deems a valid process of deduction is accepted, and the contradictory of any such proposition is rejected" (*Plato's Phaedo*, p. 139). The contradiction of a proposition deduced from an hypothesis is inconsistent with the hypothesis. Nonetheless we can scarcely suppose that Socrates' instructions to reject as false whatever does not agree with the hypothesis are intended to require deduction of an indefinite number of consequences of the hypothesis until one is found which is contradicted by the proposition to be rejected. Some more direct test of inconsistency must have been intended.

consistency.[22] Most important, however, is the fact that
συμφωνέω appears also in the companion passage 101D,
and occurs there in a fashion which makes the interpretation
'to be entailed by' quite implausible.[23] Given the proximity
of the two passages, and their obviously common subject
matter, it seems entirely unlikely that Plato should have used
the same term at 100A and at 101D to convey such markedly different meanings. This is even more emphatically
the case since σωμφωνέω appears to be the key term in
either context.[24]

For these reasons it is better to seek some alternative
interpretation of Plato's intended meaning at 100A. Without flatly ruling out the possibility we have just considered,
let us attend somewhat more deliberately to the *effect*, in
his description of the scene, that Plato probably intended
Socrates' remarks to have upon his immediate audience.

Now if we allow, as surely we must, that Socrates'
audience could be counted upon to recall the techniques of
geometrical analysis upon hearing his description of method

[22] Robinson, *Plato's Earlier Dialectic*, p. 127. Passages mentioned
include *Phaedrus* 270C and *Gorgias* 457E.

[23] The instructions at 101D are to check the consequences of one's
hypothesis for *mutual* agreement (ἀλλήλοις συμφωνεῖ) before one turns
to substantiate the hypothesis itself. Only rarely, if ever, would the
consequences of a dialectician's argument entail *each other*, and there
is no reason Plato might have for thinking that they ever should.
Surely the desideratum here is *consistency* among the consequences
instead. These remarks will require qualification in light of the discussion of 101D in the section following, but stand as a good reason
for our being less than completely satisfied with any interpretation
which makes entailment the basic meaning of συμφωνέω at 100A.

[24] Assigning different meanings to συμφωνέω at 100A and 101D appears incorrect despite the fact that ἔχω undergoes a shift of meaning
between 101D1 (ἐχόμενος: cling to) and 101D3 (ἔχοιτο: fasten upon),
for the latter is scarcely a central term in either context. Hackforth
takes this dual use of ἔχω as a piece of careless writing (*Plato's
Phaedo*, p. 135n), and Robinson calls it an outrageous case of ambiguity (*Plato's Earlier Dialectic*, p. 130). It seems rather more
likely to be a lighthearted play on words. See also John Burnet,
Plato's Phaedo (Oxford: Clarendon Press, 1911), p. 101.

at *Phaedo* 100A, interesting results follow for the interpretation of this latter passage. Cebes and Simmias in the prison audience and Echecrates in the "outer dialogue," being Pythagoreans, would listen to the remarks at 100A and 101D with a familiar ear and would naturally think of the hypotheses and related assertions that Socrates was discussing as convertible propositions.[25] But if we think of the relationship of agreement at 100A as holding between convertible propositions, then the difficulties above disappear and Socrates' comments on method become perfectly lucid.

Commentators recall too infrequently the emphasis laid in the Academy on mathematics as a necessary prelude to philosophy.[26] Several of Plato's students were, or were to become, prominent mathematicians, and Plato himself seemed to enjoy some reputation in this direction among ancient historians of the subject.[27] There is no probable doubt, at any rate, that Plato was aware of current mathematical developments, and that he frequently alluded to such matters in philosophic discussion. It is entirely unlikely that Plato should have written on the subject of philosophic methodology without considering, in the process, comparable methods which had already proven fruitful in contemporary mathematics. There is good reason to think, in particular, that Plato was guided by such considerations in

[25] See A. E. Taylor, *Plato: The Man and His Work* (London: Methuen & Co., 1926), p. 176, for a discussion of the persons present at the death scene. That Cebes and Simmias were "mathematical" rather than "religious" Pythagoreans is indicated by Simmias' preference (92C), and Cebes' concurrence (95A), of the theory of recollection over the attunement theory of the soul.

[26] There is the (perhaps apocryphal) story, from Tzetze's *Book of Histories* 8 (972–73), that Plato had written over the door of the Academy "Let no one unversed in geometry come under my roof." See Ivor Thomas, ed., *Greek Mathematical Works* (Cambridge: Harvard University Press; London: Loeb Classical Library, 1941), 1:387.

[27] See Proclus' *Commentary on Euclid*, reproduced in part in Ivor Thomas, *Greek Mathematical Works*, pp. 151–55.

his thought behind the methodological passages at *Phaedo* 100A and 101D.

A heuristic technique well known among mathematicians of Plato's day was the so-called "method of analysis," in which proof of a given proposition is sought by deducing consequences from it until one is reached which is known independently to be true. Since, as a point of procedure, geometers typically are concerned with deductions in which both premises and conclusions are statements of equality which are mutually convertible, a demonstration of the proposition in question often could be produced subsequently by a deductive movement in the opposite direction.[28] This opposite movement, starting with the proposition already known to be true and ending with the proposition to be demonstrated, was known as "the method of synthesis." In this fashion, the "causes" or premises with reference to which a proposition could be demonstrated often could be found among the consequences of the proposition itself.

Now, in discussing recourse to λόγοι (99E) as part of a method in terms of which the Socratic investigation into causes might be put on a precise logical basis, it is natural that Plato should have thought of the method of geometrical analysis and have been intrigued with the possibility of applying some similar method to problems of "natural" as against mathematical causality. A forceful indication that the method (or methods) described at 100A and 101D is considered by Plato to be familiar to the mathematicians of his day is found in the combination of facts (1) that

---

[28] There is, of course, no necessity that this characteristic of convertibility was part of *all* geometrical methods referred to as "analysis." This is thoroughly discussed in N. Gulley's "Greek Geometrical Analysis," in *Phronesis*, 3, no. 1 (1958): 1–14. Gulley allows, nonetheless, that "there is at least no doubt that Greek geometers were aware that a large number of geometrical propositions were convertible . . . , that they practiced a method of analysis where the steps were in fact convertible, and that before the time of Pappus a formulation of this method had been made representing the analysis as deductive" (p. 4).

Socrates' listeners are pictured as finding the description
"extraordinarily clear" (102A) after the second statement
at 101D, and (2) that all the speakers involved in this
portion of the dialogue (with the exception probably of Phaedo
and possibly of Socrates himself) were Pythagoreans, and
hence likely to be familiar with current mathematical
developments. With this in mind, let us examine more
closely the method of geometrical analysis.

Our main source of information about geometrical analysis
as practiced by Plato's contemporaries is in Pappus' account
of the so-called "Treasury of Analysis," which is described
as a "special body of doctrine furnished for the use of those
who, after going through the usual elements, wish to obtain
power to solve problems set to them involving curves. . . ." [29]
The power provided by this method is for the discovery of
proofs of theorems which did not easily bend to the customary methods of proof treated in Euclid's *Elements*. The
technique was to treat the proposition to be demonstrated
as an hypothesis, and then to draw consequences from it,
and further consequences from these, and so forth, until
a proposition was reached which was already accepted as
true, or which was recognized as independently demonstrable.
This in itself, of course, does not amount to a proof of the
proposition with which the problem originated. But it is a
feature of geometry, not shared by logic either now or then,
that it deals for the most part with assertions of equality in
which equals can be added to or divided by equals, and in
which any component term could be replaced by an equivalent term, without change in truth value of the original
equations. Thus, for example, if we begin with the assertion
(in terms of line segments) that $AB + BC = 2CD$, we can
deduce $AB = 2CD - BC$ by the subtraction of BC from

---

[29] This can be found most readily perhaps in Thomas, *Greek Mathematical Works*, 2:597. The following statement of the method
itself, part of which is quoted, is found there also (pp. 597–99),
but is frequently quoted elsewhere in works on this general topic.

either side. In a similar fashion, however, the former can be deduced from the latter as well. Thus the propositions $AB + BC = 2CD$ and $AB = 2CD - BC$ are mutually deducible, or convertible.[30] This is the feature which made the process of analysis a method of discovering proofs. If not all the successive consequences leading from the original proposition to one independently known to be true are convertible with their antecedents, then of course nothing is gained for the proof of the proposition in question. But if the consequences are all convertible, which would frequently turn out to be the case, then the construction of the desired proof of the original proposition is a matter merely of reversing the order of the propositions derived during analysis. This backward movement, accordingly, begins with the proposition previously accepted as true, and yields a deductively sound proof of the proposition originally in question.

"Analysis," Pappus says, "is a method of taking that which is sought as though it were admitted and passing from it through its consequences in order to something which is admitted as a result of [some previous] synthesis."[31] Synthesis, however, proceeds in the opposite direction, for there "we suppose to be already done that which was last reached in the analysis, and arranging in their natural order as consequents what were formerly antecedents and linking them one with another, we finally arrive at the construction of what was sought. . . ."[32] Pappus then distinguishes between two sorts of analysis having to do with proofs of theorems and constructions respectively, and reiterates in connection with the first that we begin with something "we suppose . . . to exist and to be true," and then pass through its consequences until something is reached which is admitted;

---

[30] See, for example, the reconstructed proof of Euclid XIII.I, in which both procedures of analysis and of synthesis are apparent, reproduced by R. Robinson in *Mind*, 45 (1936): 470.

[31] Thomas, *Greek Mathematical Works*, 2:597.

[32] *Ibid.*

"then, if that which is admitted be true, that which is sought will also be true, and the proof will be the reverse of the analysis, but if we come upon something admitted to be false, that which is sought will also be false." [33]

Now there seems to me to be no reasonable doubt that Plato was intimately acquainted with this method of analysis. There is a passage in Proclus, in fact, where Plato apparently is credited with its invention.[34] And Cornford comes to the qualified conclusion, in the course of examining the relation between analysis and the dialectical method described in *Republic* VI, that "it is quite possible to accept the statement that Plato 'discovered' the method of Analysis, in the same sense as Aristotle discovered the syllogism. . . ." [35] Questions of origin aside, we have additional evidence that Plato was aware of the method in *Meno* 86E.[36] Having protested to

[33] The reader may note the considerable similarity between this statement and what Plato says at 100A.

[34] See Sir Thomas Heath's *A History of Greek Mathematics* (Oxford: Clarendon Press, 1921) 1:291. Gulley, " Geometrical Analysis," p. 7, also cites Diogenes Laertius (III, 24) in support of this point.

[35] "Mathematics and Dialectic in the *Republic* VI–VIII," *Mind*, n.s. 41 (1932): 47. H. Cherniss, "Plato as Mathematician," *Review of Metaphysics*, 4 (1950–51): 395–425, should be read in this connection for criticism of Cornford's interpretation of geometrical analysis. Also see Gulley, "Geometrical Analysis."

[36] R. S. Bluck, in *Plato's Meno* (London: Cambridge University Press, 1961) reviews reasons, mostly deriving from comments by Aristotle, for thinking that the method reflected in the hypothetical reasoning at *Meno* 86D ff. is not of the sort involving convertible propositions exclusively. Robinson (*Plato's Earlier Dialectic*, p. 121) also raises doubts whether the method in this passage is comparable to that of the so-called "method of analysis." The facts of the matter are that the proposition that virtue is knowledge is treated as convertible with the proposition that virtue is teachable at 87C, but that no other convertible propositions are involved in the sequel. Also, the geometrical example (for details of which see Thomas, *Greek Mathematical Works*, 1:396–97) is one in which both necessary and sufficient conditions are laid down for the inscription of a triangle in a given circle. This certainly smacks of convertibility. It would appear that Robinson is wrong when he says that the geometrical method of analysis and the method in the *Meno* have nothing in common ex-

Meno once again that one should not attempt to answer the
question whether virtue can be taught until one knows what
virtue is, Socrates in this passage consents to face the question
by "use of a hypothesis—the sort of thing . . . that geometers
often use in their inquiries" (86E).[37] The geometer's answer
to the question whether a given area can be inscribed as a
triangle in a given circle, for example, will be that it depends
upon whether certain conditions are met. These conditions
can be considered *hypothetically* as met, and the desired
consequences drawn from them. "If the area is such that, when
one has applied it [sc. as a rectangle] to the given line
[i.e., the diameter] of the circle, it is deficient by another
rectangle similar to the one which is applied, then, I should
say, one result follows; if not, the result is different." (87A)[38]
The upshot is that the area can be inscribed in the circle if
and only if it can be contained within a rectangle, one side
of which is along the diameter and the other of which is
extended perpendicular to the diameter terminating at the
circumference, such that this rectangle is similar (i.e., the
sides relate in the same ratio) to the rectangle the longer side
of which is the shorter of the former and the shorter side of
which is the remainder of the diameter. Socrates could have
gone on to point out what his mathematically informed readers
would recognize anyway, that the first result follows if and

---

cept their use of hypothesis (*Plato's Earlier Dialectic*, p. 121). They
also have in common their use, limited as it may be in the *Meno*, of
convertible propositions. Nothing is at stake for present purposes, however, in the issue whether Plato's reasoning at *Meno* 86D ff. follows
exactly the pattern of geometrical analysis. It is enough that we are
able to agree with Bluck that "certainly it is to mathematicians that
Plato seems to be indebted for his own conscious practice and development of a 'hypothetical method' " (*Plato's Meno*, p. 85).

[37] The translator of the *Meno* quoted is W. K. C. Guthrie, as in
Plato: The Collected Dialogues, E. Hamilton and H. Cairns, eds.
(New York: Pantheon Books, 1961).

[38] A complete explanation of this geometrical example is given in
Thomas, *Greek Mathematical Works*, 1:395–97. Other interpretations
have been offered, but this seems to be the most plausible. For a survey, see Bluck, *Plato's Meno*, pp. 441–61.

only if the rectangle can be so applied, and the other result follows if and only if the conditions are otherwise. This seems clearly to be an example of analysis to test the constructibility of certain figures (Pappus' second kind, called "problematical"). Socrates then proceeds to test the thesis that virtue can be taught by assuming the further proposition that virtue is knowledge, making quite explicit (87C) that the two propositions are mutually implicative, or convertible.

Consider, as a simple illustration of the relationships under discussion, the three equations below, in which the variables represent line segments:

(H) AB + BC + 3CD = 5CD
(P) AB + BC = 2CD
(R) AB = 2CD − BC

These equations are convertible in that any one can be deduced from any other by the general rule that addition of equals to equals yields equals. This being the case, any two of the equations are consistent and any two are mutually implicative. Thus it is correct to assert: MHP, MPR, etc., and LCHP, LCPH, etc. But consider the further equation (Q) AB + BC = CD, with CD ≠ O. Although H and Q might both be false, they cannot both be true; hence H and Q are inconsistent. It is apparent also that H and Q are not mutually implicative. Hence we may assert NMHQ and both NLCHQ and NLCQH. But in general, any equation expressed in the same terms as H is related to H either as P or as Q. Hence the only two alternatives for such equations is that they be both consistent with and mutually implicative with H or that they be both inconsistent and not mutually implicative with H. This being the case, *any* proposition which, like P, is consistent with H also is entailed by it.

The application of these relationships to the passage at 100A is entirely perspicuous. Socrates has stated that he first lays down as true the proposition (h) he judges strongest, and then posits as true whatever (other proposition p) agrees with it and as false whatever (other proposition q) does not.

If we read the term for 'agrees with' to mean 'is consistent with', and conceive the propositions in question according to the analogy of the convertible propositions employed in geometrical analysis, these methodological instructions make perfectly good sense. Since q is not consistent with h, its falsehood is deducible directly from the truth of h. But any proposition (expressible in common terms with h) is either inconsistent with h or entailed by h. Since p is consistent with h, it is entailed by h also, and its truth is deducible from the truth of h. Thus the relationships LChp and NMhq are left intact, and these are just the relationships necessary for a logically intelligible interpretation of the passage in question.

Thus we have available two possible interpretations of συμφωνέω and its denial, either of which nullifies any charge of logical absurdity against Plato regarding *Phaedo* 100A. (1) We may construe συμφωνέω to represent the relationship of entailment, and the denial of this relationship (contrary to our intuitions conditioned by propositional logic) to represent inconsistency; or (2) we may construe συμφωνέω to represent the relationship of consistency, and assume in our understanding of 100A, as Socrates' immediate audience would likely have assumed, that any proposition consistent with the hypothesis is also entailed by it. We have already examined factors unfavorable to the former possibility. Since these considerations involve a particular reading of ἀλλήλοις συμφωνεῖ at 101D, however, let us turn to a more detailed examination of this latter passage before attempting a final arbitration between these two possible interpretations.

3 / The Method of Defense at 101D

Continuity between 100A and 101D is furnished by Socrates' discussion of the Forms as "causes," concluding with the advice to his listeners to "cling to the safety of your hypothesis" (101D) and answer questions about the "causes" of things accordingly.[39] But if anyone should attack the hypothesis itself,

you would disregard him, and refuse to answer until you could consider the consequences of it, and see whether they agreed or disagreed with each other [ἀλλήλοις συμφωνεῖ ἢ διαφωνεῖ]. But when the time came for you to establish the hypothesis itself, you would pursue the same method [ὡσαύτως]: you would assume some more ultimate [ἄνωθεν] hypothesis, the best [βελτίστη] you could find, and continue until you reached something satisfactory [τι ἱκανόν]. (101D–E)

The mistake of discussing both the hypothesis and its consequences at the same time is one to be avoided by anyone who "wanted to discover a truth" (101E).[40]

[39] The hypothesis immediately in question here must be the principle claimed to follow from the theory of Forms hypothesized at 100B—namely the principle that the presence of the Forms in particular things is the "cause" of their being what they are. No other interpretation of 101C seems possible. At 101D, however, Socrates seems to lose sight of this particular example and speaks of the defense of hypotheses in general.

[40] This mistake seems to have been committed by Socrates himself in the *Meno* where, after introducing the hypothesis that virtue is knowledge (87B), he proceeded at once to attempt to *establish* that hypothesis by deduction from other hypotheses (87C–88D), only to find later (89D–96C) that the hypothesis appears to be inconsistent with the fact that there are no teachers of virtue. In outline, the argument to establish the hypothesis that virtue is knowledge proceeds as follows. All good things are advantageous (granted by Meno at 87E). All advantageous things become so by wisdom (granted at 88D). It follows that all good things are accompanied by wisdom. But virtue is a good thing (accepted at 87D). Therefore virtue is accompanied by wisdom, or as put at 88D, virtue is a sort of wisdom. I take it that the shift from ἐπιστήμη at 87D to φρόνησις at 88D is an intimation of the forthcoming conclusion that the virtue of good citizenship comes from right opinion rather than from knowledge. This argument is overturned, however, when Socrates at 89C himself challenges the hypothesis that virtue is knowledge on the grounds of incompatibility between its consequence, that there are teachers of virtue

Among the few things that are entirely clear about these instructions are that there are two distinct sets of procedures to be followed when one's hypothesis is attacked, and that one set is to be completed before the other is begun. First is the procedure of testing the consequences of one's hypothesis for mutual agreement. Only when a satisfactory outcome has been established in this respect should one turn to the question of establishing the hypothesis itself. Having turned to this question, however, one should "pursue the same method," assuming the "best" of the "higher" hypotheses one can find, and continue in the same procedure until "something satisfactory" is reached.

Less clear, in these instructions, is (1) what is meant by speaking of mutual agreement between the consequences of one's hypothesis. That is, what must be established about these consequences before one is entitled to proceed to a justification of the hypothesis itself? This is a recurrence of the problem of interpreting συμφωνέω which we have encountered already in connection with 100A. Further is the problem (2)

(89D), and the apparent fact emerging in further conversation with Meno and Anytus that there are no such teachers. (Robinson is wrong in saying that "it is not possible to hold that he [Plato] goes on to infer something from virtue's being knowledge" (*Plato's Earlier Dialectic*, p. 121). Plato reasons at 89D that if virtue is knowledge it is teachable, and if teachable there must be teachers of it. The falsehood of the latter entails the falsehood of the proposition that virtue is knowledge. Robinson is right, however, in his implicit suggestion that the order of these various inferences in the dialogue is not what one would expect in thinking of the reasoning as modeled after the method of geometrical analysis.) If the reader senses a rebuke of Socrates at 101D, in light of the fact that the whole proceedings at 100A–101D are bound to evoke thoughts of this sequence in the *Meno*, it should be pointed out that Socrates says only that *it seems likely* to him that the next step after hypothesizing that virtue is knowledge is to find out whether the hypothesis is true, and this may have been intended only to lead Meno on. Readers intrigued by the possibility of a criticism of Socrates here, however, may bear in mind that the disputants (ἀντιλογικοί: 101E) who muddle hypothesis and conclusion resemble the "Sophist of Noble Lineage" in the *Sophist*, among which class Socrates would likely be numbered. In this latter connection, see chap. III, sec. 3.

of identifying the method one is to follow in the same way in establishing the hypothesis itself. The expression "in the same way" (ὡσαύτως) surely refers to something described previously. Yet the only instructions thus far mentioned in the passage are to check the consequences of the hypothesis for mutual agreement, and this suggests little by way of a positive procedure for justifying the hypothesis in turn. Plato thus must be presumed to be referring not only to the check for mutual agreement at 101D, but also to the instructions at 100A. This is one more reason for considering the remark about consistency at 101D as an extension of what was said at 100A, and for rendering parallel interpretations of συμφωνέω in the two passages. This problem is further complicated, moreover, by the description of the circumstances under which one is to *stop* applying that method—namely when some "higher" hypothesis is found which can be deemed "satisfactory." Now, what one will find "satisfactory" obviously depends upon what one has been trying to do all along, so the interpretation to be given τι ἱκανὸν depends upon the answer to problems (1) and (2). But there is the apparently independent issue concerning what Plato meant in referring to the stages through which one proceeds in justifying a given hypothesis as ἄνωθεν. Since one apparently is to continue seeking "from on high" until something "satisfactory" is reached, presumably at each stage an hypothesis is to be assumed which is in some sense ἄνωθεν as regards previous stages. Let us begin with the problem (3) of interpreting the sense in which the hypothesis assumed at the second stage of the procedure at 101D is "higher" than the hypothesis to be justified.

According to one way of rendering ἄνωθεν, the hypothesis justifying the original is "higher" than the original in the sense of being more general and perhaps more self-evident.[41] *Phaedo*

---

[41] Bluck, in *Plato's Phaedo*, pp. 15–16, 112, is of the opinion that the "higher" hypotheses are more ultimate and that there may be an intimation of the dialectical process of the Divided Line at *Phaedo* 101D. See also Taylor, *Plato: The Man and His Work*, p. 201, and Robinson's comments on Archer-Hind, *Plato's Earlier Dialectic*, p. 137.

101D, according to this interpretation, anticipates *Republic* 511B. If this interpretation is accepted, it carries with it answers to various of the other problems associated with *Phaedo* 101D mentioned above. The "best" and finally "satisfactory" hypothesis, for example, would be one which is more universal than the one to be justified and itself beyond need for justification, and the method of reaching this hypothesis would be the "upward path" of the highest section of the Divided Line. There are several reasons, however, why this interpretation should be resisted. For one thing, the procedure at *Phaedo* 101D shows no promise of culminating in "unhypothetical beginnings." To the contrary, Plato quite clearly suggests that each stage in the procedure of justification involves *hypothesizing* another *hypothesis* and that the procedure is terminated only when something satisfactory is reached. Although it is not explicitly denied in these instructions that this satisfactory terminus itself should be something other than an hypothesis, there is not the slightest hint in the *Phaedo* that this is the case. Moreover, if the procedure were that of *Republic* 511B and 533C–D, then it obviously could not be described as the "same way" as anything mentioned *before Phaedo* 101D. For these reasons, indeed, "more ultimate" as a translation of ἄνωθεν seems open to question in itself, since justification for this translation seems to fall back upon an appeal to the way the term is used in the *Republic* and in Aristotle's *Posterior Analytics*.[42] Reference intended by ἄνωθεν could reasonably be construed merely as to "the above," in the sense of "what had come before." This being the case, it seems that the interpretation of ἄνωθεν depends upon the interpretation of 101D generally, rather than the other way around. Given the quite indirect way

---

[42] Liddell and Scott give "higher more universal principles" as one possible reading of ἄνωθεν, citing *Phaedo* 101D and *Posterior Analytics* 97a 33. But the latter use would seem to bear interpretation at best as "logically prior," while the former will not support one particular interpretation of its own occurrence against another. See *Greek-English Lexicon*, rev. ed. (Oxford: Clarendon Press, 1925), p. 169. Archer-Hind also cites *Posterior Analytics* 82a 23 in defense of this interpretation.

in which mention of the "higher" is introduced into the context, this is only as it should be.

I have argued that either of two renditions of συμφωνέω enable us to interpret Plato's methodological remarks at *Phaedo* 100A. (1) It may be that the agreement of h with p amounts to entailment, while lack of agreement of q with p means, not the absence of entailment, but the presence of disagreement or inconsistency. Or (2) it may be that the relationship of agreement between two propositions is merely one of consistency and that Socrates' immediate audience is relied upon to understand, as in the context of geometrical analysis with which they surely were familiar, that a proposition which is consistent with another also entails that other proposition.[43] It may be said, in partial response to the question of what is meant by speaking of mutual agreement between the consequences of one's hypotheses, that the same two interpretations also can be made of Plato's use of συμφωνέω at 101D. The consequences of the two interpretations, however, are more divergent in this latter application.

The first step in defense of a challenged hypothesis is to determine whether its consequences agree or disagree with one another (ἀλλήλοις συμφωνεῖ ἢ διαφωνεῖ). Now if agreement and disagreement respectively mean entailment and lack of consistency, according to the first interpretation above, then for two propositions to be in disagreement (διαφωνεῖ) is for them to be inconsistent. This is neither unexpected nor unwelcome in light of the customary reading of 101D. For two propositions mutually to agree, however, is for them to be mutually implicative or convertible. And agreement obviously is the desideratum in this phase of the method. What, under this interpretation, would the instructions at 101D then amount to? In the first place, the consequences in question (ὁρμηθέντα) [44] must be conceived as themselves convertible with the hypoth-

---

[43] These two alternatives are examined in detail in the preceding section.

[44] See Robinson's discussion of this term, *Plato's Earlier Dialectic*, pp. 129–31. Also see Hackforth, *Plato's Phaedo*, pp. 139–40.

esis under consideration, for if all conceivable consequences of
a proposition are equivalent, then each consequence in turn
must be equivalent to the hypothesis itself.[45] Under this interpretation, the method obviously is patterned after geometrical analysis, in which the propositions involved at each stage
are convertible. The first step in defense of an hypothesis,
therefore, may be viewed as one of testing whether the consequences of the hypothesis are convertible with it, since in
general if two propositions (in this case the consequences) are
convertible with a third (the hypothesis) then they are convertible with each other.[46] The next step, Socrates informs his listeners, is to assume some other hypothesis, the "best" you can
find, and to pursue "the same method" with respect to the hypothesis originally in question. By pursuing "the same method"
(ὡσαύτως), in this rendition, Plato would have to mean pursuing the method of deducing the hypothesis in question from
the ("best") hypothesis, with which however the former hypothesis would have to be convertible. But if the hypothesis in
question is convertible with the "best" hypothesis assumed to
justify it, then the latter could not be "more ultimate" in the
sense of being more general or more "self-evident" than the
former. I have suggested, however, that the term ἄνωθεν in this
connection might mean merely "above," in the sense of "having been mentioned before," and this is the sense to be relied
upon under the present interpretation. The second stage in the
defense of a challenged hypothesis, then, would involve finding
another hypothesis which, as before, was convertible with the
hypothesis in question but which was "best" in comparison with
other possible hypotheses in being least open to question in the
context in which the original hypothesis was challenged. This
procedure would continue until an hypothesis was found which

[45] Among the consequences of the hypothesis h is h itself.

[46] As Robinson points out, *Plato's Earlier Dialectic*, p. 130, this
interpretation puts undue emphasis upon the "minor activity of check-
ing one's logical calculations." I am arguing, however, only that this
is a possible interpretation, not that by itself it is the best interpretation.

was satisfactory to all participants in the discussion, including those who had challenged the original hypothesis.

A peculiar result of this interpretation of συμφωνέω, which the reader may recall was introduced in connection with 100A without any mention of geometrical analysis, is that its application to 101D requires the assumption of convertibility between the consequences of the hypothesis to be established. As long as the relation of agreement is construed as implication, there is no other way to interpret the instruction that the consequences are to be tested for mutual agreement.[47] As the other side of a somewhat paradoxical situation, it appears that the only way the interpreter of 101D can avoid relying upon the analogy of geometrical analysis is by the second rendition of συμφωνέω, the introduction of which at 100A depended entirely upon this very analogy. Let us see how this is the case.

According to this second interpretation of συμφωνέω, for two propositions to be in agreement is for them to be consistent. This makes entirely credible Socrates' remark that he posits as false whatever does not agree with the hypothesis he assumes to be true. The other half of the methodological statement at 100A—that whatever agrees with the hypothesis is posited as true—is accommodated by the assumption that members of Socrates' audience are intended to draw upon an acquaintance with geometrical analysis in understanding that any proposition consistent with the hypothesis is also convertible with it and hence entailed by it. Thus, in line with this assumption, we may read 100A as a *reminder* of the two relationships by which (1) the truth of a proposition has, as a consequence, the truth of another (entailment), and (2) the truth of a proposi-

---

[47] It is doubtful whether commentators who suggest that συμφωνέω at 100A means "to be entailed by" have always recognized this implication of their interpretation. Hackforth, for example, considers that any proposition agrees with the hypothesis which is "arrived at by what the inquirer deems a valid process of deduction" (*Plato's Phaedo*, p. 139), but seems to go on to interpret the relation of *mutual* agreement at 101D as involving only a one-way entailment (see pp. 139–40).

tion requires the falsehood of another (inconsistency). Read this way, the purpose of 100A will appear to be that of separating these two propositional relationships for further discussion with an audience thus knowledgeable of geometrical analysis. With this understanding of the two relationships, it will be natural for us, as well as for Socrates' immediate audience, to construe συμφωνέω at 101D in the same fashion as at 100A, indicating *consistency* between propositions found to be in mutual agreement. The sense of *entailment*, however, which at 100A is suggested by analogy with the consistent and hence convertible propositions in a proof by geometrical analysis, is indicated at 101D by mention of the *consequences* of the hypothesis to be established. The propositions the consistency of which is to be tested are referred to as τὰ ὁρμηθέντα, as "based upon" the hypothesis. This reference in itself should be enough to remind the audience of the relationship carried over from 100A, according to which the truth of another proposition follows from the truth of the hypothesis "judged to be soundest."

According to this second interpretation, the method described at 101D is as follows: The first step is to test whether or not the consequences of the hypothesis to be established are consistent with one another, regardless of how numerous these consequences might be. When and if consistency is established, the next step is to proceed by the same method in seeking some "more ultimate" hypothesis, not resting until something "satisfactory" is reached. In this rendition, the method referred to as "the same" is that involved in the consistency-check, and that foreshadowed at 100A. It involves two phases: (1) drawing consequences from the "more ultimate" hypothesis and (2) testing these consequences for mutual consistency. This rendition is thus entirely in accord with the customary way of interpreting 101D. Another advantage is that ἄνωθεν now may be taken to mean "more ultimate" in the sense of "more comprehensive." That is, the "higher hypotheses" may be conceived as higher in that they imply, but are not necessarily implied by, the hypothesis originally calling for justification. The "satisfactory" higher hypothesis, finally, is one which is no longer open to challenge in the context in question.

Now both of these renditions are plausible, and either absolves Plato from any charge of logical nonsense in what he says at *Phaedo* 100A and 101D. The question to be faced at this point is which interpretation Plato intended. Each interpretation, relative to the other, has its own advantages and disadvantages. The major disadvantages of the first interpretation, in which συμφωνέω indicates implication, are the following: (1) Its results in connection with 101D, which require convertibility between the consequences of the hypothesis to be tested, make no sense as a philosophic methodology. Philosophers, being essentially logicians rather than mathematicians, do not deal typically with convertible propositions, and any description of their method which suggests otherwise is deficient for this very reason. Also (2), the method emerging from 101D under this interpretation would be difficult if not impossible to reconcile with the dialectical method described in *Republic* 511B, in connection with the uppermost section of the Divided Line. Further, there are the difficulties (3) of explaining why Plato would put so much emphasis in 101D on merely testing the accuracy of one's deductions, and (4) of explaining why συμφωνέω in this context should be used to indicate *deducibility* while elsewhere in Plato's writing it seems to mean merely *consistency*.[48] Yet a further disadvantage of the first interpretation is (5) that the proof of the immortality of the soul which follows 101D shows no involvement whatsoever of convertible propositions. One might well wonder why this is so if that proof is an illustration of the method and if the method relies so heavily upon the convertibility of the propositions involved in its application.

The advantages of the first interpretation, in turn, are the disadvantages of the second. And the main disadvantage of the

[48] See Robinson, *Plato's Earlier Dialectic*, p. 130, for these last two difficulties mentioned.

second seems to be (1) that the sense of entailment carried (indirectly) at 100A by the term συμφωνέω is entirely divorced from that term at 101D and left instead to be carried by the term ὁρμηθέντα. At 101D, in other words, agreement means *solely* consistency, whereas at 100A under the second interpretation it suggested both consistency and entailment. The strength of this difficulty, it should be admitted, is not overwhelming, since Plato never seemed much attracted by the ideal of one technical term for one technical concept. Yet neither is the difficulty minimal, since Plato did make a point of using συμφωνέω in both contexts, where different terms might have done the job as well. A second difficulty has been raised by Robinson, to the effect that no hypothesis of the sort Plato would envisage being tested by the method at 101D would be complex enough to have inconsistent consequences.[49] Now indeed there is nothing logically amiss in the notion that a proposition might have contradictory consequences, since any consequences whatsoever can be deduced from a statement which is itself inconsistent. Yet it is unlikely, as Robinson points out, that any dialectician would ever find himself working with an hypothesis which could be shown inconsistent without the help of auxiliary assumptions or principles. Robinson's suggestion, which seems sound, is that the consistency check which Plato mentions at 101D pertains not merely to the direct consequences of the hypothesis itself but to the "standing assumptions" as well of the context in question.[50] Thus this difficulty, too, admits a response. Yet the fact remains that if this second interpretation is correct then Plato is assuming far more than he says at 101D; and it is the case in general that the fewer as-

[49] *Plato's Earlier Dialectic*, pp. 129–32.
[50] *Ibid.*, p. 133. This is just what Plato does in the *Theaetetus*. As we shall see, one of the primary roles of the theory of perception in this dialogue is to provide a background of accepted theses against which the hypothesis that knowledge is perception can be shown inconsistent.

sumptions one requires the better one's stance as an interpreter of a disputed passage.

Now granting the advantages of either interpretation, someone might persist in asking which interpretation Plato himself intended in writing *Phaedo* 100A–101D. I think the proper response to this question is to refuse its implication that only one interpretation is acceptable. For the consumption of the mathematicians in his audience, there is no reason why Plato should be unhappy with those parts of either interpretation which lean heavily upon the analogy of geometrical analysis. What better sense, indeed, can be read into the laudatory remarks of Cebes, Simmias, and Echecrates at 102A, where all profess to find Socrates' description of method "wonderfully clear even to a feeble intelligence"? [51] At the same time, those aspects of the two interpretations which seem best to accord with what Plato says about dialectical method in the *Republic* can just as well be allowed the reader with specifically philosophic interests in mind. What I suggest, then, is that *Phaedo* 100A–101D, although not at all a piece of logical nonsense, remains vague as to how exactly it should be interpreted, and that this is as Plato intended it to be. Perhaps Plato was not entirely clear himself at this point about the exact propositional relationships to be exploited in a successful philosophic method, or perhaps he felt that no more explicit statement was called for in the context of the *Phaedo*. Whatever Plato's attitude in this connection, however, the task remains of separating out the uniquely philosophic from the merely mathematical strands of the methodological remarks between 100A and 101D. Perhaps it is no coincidence that this is just what is accomplished

---

[51] This remark of Echecrates should cause considerable embarrassment to the commentator who is unable to find a coherent methodology in *Phaedo* 100A–101D. The alternatives open in such a case are (1) that Simmias and Cebes are confused, (2) that Plato is confused, and (3) that the commentator himself is confused. But Simmias and Cebes have shown themselves remarkably clearheaded throughout the dialogue.

by the subsequent description of dialectical method in the *Republic*.

4 / The "Upward Way" at *Republic* 511B

Our examination of *Phaedo* 100A–101D has isolated two possible interpretations of the method therein described, neither of which Plato appeared to encourage more strongly than the other. If συμφωνέω at 100A and 101D is taken to indicate entailment, then the method is one of testing the consequences of the challenged hypothesis for mutual entailment and, subsequently, of attempting to find some further less questionable hypothesis which is related to the former "in the same fashion," that is by mutual entailment. This interpretation accords nicely with the suggestion that Plato here is describing the method of geometrical analysis. If, on the other hand, συμφωνέω is taken to indicate mere lack of contradiction, then the method is one of testing the consequences for mutual consistency and, subsequently, of attempting to find other less questionable hypotheses from which the original hypothesis can be deduced. This interpretation accords with the usual construction put upon *Phaedo* 100A–101D as a description of philosophic methodology. The relative advantages and disadvantages of the two interpretations have been discussed in the previous chapter. Neither interpretation seems overwhelmingly more likely than the other to express Plato's own intentions for the passage, and the conclusion recommended is that Plato indeed did not intend one interpretation to the total exclusion of the other.

It is conceivable, of course, that Plato was not aware of the ambiguity which makes these two interpretations possible. My conjecture, however, is that Plato was more interested at the time the *Phaedo* was written in the similarities than in the differences between mathematical and philosophic methodology.[52] In view of this conjecture, it is interesting to compare the two alternative interpretations with an eye for their common features. Both emphasize, as readings of *Phaedo* 100A, (1) that a proposition can be either justified or defeated with reference to its relationships with other propositions. Both require (2) that the consequences of an hypothesis to be justified should at least be determined to be consistent as a preliminary part of the justification. And both specify (3) that the procedure of justifying the hypothesis itself should be carried out "in the same way," namely that it should rely upon the same propositional relationships by which consequences were drawn from the original hypothesis and found consistent. The fact that this common ground is enough on which to base the proof of immortality following 101D, which relies on the quite conventional relation of one-way entailment between propositions,[53] reinforces the suggestion that if Plato was aware of the two possible ways of construing 100A–101D he had no particular reason for being more specific about the differences.

Be this as it may, the main burden of Plato's methodological remarks in that most methodological of all passages in the *Republic*, the Divided Line, is to strike an unbridgeable distinction between the procedures of the mathematician and those of the philosophic dialectician. Mere conformity and

---

[52] Whatever else one makes of it, the *Phaedo* emerges as a powerful call in the older Pythagorean style for a *rapprochement* between the ideals of mathematics and of the good life. Philosophy is depicted as the discipline in which these two ideals are merged. In such a context, there would be no point in emphasizing the differences between philosophy and mathematics.

[53] The proof of immortality of the soul can easily be interpreted as being deductively sound. As Socrates remarks to Simmias and Cebes, however, the "original assumptions, acceptable as they are to you both, ought nevertheless to be more precisely examined" (107B). Mere deductive soundness is not enough to assure the truth of the conclusion. The premises themselves must be subjected to dialectical examination, which Socrates in the *Phaedo* does not attempt to provide.

agreement (510D) or hanging together (533C) [54] of propositions, as in mathematical reasoning, does not amount to knowledge of the sort to which the philosopher aspires. Mathematics,
accordingly, although conducive to the apprehension of truth
(525B), falls short of the top in the hierarchy of mental states
symbolized by the Divided Line.

Plato's description of dialectical method is contained in *Republic* 510B, 511B–C, and 533C. An interesting thing about
this description is that it is accomplished almost exclusively
by pointing out aspects of geometrical reasoning which dialectic does not share.

> Now consider how we are to divide the part which stands
> for the intelligible world. There are two sections. In the
> first [55] the mind uses as images those actual things which
> themselves had images in the visible world; and it is com-
> pelled to pursue its inquiry by starting from assumptions
> [ὑποθέσεων] and travelling, not up to a principle, but down
> to a conclusion. In the second the mind moves in the other
> direction, from an assumption up towards a principle which
> is not hypothetical [ἀρχὴν ἀνυπόθετον]; and it makes no use
> of the images employed in the other section, but only of
> Forms [εἴδεσι], and conducts its inquiry solely by their
> means. (510B)

Dialectic here is contrasted with mathematical reasoning in
two respects. (1) Whereas the latter proceeds downward (deductively) from its hypotheses to conclusions that are equally
hypothetical, dialectic proceeds "in the other direction" from
hypothesis to starting points which are not hypothetical. And
(2) dialectic, unlike mathematics, does not rely upon images
(diagrams and illustrations), but moves solely among ideas or

[54] The term ὁμολογουμένως at 510D is translated in a form equivalent
to 'consistent(ly)' by Cornford, and συμπέπλεκται at 533C comes out
'consistent with itself'. All passages quoted from the *Republic* are
from Cornford's translation.

[55] Symbols relating to Cornford's schematization of the Divided
Line are omitted from this quotation.

Forms. The same points are made at 511B–C, but with an important addition. Whereas the mind, in studying the objects of mathematics, first "is compelled to employ assumptions, and, because it cannot rise above these, does not travel upwards to a first principle; and second . . . uses as images those actual things which have images of their own in the section below them . . ." (511A), the mind engaged in dialectic, proceeding by "unaided reasoning" (without images), "treats its assumptions, not as first principles, but as *hypotheses*[56] in the literal sense, things 'laid down' like a flight of steps up which it may mount all the way to something that is not hypothetical, the first principle of all; and having grasped this, may turn back and, holding on to the consequences which depend upon it, descend at last to a conclusion, never making use of any sensible object, but only of Forms, moving through Forms from one to another, and ending with Forms" (511B–C). The important addition in this passage is that dialectic itself includes a "downward movement," like mathematical reasoning. The difference is that, while the conclusions reached by the latter means are no less problematical than the hypotheses from which they are derived, the conclusions reached by the deductive movement of dialectic share the nonhypothetical character of the first principle previously reached by the "upward" dialectical movement. It is emphasized again, however, that the entire dialectical procedure remains solely on the level of ideas or Forms. The deductive movement begins with Forms, moves through Forms, and ends with Forms. It is in this fashion that the dialectician is able to exact "an account [λόγον] of the essence of each thing" (534B) he sets out to study.

[Geometers] leave the assumptions they employ unquestioned and can give no account [λόγον] of them. [For if] your premiss is something you do not really know and your conclusion and the intermediate steps are a tissue of things

[56] Translator's emphasis.

you do not really know, your reasoning may be consistent with itself, but how can it ever amount to knowledge? (533C)

The method of dialectic, on the other hand, is "the only one which takes this course, doing away with assumptions and travelling up to the first principle of all, so as to make sure of confirmation there" (533C–D).

In sum, there are two points of similarity between geometry and dialectic, and three points of essential difference. These methods are similar in that (1) they both begin with hypotheses and (2) they both include the deduction of consequences from appropriate starting points. They are dissimilar in that (1) geometry involves *only* deduction, while dialectic first proceeds "upward" to nonhypothetical beginnings; hence, (2) both starting points and conclusions of geometry are problematical, while dialectic achieves unproblematical beginnings and conclusions; and (3) geometry but not dialectic involves perceptible images.

Both the problematical aspects of geometry and its use of images have been illustrated in passages from earlier dialogues which we have already discussed. The brief geometrical illustration of hypothetical reasoning at *Meno* 86D–87A quite obviously suggested the necessity of constructing a figure to achieve the desired proof. And there is a clear sense in which a series of convertible propositions, such as those Plato most likely had in mind in writing *Phaedo* 100A,[57] illustrates a propositional relationship in terms of which the geometer is intrinsically unable to give an *account* of the hypotheses he initially accepts as true. If two propositions imply each other, they are equivalent, and neither can serve as an explanation or account of the other. Thus 'this man is married' in no sense explains or is explained by 'this man has a wife', and there is no sense of 'account' in which either of the two convertible assertions $AB + BC = 2CD$ and $AB = 2CD − BC$ is able to provide an account of the other. While confined to dealing

[57] This is argued in section 2 above.

with convertible propositions, the geometer is unable to "rise above" the hypotheses with which he begins; his only mode of inference is deductive, and he will not feel called upon to provide any account of his procedures beyond showing that no inconsistency is involved in any of his deductions. Thus we are equipped with illustrations, if any are needed, of the main respects in which geometry differs from dialectic. There is no doubt, in general, what procedures Plato is claiming *not* to be part of dialectical reasoning.

But everything unproblematical about this method has been said when dialectic has been denied these characteristics of mathematical reasoning. Granted that dialectic is not limited to deduction from hypotheses but involves an "upward way" as well, the question remains just what this "upward" motion of thought was supposed to be. And granted that the dialectician is able in some fashion to move "upward" from hypotheses to a nonhypothetical starting point, it is by no means clear what such a starting point would be found to be like once it had been achieved. There is room for endless speculation on either issue, and no unquestionably authentic illustration of dialectical reasoning either to or from nonhypothetical beginnings is available in any dialogue prior to the *Republic* which would temper such speculation with immediate evidence.[58]

---

[58] When Socrates is not engaged in showing other people's presuppositions untenable, but rather is drawing out consequences of his own hypotheses, he usually takes pains to emphasize their tentative character. Thus at the end of the argument for immortality of the soul at *Phaedo* 107B, Socrates says to Simmias and Cebes, "our original assumptions, acceptable as they are to you both, ought nevertheless to be more precisely examined." Another urging of caution too often overlooked by zealous commentators is at the beginning of the discussion of justice in the *Republic*, based on the notion of the tripartite soul. At *Republic* 435, just after the notion is introduced, Socrates says "it is my belief that we shall never reach the exact truth in this matter by following our present methods of discussion; the road leading to that goal is longer and more laborious. However, perhaps we can find an answer that will be up to the standard we have so far maintained in our speculations." (435C–D) This warning is repeated at 504B.

One major problem regarding the nature of the nonhypothetical beginning has been whether the "first principle of all" mentioned at 511B is the Good, and whether this means that the Good in some sense is a starting point from which "an account of the essence of each thing" (534B) can be deduced. Now I find no direct evidence in the *Republic* that the Good was considered to be the sole nonhypothetical beginning toward which the "upward bound" dialectician proceeds and from which he deduces his conclusions about the true nature of things.[59] At 532B, it is stated that the dialectician makes "his way in every case to the essential reality and perseveres until he has grasped by pure intelligence the very nature of Goodness itself." But this is not to say that the essential reality of a thing is not realized *until* the nature of the Good itself has been grasped. It is to say, rather, that the dialectician, and particularly the philosopher charged with the well-being of a

[59] In the opinion of Robinson, "[m]ost students of Plato believe that he thought there was really only one [genuine beginning], namely, the Idea of the Good." (*Plato's Earlier Dialectic*, p. 159) Without mentioning names, Robinson offers his guarded agreement (p. 160). A case in point is Bluck, who believed that Plato thought "the existence and nature of the whole world of reality can be verified and confirmed by the philosopher in the light of the Form of the Good" (*Plato's Phaedo* [London: Routledge & Kegan Paul, 1955] p. 12), and construes the Divided Line as describing a procedure for reaching "ultimate teleological cause[s]" (p. 166). The hypotheses with which the dialectician deals are "provisional notions of Forms" (p. 162). Although it may be, as Bluck claims, that Plato never abandoned "the search for the kind of cause that Socrates had hoped to find in Anaxagoras" (p. 202), I see no way in which the "notion" of the Good or of any other Form could serve as an hypothesis from which consequences can follow and conclusions can be deduced (511B). It is reasonably clear that Plato thought that the dialectical procedure could be applied in teleological reasoning apropos of the Good (534B–C). But it is totally unclear how the Good, or any other Form in itself, could serve as a "first principle" from which truths about other things could be drawn. In support of the statement that "the seeker after truth continues to work upwards to higher and higher principles, until he reaches the Form of the Good itself, the ultimate principle of all things" (p. 147), Bluck cites *Republic* 510B; but at 510B there is no mention of the Good.

city or state, will not stop until he has grasped the nature of the Good as well as the nature of other things in themselves. This is born out at 534B, where the dialectician is named as one "who demands an account of the essence of each thing," whereas with one unable to do this "his intelligence is at fault"; and this is claimed to "apply to the Good" as well as to other Forms. For our purposes, it is enough to allow that teleological reasoning involving the Good might be implemented by the dialectical method of the Divided Line, but that there is no apparent necessity, and indeed no apparent sense, in the suggestion that all applications of this method in order to be successful must in some way culminate in the Form of the Good.[60] All that can be said of a positive sort about the objects of the mental acts involved in the "upward way" is that they are Forms alone, for reason in these operations never makes "use of any sensible object, but only of Forms, moving through Forms from one to another, and ending with Forms" (511C). If we need an example of Forms as objects of actual dialectical reasoning, we must wait for the *Sophist*. But in the *Sophist* there is no mention of the Good.

The other major problem with Plato's description of dialectic is that no indication is given in the *Republic* of the nature of the "upward way" from hypothesis to a nonhypothetical starting point. I shall maintain that there are clear illustrations of this procedure in the *Sophist* also. But it must be admitted that none are offered in the *Republic*, and none apparently in earlier dialogues. Numerous interpretations have sprung up regarding the nature of the "upward way," the more cogent of which have been reviewed by Robinson.[61]

One clear thing about the "upward path," I believe, is that it includes the method of justifying hypotheses that emerges from the second interpretation of the relation of "agreement" at *Phaedo* 101D examined in the previous section. According

---

[60] The method at *Phaedo* 100A, after all, was to apply to questions "about causes or anything else."

[61] *Plato's Earlier Dialectic*, pp. 160–79.

to this rendition, to say that two propositions are in mutual agreement is merely to say that they are consistent, and the first step of the method is to establish consistency among the deductive consequences of the hypothesis to be justified. The second step is to attempt to provide grounds for the hypothesis by deducing it, in the same fashion, from some other hypothesis "above" which itself can be shown to yield only mutually consistent consequences. The procedure of justification is complete when an hypothesis has been reached which is "satisfactory," in the sense presumably of not itself requiring justification in turn. This interpretation was contrasted, we recall, with another in which "agrees with" is taken to mean "is deducible from," and in which the various hypotheses involved in the procedure at *Phaedo* 101D all are convertible with one another. This latter interpretation (the first examined in the preceding section) makes *Phaedo* 101D yield a method which quite plainly fits the mathematical level of the Divided Line. I have argued that the method indeed was one actually practiced by geometers among Plato's contemporaries, and that one of its features is that none of the chain of propositions deriving from its application is in a position to serve as a systematic justification of any other. This method accordingly is unable (as is mathematics generally, by Plato's description) to "rise above" and to provide an account of its own assumptions. Just as clearly as it fits the third level according to this interpretation, however, the method according to the other interpretation belongs to the top level of the Divided Line. Although the dialectician is not satisfied with mere consistency,[62] he is not satisfied either with anything less. Given that the necessary condition of consistency is met, the dialectician proceeds, according to *Phaedo* 101D (under this interpretation) as well as *Republic* 510B, to seek a justification of his hypothesis. And this justification involves, in some sense or another, the achievement of "higher" principles from which those to be

---

[62] *Republic* 510D, 533C.

justified follow as logical consequences.[63] To this extent, then, the method of *Phaedo* 101D and that of the dialectician of the Divided Line are indistinguishable. Thus one role served by the methodological descriptions in the *Republic*, whether Plato intended it this way or not, is to distinguish sharply between the two interpretations admitted by *Phaedo* 100A–101D. Left unclear in the *Phaedo* itself, the relation between these two interpretations is just the relation between the two top levels of the Divided Line.

For all this, we cannot simply identify the dialectician's procedure with the nonmathematical interpretation of *Phaedo* 101D and expect thereby to remove the puzzle about the nature of the reasoning involved in the "upward way." For one thing, more is involved in the dialectical method as described in the *Republic* than in the description at *Phaedo* 100A–101D. The former, unlike the latter, is claimed to rely only upon Forms or ideas (510B) as grounds for its treatment of hypotheses. And the former, unlike the latter, terminates in principles (or a principle) which are themselves nonhypothetical. Because of this, the dialectical method lays claim to a degree of certainty in its results that does not seem to belong to the method described in the earlier dialogue. Another reason is that the nature of the movement from challenged hypothesis to "higher" supporting hypotheses is not clear in the *Phaedo* description either. The problem remains of reaching some insight into what Plato was thinking about when he spoke of the mind's moving "upward" from its hypotheses to nonhypothetical first principles.

Robinson has distinguished, among other interpretations of this "upward" movement, what he calls the "mathematical theories," the "synthesis-theory," and the "intuition-theory." [64]

[63] *Phaedo* 101D; *Republic* 511B–C.

[64] *Plato's Earlier Dialectic*, pp. 162–77. A fourth, the "Phaedo-theory," that the "upward path" is identical with the method at *Phaedo* 101D, has already been discussed. After reviewing these several interpretations, Robinson comes to the same general conclusion as above: the

One form of mathematical theory is that the "upward path" is nothing more nor less than the method of geometrical analysis.[65] This has been effectively rebutted by Cherniss.[66] A more attractive suggestion of this sort is that what Plato had in mind is analogous to the process of axiomatization practiced by mathematicians, logicians, and to some extent by physical scientists today.[67] In this interpretation, the dialectician's procedure is to seek out a set of axioms or fundamental principles from which the propositions he hopes to justify can be deduced as consequences. The axioms themselves, however, would be nonhypothetical, in the sense that it would not be intelligible to question their adequacy within their own particular formal context. To justify the axioms themselves would be to establish a more inclusive context within which they in turn could be deduced. The "first principle[s] of all" (511B), accordingly, would be the axiom or set of axioms within a given context for which no further justification could intelligibly be sought. Attractive as this interpretation may seem, however, it scarcely could be what Plato had in mind. As Robinson points out,[68] the ideal of formal axiomatization was unknown in Plato's day, and those who practice it today have no concern, as Plato did, with the factual truth or falsehood of the axioms with which they begin. Axiomatization, moreover, is formal not only in the sense of being deductive but also in the sense of being indifferent to the particular meanings that

---

"upward way" *includes* the method at *Phaedo* 101D, but is not exhausted by it (p. 172).

[65] This has been argued by F. M. Cornford in "Mathematics and Dialectic in the *Republic* VI–VII," in R. E. Allen, *Studies in Plato's Metaphysics* (New York: Humanities Press, 1956).

[66] "Plato as Mathematician," *Review of Metaphysics*, 4 (1950–51): 395–425. A partial defense of Cornford in this regard may be found in Gulley's "Greek Geometrical Analysis." *Phronesis*, 3 (1958).

[67] Robinson, *Plato's Earlier Dialectic*, p. 168, attributes this theory to Stenzel.

[68] *Ibid.*, pp. 168–69.

might be attached to the symbols involved in the formalization. For Plato, on the other hand, what is important to the dialectician is not the linguistic symbols with which he operates but the meaning behind them.[69] It is the Form and not the formalization in which Plato's dialectician finds the ground upon which the truth of his conclusions is established. Moreover, there is not the slightest hint of axiomatization in any of the dialogues. If the method described in the heart of the *Republic* is to be conceived as more than a curious and dispensable excrescence, we are entitled to expect some evidence that Plato himself employed it, or tried to employ it, either in the dialogues themselves or in the teaching which the dialogues were intended to implement.[70]

Robinson's own interpretation is what he calls the "intuition-theory of the upward path." According to this theory, the dialectician's discovery of a nonhypothetical starting point amounts merely to an intuition of the truth and is the natural result of long and continued labors with the hypothetical procedures adumbrated at *Phaedo* 101D. The main difference between the dialectician of the *Republic* and the practitioner of the method of the *Phaedo* is that the former is concerned to reach certainty in his starting point; but the mode of procedure is essentially the same. As Robinson describes it, Plato

[69] Plato's mistrust of the written and spoken word is amply attested in the *Phaedrus* and the (perhaps spurious, but nonetheless informative) *Seventh Letter*.

[70] I would contend nonetheless that the dialectical method stemmed ultimately from considerations of mathematical reasoning, but I do not mean to imply either of two "unpleasant things" Robinson says must follow from this view (*Plato's Earlier Dialectic*, p. 167). Despite its origin, Plato's method at the top of the Divided Line obviously is not mathematical, and it is inconceivable that Plato thought it was. At the same time, I would deny that Plato "was dishonourably denying the mathematicians a credit he knew to be their due" (*ibid.*). *Phaedo* 100A–101D and *Meno* 86E–87A, according to my interpretation, give full credit to the mathematicians by being intelligible only against the background of geometrical analysis.

conceives that the dialectician takes an hypothesis and deduces its consequences, trying his hardest to discover some contradiction in those consequences. If he does discover one, the hypothesis is thereby refuted. He then takes another hypothesis, usually a modification of the first one designed to avoid the contradiction which refuted that. He then deduces the consequences of this second hypothesis, again trying his hardest to make it lead to a contradiction. He continues this process for a long time, making a great effort to be patient and thorough. Some day, after months or years of labour, he reflects that he has now been attempting to refute the same hypothesis for many weeks, and that this last hypothesis has endured every test and stood consistent in all its consequences, which he has deduced on every side as far as it seems possible to go. With this reflection (if he ever gets so far) it dawns on him that this hypothesis is certainly true, that it is no longer an hypothesis but an anhypotheton. (p. 173)

But this theory is obviously deficient. As a statement of formal procedure, Robinson's suggestion is indefensible, since no number of frustrated attempts to disprove an hypothesis amount to a demonstration of its truth. After many failures to detect an inconsistency in a hypothesis, the mathematician, logician, or dialectician might become *convinced* of its truth; but it might be false anyway. And this basic fact about demonstration surely was within Plato's grasp. Moreover, as a statement of informal procedure, Robinson's suggestion amounts merely to saying that the dialectician, after long study of an hypothesis, finally sees that it is true. And this scarcely amounts to a description of how the dialectician reaches a nonhypothetical starting point. If the word 'intuition' is felt to be pertinent here, its use at best accomplishes little more than a reformulation of the problem. If the dialectician's grasp of first principles is intuitive, our problem remains one of describing the procedure—the "upward way"—by which the intuition is to be achieved.

The "synthesis-theory," which Robinson attributes to Zeller among others, is that the "upward path" is the same as the method of synthesis or collection described in several later dialogues, and that the deductive "downward way" in some sense corresponds to the method of division.[71] The basis given for this opinion is that Plato would scarcely distinguish an upward and a downward path in the *Republic*, and two similarly opposed procedures in the *Phaedrus* and elsewhere, and mean something different in the two different contexts. Added to this is the fact that the *Republic* in various places uses language suggestive of collection and division.[72] Robinson, however, finds several reasons for disagreement with the synthesis-theory, the most important of which is that it provides no room within the Divided Line for the companion activity of division as actually practiced in the later dialogues.[73] The "downward path" in the *Republic* seems to be deductive; yet division in some sense is a matter of classification, and scarcely a matter of deductive proof. Moreover, Plato's statement at *Republic* 534B–C, that the dialectician "must be able to distinguish the essential nature of Goodness, isolating it from all other Forms," suggests strongly that division is part of the

[71] Collection and division are discussed extensively in chapters 3 and 4.

[72] Robinson, *Plato's Earlier Dialectic*, pp. 162–63.

[73] Several of Robinson's objections to the synthesis-theory are based on assumptions about the nature of collection and division which I cannot accept. He objects, for example, that the Good, as terminus of the "upward path," is probably not to be conceived "as being the *summum genus*" (p. 163); but I argue later that the outcome of collection is not to arrive at *genera* at all, and I have argued already that the Good is not the only proper terminus of the "upward way." He contends also that collection, being a form of generalization, "would surely have to be empirical. Generalization picks the universal out of the particulars given to sense." (*ibid.*) This opinion is flatly countered by the examples of collection given in the *Sophist*.

"upward way"; and various authorities are cited as being of this opinion.[74] But if division joins synthesis as part of the "upward way," then the analogy upon which the theory is based disappears. Robinson seems justified in his conclusion "that it would be very wide of the mark to say that the upward and downward paths mentioned in the Line were thought of by the author as consisting either essentially or mainly in synthesis and division respectively."[75]

What then are we to say regarding the nature of the "upward way"? I think it would be a mistake to seek clever new theories where the cleverest of the old have failed because they are far more *specific* than the text will support. The answer, it seems to me, is that Plato himself was not clear about what was involved in this phase of the dialectician's procedure. Just as, while writing *Phaedo* 100A–101D, he probably was not aware of the ambiguities which give rise to conflicting interpretations of that passage, so too in describing the Divided Line he probably was not prepared to say more precisely than he did just what procedures are involved in the "upward way." If, to the contrary, we assume that he was aware of the problems that have proven so perplexing to recent commentators, then we may assume also that he found no reason to anticipate these problems with specific answers in a context given over to a discussion which, from the beginning, is not expected to "reach the exact truth" (435D). Anyone convinced that Plato knew precisely what the technique of the "upward way" amounted to could do no better than seek evidence of Plato's thought in his practice in the later dialogues. It will not do, for such a person, to limit attention to prior dialogues, since Plato's thoughts on methodology obviously were undergoing considerable change between the time of the *Meno* and the time of the *Republic*. But in the later dialogues the "upward way" as such is not illustrated.

My suggestion is that the *Republic* represents a later and

---

[74] Proclus and Maier; Robinson, *Plato's Earlier Dialectic*, p. 164.
[75] *Ibid.*, p. 165.

more mature methodological phase than we find in the *Phaedo*, but that Plato while writing the *Republic* still was uncertain about matters of philosophic procedure. Although I agree with Robinson that Plato did not have collection and division precisely in mind in writing about the Divided Line, I agree also with his observation that

> it is clear from certain passages in the *Republic* that Plato was already thinking of something at least faintly like the synthesis and division of the *Phaedrus* as being activities proper to the dialectician; and it is fairly likely that he would have agreed, if asked, that these activities might sometimes aid the activities of the upward and downward paths.[76]

The path along which Plato is heading, in these discussions of method in the middle dialogues, leads directly to the method of collection and division. Evidence for this will come with an examination of important methodological developments in the *Theaetetus* and the *Sophist*. If we were to answer the question of the nature of the "upward path" in the *Republic* from the vantage points of these later dialogues, the answer would have to be that *both* collection and division are necessary parts of the procedure that enables the dialectician to render an "account of the essence of each thing" (534B) he undertakes to explain.

Where do we stand with Plato, methodologically, at the end of the middle period of philosophic activity? We are instructed by the *Phaedo* (1) that propositions (considerations, verbal formulations) can be justified or refuted on the basis of their relationships with other propositions (hypotheses) and that there are two relationships on the basis of which such criticism is possible, corresponding to what we call "entailment" and "consistency." We are told further (2) that the first step to take in defending an hypothesis that has come under ques-

---

[76] *Plato's Earlier Dialectic*, p. 165.

tioning is to make sure that the hypothesis admits no inconsistency among its consequences. And we are instructed (3) that the hypothesis should be justified by deducing it from other less problematic hypotheses which themselves can be shown to be consistent. Whether the relationship among consistent propositions in this method also includes mutual entailment is left ambiguous in the *Phaedo* but is cleared up emphatically in the *Republic*, where we are told (4) that the "higher" propositions which provide the account of one under question entail the latter but are not entailed by it in turn (as is the case with some forms of mathematical reasoning). Finally, we learn from the *Republic* (5) that the terminus of the dialectical procedure is in a starting point which itself stands beyond need of justification. No more than this is present in the methodological passages we have examined. But this is considerable in itself.

During the remainder of this study I shall refer to the procedure defined by these five points as "Plato's early method of hypothesis," or simply "the hypothetical method."

Let us follow in detail the workings of this method as Plato in the *Theaetetus* attacks the formidable problem of providing a defensible analysis of the concept of knowledge. If the method is adequate, it should be able to define the results of its own application. As we shall see, however, this test is satisfactorily met only by a refined procedure, described and illustrated in the *Sophist* as the method of collection and division. These matters are the concern of chapters II and III.

I I

The *Theaetetus*

1 / The Division of the Surds

A point too often overlooked in commentaries on the *Theaete-tus* is that an example of knowledge (contrasted with true opinion) is given at the beginning of the dialogue. The example is supplied not by Socrates but by his respondent, which in itself marks Theaetetus off from the respondents of the earlier dialogues. Meno, for instance, not only is unable to provide a definition of the sort Socrates asks for, but is unable even to understand the point of the examples Socrates offers. Theaetetus, on the other hand, not only is able to grasp immediately Socrates' distinction between giving instances and giving a definition, but is able to supply an example of such a definition out of his own mathematical experience. This sharp contrast in intellectual capacity between the soldier and the mathematician is a reflection of the contrast in accomplishment between their namesake dialogues. Apart from its forceful presentation of the doctrine of recollection, the *Meno*'s primary achievement is true opinion about the relation between virtue and true opinion.[1] The *Theaetetus*, on the other hand, aims at

---

[1] Both the "inner" dialogue with the slave boy and the "outer" dialogue with Meno himself end with the replacement of false by true (or somewhat truer) opinion in the mind of the respondent. The

and nearly achieves knowledge about the nature of knowledge itself.[2] This high aim is symbolized in Theaetetus' opening division of the lengths and surds (147E–148B).

Theaetetus and his friend, the young Socrates, have been listening to a demonstration by Theodorus that the sides of squares three and five square units in area are not commensurate in length with the unit itself, and that the same is the case with the sides of other areas through seventeen square units with the exception of four, nine, and sixteen. Discerning a common property which marks the former off from the latter, Theaetetus and young Socrates set about to define this property in a way which permits attribution to all lengths not commensurable with the unit which measures their squares.[3] Their procedure first was to divide all numbers into those which are equal to the product of a number multiplied by itself and those which are not. Numbers of the first sort were

---

absence of knowledge in either case is remarked at 85D and 100B. Plato warns us repeatedly throughout the *Meno* (71B, 79C, 79D, 86D–E) that the conditions of achieving knowledge about the subject under discussion are not met in the dialogue: one cannot inquire constructively about virtue, in its relation to learning, knowledge and opinion, until one knows what virtue itself is. Another warning that the results of the *Meno* fall short of knowledge is that Socrates "muddles matters" by "simultaneously discussing premiss and consequences" (*Phaedo* 101E) when he sets out to justify the hypothesis that virtue is knowledge before testing whether its consequences are consistent (see note 40, chapter I).

[2] It is argued in the following text that the *Theaetetus* fails to achieve a definition of knowledge that Plato could accept only because it fails to consider a fourth and entirely plausible sense of the term λόγος, according to which knowledge could be equated with true judgment accompanied by an account. By saying that Plato aimed at knowledge about knowledge, I mean to suggest only that he could scarcely have come so close without trying. Yet in another sense, he obviously was not trying, since he obviously was aware of this fourth meaning, carrying with it implications of the Forms.

[3] Discovery of the theorem on incommensurables in Euclid X.9 is attributed to Theaetetus alone, for which see Sir Thomas Heath, *A History of Greek Mathematics* (Oxford: Clarendon Press, 1921), 1:155.

conceived to be analogous to a square figure and were designated "squares," while those of the second were likened to what the Pythagoreans had called "oblong figures" and were designated "oblong numbers." Names then were given to the square roots of the numbers in the two classes thus distinguished. The numbers corresponding to the sides of the square figures with *squares* as areas were called "lengths," while numbers corresponding to the sides of square figures with *oblong numbers* as areas were called "roots." Thus the sides of squares with areas three, five, six, and so forth, in Theodorus' proofs would be classified as roots, and the sides of squares with areas four, nine, and sixteen would fall within the class of lengths. Theaetetus' achievement at first glance may appear to be little more than the provision of a general terminology. Yet he has pointed out necessary and sufficient conditions both for belonging to a class of integers (the "lengths") each member of which is commensurable with any other member, and for belonging to the complementary class (the "roots") no member of which is commensurable with any member of the former.[4] In the language of the *Sophist*, it may be said that Theaetetus has achieved a division of numbers according to Kinds. Such an achievement is knowledge in its most proper form, the prized result of the dialectician's skill.

It is important to note that the "roots," although not commensurable with the "lengths" in themselves, become commensurable with the "lengths" in their squares. The "roots" thus have the *power* to become commensurable with the "lengths," and the squares of members of the two classes com-

---

[4] A. E. Taylor says that the "roots" or "powers" have no common measure among themselves (*Plato: The Man and His Work* [London: Methuen & Co., 1926] p. 324). This is mistaken, since $\sqrt{3}$ and $\sqrt{27}$, for example, have a common measure, namely $\sqrt{3}$. It is true, of course, that the square roots of the prime numbers share no common measure, and Taylor considers only $\sqrt{3}$ and $\sqrt{5}$. But the square roots of *all* numbers save squares are included among the "roots."

prise the class of all integers. It is for this reason, probably, that Plato chose the term δύναμις to represent the "roots."

Now this use of δύναμις seems to be peculiar to Plato, and peculiar in particular to the *Theaetetus* itself.[5] It is reasonable to surmise that Plato chose this term for the "roots" in this context because of their capacity to take on an important characteristic when considered from a higher level which they do not possess on their own level alone.[6] The "roots" have the power to become commensurate with the "lengths" when raised to the *second* power (as we would say), or squared. And as Theaetetus remarks, somewhat as an afterthought, another distinction of the same sort can be made "in the case of solids" (148B). This is to say that another natural division can be made between numbers which are commensurable among themselves (the cube roots of eight, twenty-seven, and so forth), and those which are commensurable with the others only in their third powers (the cube roots of all integers not themselves cubes of integers). These "solid numbers" (three powers corresponding to three "dimensions") also have the *power* to take on characteristics relative to a higher level which they do not have in themselves.

A further indication that this use of δύναμις was deliberately chosen comes with its next occurrence, for the context of this second occurrence parallels Theaetetus' example of the "roots" in a respect which is essential to the interpretation of the first section of the dialogue. In the "esoteric" theory of perception ironically attributed to Protagoras (156A–157C), the two kinds of motion which alone constitute the perceptible

---

[5] Taylor observes that this use of δύναμις "was presumably an experiment in language which did not perpetuate itself." (*ibid.*) When the term appears again at *Sophist* 247E, it carries no apparent mathematical connotation.

[6] Although Plato puts the words in the mouth of the discoverer of the general formula for the "roots," the discovery is represented as having been quite recent (147D), and there is no reason to make Theaetetus use the same terminology as would come to be used commonly in later discussions of his finding. Plato is free to use a term to designate the "roots" which serves his purposes at the moment.

universe are described as being nothing but powers of acting and powers of being acted upon. It is a feature of this theory that these powers in themselves are totally irrational, and can be "given an account" only from the vantage point of a higher context. Let us turn to examine this theory in detail.

2 / Constitution of the Theory of Perception

Theaetetus' tentative proposal (α) that knowledge is identical with (nothing but) perception is immediately compared with the famous saying of Protagoras, (β) "man is the measure of all things—alike of the being of things that are and of the not-being of things that are not" (152A).[7] Both hypotheses are introduced to be eventually rejected, and their relationship at the outset appears obscure. Even if it could be established that man is the measure of all things, in some plausible sense of the epigram, it would not follow immediately that perception is knowledge. Nor, conversely, could the falsehood of (α) be deduced from the falsehood of (β). Thus there is no immediate logical relationship of consequence between the two. Moreover, the saying of Protagoras, introduced as it is within the dialogue soon after Theaetetus' discussion of his proof that there are two classes of things which have *no* common measure, is made to seem improbable from the first.[8] What purpose is served by shifting attention from the hypothesis to be tested, that knowledge is perception, to another hypothesis which not only is logically independent of the first but which moreover is not even initially tenable in the context of the dialogue?

The answer here is that the two hypotheses have at least one

[7] The translator of passages quoted from the *Theaetetus* and the *Sophist* is F. M. Cornford.

[8] If the statement that man is the measure of all things is taken literally, it follows that man is the measure both of "lengths" and "roots." Hence, contrary to what Theaetetus had shown, "lengths" and "roots" would have a common measure. This consequence is absurd; so, accordingly, is a strict interpretation of (β).

of their necessary conditions in common.[9] There are certain
assumptions about the nature of perceptual objects, and of
the perceiver's relation to them, which must be granted if
Protagoras' saying is to take on even an initial plausibility.
These same assumptions are necessary also to any conception
of the perceptual act and its object that will provide a credible
rendering of Theaetetus' hypothesis that knowledge is perception. The truth of a statement of these assumptions is thus a
necessary condition of the truth of either hypothesis. To say
that the two hypotheses have a necessary condition in common, of course, is not necessarily to say anything about equivalence or even about logical compatibility. Two assertions
might share necessary conditions but have entirely different
(even incompatible) sufficient conditions, and hence be entirely
distinct in their claims. That the two share a necessary condition, however, is enough warrant for their juxtaposition,
since uncovering this condition for Protagoras' hypothesis provides the same service for that of Theaetetus.

The necessary condition in question here is one regarding
infallibility. As Socrates remarks in his speech following
(152C), perception, insofar as it is knowledge, must be infallible. That is, one of the "marks" of knowledge [10] is that

[9] Taylor seems to have seen something of this (*Plato: The Man
and His Work*, p. 330), although he is wrong in saying both are
justified by the same considerations of perceptual relativity. Gulley
may have seen this also, as indicated by his remark that it follows
from Protagoras' thesis "that perception is infallible, which is assumed in the claim that knowledge is perception." (N. Gulley, *Plato's
Theory of Knowledge* [London: Methuen & Co., 1962], p. 77) But
he is probably wrong in reading 152A as a statement of equivalence
between the two hypotheses. It is shown below that the two are
distinct in their consequences; hence Plato probably would not have
agreed "that the claim that knowledge is perception implies acceptance of the thesis of Protagoras that 'man is the measure of all
things'" (*ibid.*).

[10] To mention a "mark" of knowledge is not to define it, but to set
a requirement which an adequate definition must meet. A mark may be
discerned where a definition is unobtainable, as δύναμις is established as
a mark of the real (τὰ ὄντα) at *Sophist* 247E.

it is infallible, and if we are to uphold the claim that knowledge is perception then we must be prepared to maintain also
that perception is infallible with regard to its object. A similar
requirement holds for the defense of Protagoras' thesis. If
man indeed is the measure of all things, then all things are
determined in their properties by their relationship to man
(a man, or men), and there is no criterion more ultimate
which can override what is disclosed in that relationship. Thus,
again, the maintenance of Protagoras' thesis requires that we
admit an infallibility of some sort in man's relationship to objects of which he becomes aware. The requirements of the two
theses are merged into one by Plato's limitation of Protagoras'
claim, in the immediately following passages, to the range of
perceptual awareness. Both (α) and (β), thereby, are made
to rely upon the further thesis (σ) that man's awareness of
perceptual objects is infallible with reference to the properties
which it discloses.

Now the conception which blocks acceptance of (σ) most
forcefully is the conception that objects might have determinate properties which are independent of what appears to man
in his awareness of them. If, for example, we think that the
wind "really is" warm, then when it appears cool in our perception of it we consider this perception to be deceptive and
thereby fallible. The only way to assure that perception is infallible is to abandon the conception that objects might have
properties the determination or "measure" of which is independent of man's awareness. By this stage, the reader may
have become impatient with vague references to "man's awareness," as if all men had the same perceptual awareness, and as
if every man had the same awareness from moment to moment. The reaction of common sense to considerations of this
sort, indeed, would be to insist that any normal person has
reliable as well as deceptive perceptions, and has both quite
frequently. If this is the case, then some perceptions may qualify for the title "knowledge" and others may not; but there is
no need in any case to question the general conception that

perceptual objects have determinate properties independently
of our perception of them. The answer to this potential objection is that Plato too will limit the range of perception which
might be identical with knowledge, but that he has not yet
done so. It is part of Protagoras' claim, however, that a man
is infallible in *all* his perceptions and, moreover, that *all* men
are thus infallible. And the consequence of this general claim
is that all (human) perceptions are infallible, which in turn
requires the rejection of the conception that objects might have
properties other than those disclosed in our perceptual awareness of them at some given moment.

There follows in the text, accordingly, a series of arguments in favor of the conception that feelings of chill (152B),
colors (153D–154B), and the so-called "primary qualities"—
or "quantities"—of size and equality (154C–155C) are dependent for their determination upon the perceiver as well as
upon the perceived object. These are arguments, in short,
against the common notion that objects of perception have
properties which are independent of all perceptual circumstances. There is no pretense that these arguments *prove* the
contrary of that notion. And there is no conclusive reason in
the immediate context to believe that Plato accepts the relativity of perceptual objects indicated by these arguments in
anything more than a provisional way.[11] The point of these

---

[11] F. M. Cornford argues, in *Plato's Theory of Knowledge* (London: Routledge & Kegan Paul, 1935), p. 49, that Plato himself must
accept the theory of perception developed in 156A–157C, because
it would have been pointless for Plato to show that knowledge is
not perception in terms of a conception of the latter other than his
own. This reasoning is shown inconclusive below. Runciman, on the
other hand, argues that Plato could not have accepted this theory,
since a "Berkeleyan position of this kind . . . would be incompatible
with the Theory of Forms" (W. G. Runciman, *Plato's Later Epistemology* [Cambridge: Cambridge University Press, 1962], p. 19). His
argument is that Plato "certainly never thought that, for instance, the
whiteness of snow did not exist unless white snow was somewhere
being looked at by somebody" (*ibid.*) Runciman deserves credit for
pointing out the likeness between this theory and Berkeley's; but his
argument, insofar as intelligible, confuses the Form Whiteness with

arguments is merely to show the consequences of Protagoras' hypothesis for our conception of the nature of perception and of the nature of the perceptual object. At this stage in the dialogue we are merely examining some of the necessary conditions for maintaining Protagoras' hypothesis, and the arguments from 152B through 155C are intended to explicate important aspects of these conditions. Insofar as these conditions overlap those of the still unclarified claim that knowledge is perception, we are examining also the consequences we must be prepared to accept if we accept this latter hypothesis.

The first argument (152B–C) takes its departure from an implied distinction between the wind in itself, which can be called "the same [τοῦ αὐτοῦ]" (152B), and the chill we perceive in its presence. Cases in which the "same wind" feels different to different people, or different to the same person at different times, lead to the question of the relationship between the wind in itself and the properties which appear in our perception of it. Designating the wind itself 'X', the property of being chilly 'k', and the property of lacking chill (being warm or thermally indifferent) 'm', we may set up a series of four mutually exclusive and exhaustive ways in which m and k might relate to X. The two possibilities which have most to recommend them from a logical point of view are (1) that X is k and not-m (the wind is chilly), or (2) that X is m and not-k (the wind is not chilly). Protagoras, however, cannot accept either of these alternatives, since each gives precedence to one sensible quality over its opposite. A consequence of his position, as we have seen, is that human awareness is infallible with regard to all properties disclosed within it; and since the wind appears to have both properties k and m, neither (1),

the apparent whiteness of actual visual perception. I am inclined toward the judgment of H. Cherniss, that "Plato accepts this unceasing flux as a characteristic of all phenomenal existence" ("The Philosophical Economy of the Theory of Ideas," *American Journal of Philology,* 57 [1936]:445–56; reprinted in Allen, *Studies in Plato's Metaphysics,* p. 9).

which denies m, nor (2), which denies k, is admissible. Theaetetus' hypothesis, moreover, is bound by the same consequence of perceptual infallibility. Thus we find (1) and (2) explicitly rejected by both Protagoras and Theaetetus at 152B, where they opt for a third alternative (3) that X is both k and m.[12] From the logical point of view, however, (3) is necessarily false, which presumably leads Socrates to speak of Protagoras' thesis as a dark saying provided for the public from whom the truth of his doctrine remained a secret. (152C) The remaining alternative is (4) that X is neither k nor m, which of course is equally untenable on logical grounds. The apparent consequence is that Protagoras cannot accept any of the four alternatives and in the interests of consistency must reject the very distinction between X in itself and the properties k and m upon which the alternatives are based. This way out, in fact, is suggested by (4), inasmuch as there are two interpretations which can be put upon the denial that X is either k or m. The interpretation which lines up with the three other alternatives is to think of X as an independent and determinate object including neither k nor m among its "real properties." It is this interpretation which is logically objectionable, since m is merely the absence of k, and any determinate object is characterized either by chill or by its absence. The other interpretation, however, is logically acceptable, and this is to think of X as having no independent and determinate properties in itself, neither k nor m nor any other. If X has no "real properties," then it is not only consistent but necessary to think of X as being in itself neither k nor m.

This is precisely the point of the "secret doctrine" which Protagoras is alleged (facetiously) to have reserved for his disciples, but which in the immediately following passage is

[12] The qualification that the wind is cold or otherwise *to* the person who feels it to be so is important for the conclusion at 152C that perceptions of hot and cold are infallible. But it does not alter the contention that the same wind in this case *is* both cold and not cold. At 152B Socrates is still discussing the properties of the wind in itself, which in Protagoras' view are equated with appearances.

represented as "secret" (among philosophers and poets) only
from Parmenides. The "secret doctrine" belongs to Protagoras
only in the sense that it has been shown to be a consequence of
his dictum that man is the measure of all things. Plato's first
statement of the doctrine is an adaption instead from Heraclitus:

> All the things we are pleased to say 'are', really are in proc-
> ess of becoming, as a result of movement and change and
> of blending one with another. We are wrong to speak of
> them as 'being', for none of them ever is; they are always
> becoming. (152D–E)

The result of the distinction between X in itself and the determinate properties k and m, capable of only four possible
combinations which are equally objectionable from Protagoras'
point of view, has been the rejection from that point of view
of the very distinction itself.[13] Preparatory to a fuller and more
adequate statement of this result, Plato moves on to disclose
similar logical difficulties in connection with color and the
"primary qualities" of size and shape.

In the second argument, regarding color properties, Socrates suggests that we "follow out our recent statement and
lay it down that there is no single thing that is in and by
itself" (153E). The consequence here is that black and white
and other colors in themselves are neither in the eye of the beholder nor without it, for in either case they would have a
fixed place and hence in some sense would have being as
against mere becoming. No color exists independently of per-

[13] The "hypothesis" that the wind is distinct from its properties
leads to inconsistent consequences from Protagoras' point of view.
Socrates, in the passages immediately following, presents the different hypothesis that "nothing is *one* thing just by itself" (152D
[translator's emphasis]) and that, hence, there is nothing distinct in
itself from the various ways it appears. This may be an application
of the hypothetical method taken over from the *Phaedo* and the
Republic. If so, however, it falls short of being obvious. Clearer applications abound later in the dialogue.

ception; each color rather is the result of a momentary encounter between a particular percipient and a particular object of perception. As such, each color is a moment in a perceptual process of becoming and has no being independently of that process. "What we say 'is' this or that colour will be neither the eye which encounters the motion nor the motion which is encountered, but something which has arisen between the two and is peculiar to each several percipient." (153E–154A)

The argument for this claim in the present context is extremely concise; and it applies not only to color, but retrospectively to perceptions of hot and cold and prospectively to perceptions of size. Interestingly enough, it is an argument later to be applied by Berkeley to much the same end. The argument holds for any perceptual quality n which is claimed to be a property of X considered in itself, independently of the conditions of being perceived. If n belongs to X in itself, then a change with respect to n will be a change in X. But it is a matter of ordinary perceptual experience that n can alter without any change in what has been conceived as X in itself (apart from the way X appears). In particular, the color which appears to characterize an object can be altered in any number of ways without altering the object itself, as when we view the object with and without the intervention of colored lenses, in bright daylight or in dusk, or under the effects of jaundice; or the color can be altered merely by causing the object to be viewed by different persons under manifestly different perceptual circumstances. As Socrates says, if the thing which man measures were really "large or white or hot, it would never become different the moment it encountered a different person, supposing it to undergo no change in itself" (154B). The alternatives between which one must choose in these circumstances are (1) that n is not a property of X after all or (2) that X changes with every change in n. Insofar as n does appear to be a property of X, however, and insofar as there is available no more ultimate consideration by which the measure of what appears to man might be overruled, Protagoras cannot accept (1). Neither, for similar reasons, can Theaetetus, as long as he chooses to defend the hypothesis that knowledge is perception, with its consequence (necessary condition) (σ) that perception is infallible. Thus (2) alone is open, with its far-reaching implications regarding the nature of perception and its relation to the perceptual object. The conclusion, again under the conditions being examined, is that no distinction can be made between the way objects appear to perceivers and the way they are in themselves. Like the contents of our perceptions, the "objects themselves" which we perceive have no determinate structure independent of perception, but instead undergo variation relative to each particular set of perceptual circumstances.

The third argument, regarding quantitative comparisons of size and shape, is complex and hard to unravel, particularly in the absence of a clear conception of the purpose of the argument in its immediate context.[14] The purpose of the argument is to show that the very notion of objects remaining identical to themselves from moment to moment must be relinquished if we are to maintain consistently either that man is the measure of all things or that knowledge is perception. This purpose is achieved by stirring up a fight among common notions regarding relationships of number and size.

Propositions of two sorts figure in this set-to, neither group of which in isolation threatens to cause any trouble. On one hand, there is a series of three quite general assertions which give the appearance at first of being necessary truths, containing no reference in particular to dice or to Socrates' size, but apparently applicable to these things. On the other hand, there is a series of three particular assertions about what seems to

[14] Cornford (*Plato's Theory of Knowledge*, p. 43) asks in bewilderment: "What is the point of these alleged puzzles? Though Socrates continues: 'Do you begin to understand why these things are so, according to the doctrine we are attributing to Protagoras?' nothing more is said about them in the following context, which analyses the process of sense-perception." Cornford's question and that of Socrates are answered in the following text.

be the case regarding the quantity of a group of dice. As Socrates points out (155B), however, directly comparable assertions could be made regarding his own height, or with regard to countless other examples just as convincing as these. Since the three corresponding assertions in connection with Socrates' height are more explicitly stated, let us use these to set up a fight among the general propositions. The aim in comparing these propositions is to determine whether "they agree or are altogether inconsistent" (154E).[15]

First we may assert, on the basis of what appears to be the case (155B–C), that when compared at different times with a growing boy (a) Socrates neither gains nor loses in stature during the interval. Because of the boy's growth during that time, however, (b) Socrates becomes shorter, which in a sense is to say he becomes (either greater or) less than before. Consequently, since he is later what he was not before, (c) Socrates (in some sense) has changed.[16] All these admissions *appear* to be correct; hence none can be relinquished under the hypothesis currently being examined. Yet these admissions turn out to involve inconsistencies when thrown against three assertions we would initially want to admit, not only with respect to Socrates, but with respect to all objects which we conceive as being self-identical through space and time. We would want to admit (1) "that nothing can become greater or less, either in size or in number, so long as it remains equal to itself" (155A). We would assert moreover (2) "that a thing to which nothing is added and from which nothing is taken away is neither increased nor diminished, but always remains

---

[15] The expression ἀλλήλοις συμφωνεῖ at 154E is identical with that at *Phaedo* 101D, where Socrates outlines the first stage of the procedure for testing the adequacy of a disputed hypothesis.

[16] This last statement "fights" with the three admissions between 155A and 155B, stated in the following text, as indicated in Socrates' summary of the paradox: "For apparently I am later what I was not before, and yet have not become so; for without the process of becoming the result is impossible, and I could not be in process of becoming shorter without losing some of my bulk." (155C)

the same in amount" (155A). And we would say finally (3)
"that a thing which was not at an earlier moment cannot be at
a later moment without becoming and being in process of becoming" (155B). These latter three assertions, when applied
to Socrates in particular, may be formalized in terms of (a),
(b), and (c) above, with the one additional proposition (d)
that Socrates remains equal to, or the same as, himself. That
is, given the interpretations

(a) Socrates neither gains nor loses in stature,
(b) Socrates becomes either greater or less,
(c) Socrates is at a later moment what he was not before,
(d) Socrates remains equal to or the same as himself,

the three general propositions applied to Socrates may be formalized:

(1) (d) only if not-(b)
(2) (a) only if (d)
(3) (c) only if not-(d)

Since both Protagoras and Theaetetus are committed by their
hypotheses (entailing that what *appears* to be *is* the case) to
assert (a), they are committed by their additional acceptance
(155A) of (1) and (2) to assert not-(b). Moreover, by their
acceptance (155A–B) of (2) and (3) they are committed to
assert not-(c). But it was noted at the beginning of the argument that they must accept (b) and (c) as well as (a).
Thus, as long as Protagoras and Theaetetus accept (a), (b)
and (c), as required by their hypotheses, and in addition accept
the apparently "necessary" general assertions (1), (2) and
(3), they are caught in flat contradiction, both asserting and
denying (b) and (c).

Moving into the passage in which the three warring propositions are stated, Socrates announced his intention of studying "the notions we have in our own minds . . . [to] find
out what they are and whether, when we compare them, they
agree [ἀλλήλοις συμφωνεῖ] or are altogether inconsistent"

(154E). And now we find that these three admissions "fight among themselves in our minds when we make those statements about the dice" (155B), or when we make the corresponding statements about Socrates and his height, or when such assertions are made in connection with "countless other examples" (155C) which we would have to accept insofar as we accepted those above. After this onslaught of logical manipulation Theaetetus is left quite dizzy, so that when Socrates asks shortly whether he sees "the explanation of all this which follows from the theory we are attributing to Protagoras" (155D), he can only say that he does not. Yet when the conflicts among these propositions are explicitly formalized, the consequences are easily seen. The privileged assertion (b) could be preserved by relinquishing (1), and (c) could be saved by relinquishing (3). The two could be preserved together, however, if only (2) were rejected, and this is just what happens in the theory about to be laid out in detail.[17] Instead of admitting, as in (2), that a thing always remains the same as itself when nothing is added to or subtracted from it, Socrates will now describe a theory according to which nothing in the realm of perception, under any conditions, remains equal to itself from one moment to the next. This theory has features taken from the consequences of each of the three arguments we have been examining. From the argument about the chilly wind we obtain the conception that no distinction is to be made between the so-called object in itself and its perceived properties. The argument about color properties suggests this also, but suggests further that objects are dependent for whatever perceptual features they have upon other factors in the perceptual environment. The argument of the warring propositions, finally, suggests a conception of objects according to which they maintain no self-identity from one mo-

---

[17] Both Protagoras and Theaetetus are committed to (a), on the basis of their acceptance of the thesis (σ) that appearances are infallible. Thus the contradiction cannot be removed merely by denying the antecedent of (2).

ment to the next. These consequences are the necessary conditions for maintaining either the Protagorean thesis or that of Theaetetus, and all these consequences are built into the radical and very imaginative theory which immediately follows.[18]

The "first principle" of this theory, upon which "all that we said just now depends, is that the universe really is motion and nothing else" (156A). That is, to render consistent the various conflicting admissions Theaetetus and (supposedly) Protagoras have made, the hypothesis that the universe is nothing but motion is required. These various conflicts have been seen to stem from the initial hypotheses of these two advocates. Theaetetus' hypothesis is (a) that knowledge is identical with perception, while Protagoras is committed to the claim (β) that man is the measure of all things. Thus the theory of perception is presented as a condition under which alone the two hypotheses can be brought into logical consistency with other propositions admitted by all involved in the discussion. In short, it is a necessary condition, shared by the two hypotheses (a) and (β), that what is "real" in the world of perception is in constant change, becoming different from moment to moment, and constituted in all that it becomes so that each object of perception is infallibly coupled with its corresponding perceptual act. Thus (a) and (β) are brought into relationship with the third major hypothesis involved in this part of the dialogue, the claim attributable to Heraclitus (γ) that all things are in a process of change, or becoming.

Only these among the details of the theory are essential.

---

[18] Having found the consequences of the "hypothesis" (2) (that a thing remains the same as itself when nothing is added to nor subtracted from it) inconsistent with other theses to which both Protagoras and Theaetetus are committed by their respective doctrines, Socrates moves on to a different hypothesis under which these inconsistencies will not appear. This new hypothesis also avoids the inconsistencies disclosed in the previous arguments regarding the chilly wind and color properties. The new hypothesis, of course, is the so-called theory of perception presented at 156A–157C.

The rest of the theory may be presumed to be an intimation of Plato's own opinion regarding something of which knowledge, in his view, would be impossible—the "real nature" of the world of becoming. It appears likely, in short, that Plato subscribes to the outlines of this theory himself. But it is a mistake, nonetheless, to argue that Plato is *required* by the structure of the argument to uphold this theory of perception as his own. Cornford argues to this effect by pointing out that Plato aims to refute the hypothesis that knowledge is perception, and that for this purpose "he is bound to give us what he believes to be a true account of the nature" of the objects of perception.[19] Since it would be futile to take what someone else believes to be the nature of perception and of its object, and then to show that *this* is inconsistent with the claim of perception to be knowledge, Plato "states his own doctrine and takes it as established for the purposes of the whole subsequent criticism of perception." [20] The trouble with this argument is that it misses entirely the hypothetical character of the entire discussion up to this point in the dialogue. Let us briefly review the development of the dialogue thus far.

Theaetetus opened this dialectical sequence by proposing for discussion, in an obviously tentative fashion (151D–E), the hypothesis (α) that knowledge and perception are identical. Protagoras' famous dictum, (β) that man is the measure of all things, was introduced as a well-known thesis which is parallel to what Theaetetus has proposed in at least one essential respect: both claims have as a necessary condition that perception is infallible with regard to its object. In order to show that this is a necessary condition of both (α) and (β), Socrates has taken Theaetetus through a series of logically complex arguments, the cumulative effect of which is to provide the framework of the theory of perception which Cornford claims must, because of the structure of the argument, be Plato's own. But all that has been shown thus far is that cer-

[19] Cornford, *Plato's Theory of Knowledge*, p. 49.
[20] *Ibid.*

tain central features of the theory of perception represent the
claim (σ) that perception is infallible regarding its objects,
which is a necessary condition for the truth of hypotheses (a)
and (β). The relationship between (a) and these features of
the theory is merely that if (a) is true so must (σ) be also.
Now plainly, it is not necessary in order to refute (a) that (σ)
be taken as true in any sense whatsoever. Indeed, (a) would
be refuted if (σ) were shown false. As Cornford rightly remarks, however, (σ) is not criticized in the dialogue.[21] The
way Plato refutes (a) instead is to draw out *another* of its necessary conditions (later in the dialogue after this hypothesis
has been separated from Protagoras') and then to show that
this further condition cannot be met. It is simply a mistake,
and in fact a rather basic mistake, to think that Plato must
affirm the theory of perception in order to achieve a meaningful rejection of Theaetetus' hypothesis.

Now it is a consequence of the "first principle" of this
theory that no characteristic whatsoever can be properly attributed to "what really is." If the universe really is motion
and nothing else, then not even motion itself is a *property* of
what is. The effect of the principle, that is to say, is not to
claim with the atomists that everything real is *in* motion,
for that would be to allow that there are characteristics of
"what is" beyond motion with reference to which the things
that move might be identified. No distinction is allowed here
between motion and "what is," for only motion exists. All
properties we commonly think of as attached to "objects in
themselves"—such as color, shape, solidity, extension through
perceptual space, and even apparent motion itself—are merely
derivatives from the intercourse among motions and as such
are transitory and dependent for what existence they have upon
the basic motions themselves.

The first distinction drawn within the theory is between
two kinds of motion, one the power of acting, the other the

power of being acted upon. This distinction is not absolute, however, since a motion which acts in one encounter might be acted upon in another (157A). Thus, for example, a motion constitutive of what we call an "eyeball" might contribute passively in one perceptual encounter, when the person with the eyeball looks at a stone, and contribute actively in another, when someone else looks at the eyeball itself.[22] The result of the intercourse between active and passive motions in such perceptual situations is the production of other motions of an entirely different sort. Thus there is a second distinction within the theory between motions of the two parental types and motions which are their continually generated offspring. Motions of the first sort are termed "slow" and produce their offspring "without change of place and with respect to what comes within" (156C) their range. The generated motions, on the other hand, are "quicker, inasmuch as they move from place to place and their motion consists in change of place" (156D). The point of this distinction seems to be that the parent motions exercise their activity or passivity within a relatively fixed locale, interacting with one after another of their opposite numbers to generate offspring, while the offspring themselves not only are short-lived but appear to be forever flitting from one locale to another. The exceptional case here would be one in which an observer is staring intently at one object for an extended period of time and in which, consequently, the generated motions all appear roughly within the same place.[23]

[22] The organ which, as we might say, "does the looking" is acted upon by the seen object and hence is passive. Both organ and seen object, however, are only collections of motions.

[23] An exception in the other extreme would arise when one set of parent motions (the perceiving organ or the thing seen) is moving rapidly with respect to the other, in which case the parent motions might be as "fast" as the offspring. In the normal case, however, both perceiving organ and things seen are relatively stable, and the organ interacts with a sequence of different things, resulting in a constantly changing series of offspring.

The most important aspect of this theory in its present context, however, is the way in which the offspring motions are generated in pairs which cannot be separated into independent elements. One twin of the pair is always a perception, such as we might commonly designate 'seeing', 'hearing', and so forth. The other twin is always a characteristic, such as color or sound, which is associated with its counterpart as object of perception. Each object, moreover, occurs only with its own correlative perception, and each perception can have only its own twin as object. This is the feature of the theory which provides perception its infallibility. Since each object of perception—each color, each sound, and each shape—appears only in conjunction with its own perception, the perception itself is in turn the only source through which any aspect of its object can be revealed. Since no perception could disclose anything which could bear upon, or in any way tend to correct, what is disclosed by any other perception, each is the sole, and hence the final, criterion by which its own object is determined. Thus perception is given the infallibility with respect to its object which it must possess if it is to exhibit this necessary mark of knowledge, and Protagoras is provided a sense in which each man is the measure of what appears to him, at least in the perceptual realm.

There are at least two respects already evident, however, in which Protagoras' thesis is headed for trouble. One is that, according to the theory of perception, it is no more correct to say that man is the measure of all things which appear to him than it is to say that all things which appear to a given man are the measure of the man himself. This is a consequence of the fact that any given perception is as closely bound to its object as the object to the perception, both being "twin offspring" of the active and passive slow motions. What is perceived always is a fast motion, inseparably joined with another fast motion that is the perception in which it is revealed. Although the slow motions are the *causes* of perception, they themselves are never perceived. Thus, insofar as a thing is

conceived as perceivable, it must be conceived as nothing
more than a collection of fast motions; similarly, insofar as a
thing is conceived as capable of perceiving, it must be conceived as a collection of the "twins" accompanying these perceived objects. But since the "twins" within each pair are inseparable, one is as much the measure of the other as the other
of the one. The consequence is that a man, as a thing capable
of perception, is no more the measure of what he perceives
than the object is the measure of the man.[24] This is a consequence which Protagoras probably would not have been happy
to accept.

The second incipient difficulty for the Protagorean thesis
is that, although each object of perception has its own measure, no two objects have a common measure. Thus, insofar
as Protagoras maintained that there is one thing (a man) or
many things (men) each of which measures all things, this
claim turns out to be incompatible with the theory of perception. For the very things for which man's perception can
properly be claimed to be a measure are such that no two of
them are measured by the same perception or by the totality
of perceptions of a given man over a given time. And clearly
it is the case that all things cannot be measured by different
men with different perceptions. The objects of perception thus
share with the surds of the opening mathematical example
the feature of being without a common measure, and hence
ultimately "irrational." It is indeed likely that Plato intended
the reader to make this association, for the same word

[24] We are told at 157C that men and physical objects are assemblages of motions, but it remains uncertain whether these assemblages
include only fast motions or fast and slow motions alike. There are
passages, indeed, which indicate that slow motions are part of both
types of assemblages; for example 159C, where it is said that Socrates well and Socrates ill have different offspring. It is clear,
at any rate, that only fast motions are perceptions and objects of
perception. The man who measures the object of perception is not
the man composed of slow motions, for slow motions do not perceive. Being essentially an assemblage of fast motions, the man who
measures is measured equally by his objects of perception.

(δύναμις) used earlier for the surds is used here to name the motions in the theory of perception. This parallel will be used to support a further implicit comparison later in the dialogue. Although the surds are not commensurable on their own level, they become commensurable in their squares. Similarly, although the objects of perception have no common measure among themselves, they do become comparable on the higher level of true opinion, as evident in the images of the wax block and the aviary.

Following the statement of the theory of perception there are some fairly lengthy passages in which several possible objections of a common sort are introduced. If each perception is the sole adequate measure of its object, and hence infallible, then all perceptions are equally "correct" or "true." Yet do we not commonly suppose that madmen, dreamers, and people who are sick with various disorders, perceive what is not the case, and hence perceive "falsely" or "incorrectly"? The answer to objections of this sort is merely to draw out more explicitly the consequences of the theory, that each perceptual object is matched with one and only one perception, and vice versa. Socrates when asleep indeed becomes aware of different perceptual objects than Socrates when awake, and so again does Socrates when ill, and so forth. But by this very fact, Socrates asleep is a different person from Socrates awake, and both are different from Socrates ill and from Socrates in any other condition at any other time. For Socrates awake is a collection of motions, including his perceptions in that condition, and Socrates asleep is a collection of different motions, and hence a different thing. What appears to Socrates in one condition is just as "true" as what appears under any other condition, for there is no common measure by which these things might be compared. Thus, says Socrates, "my perception is true for me; for its object at any moment is my reality . . ." (160C). I am, moreover, "infallible and make no mistake in my state of mind about what is or becomes . . ." (160D).

Thus perception seems on first accounting to have the necessary marks of knowledge, and Theaetetus was "perfectly right in saying that knowledge is nothing but perception . . ." (160D). The hypothesis that knowledge is perception, moreover, seems to coincide with that of Protagoras, that man is the measure of all things, and both seem to fall in line with that of Heraclitus that "all things move like flowing streams . . ." (160D). What remains for this section of the dialogue is to test Theaetetus' offspring, thus fleshed out, for viability, and in the process to make it part company with the companions which have joined it in the process of delivery.

3 / Limitation of Theaetetus' Hypothesis

Exposition of the theory of perception is followed by a series of arguments, the last two of which refute Theaetetus' hypothesis that knowledge and perception are identical. There are several tasks to be accomplished by the earlier arguments, however, before this hypothesis itself is subjected to serious criticism. For one, accounts have to be settled with both the Protagorean and the Heraclitean hypotheses, thus far treated without being distinguished from that of Theaetetus. Before it can be distinguished from these others, moreover, the hypothesis that knowledge is perception must be made more specific, for there are several senses of the term ἐπιστήμη (corresponding to several senses of 'knowledge') which it would be wholly implausible to identify in meaning with αἴσθησις. At least part of the purpose behind the apparently frivolous arguments between 163A and 165E is to draw attention to certain of these irrelevant senses, and to forestall any misguided attempt to refute Theaetetus by showing that knowledge in some one of these senses is not perception.

First in the series, however, is an argument which key-

notes the entire remaining discussion up to the second section
of the dialogue. This argument not only previews the difficulties upon which each of the three hypotheses in turn will
founder, but also serves notice that in dealing with claims of
such importance we must strive for conclusive proofs and not
be satisfied with abusive arguments or arguments from mere
plausibility. The common difficulty is that the very features
which provide infallibility for perception itself render each of
the hypotheses incapable of providing a basis for *judgment* (infallible or otherwise) about the objects of perception. As
already indicated in the parallel between the surds and the
motions, individual objects of perception are incommensurable. By themselves they cannot even enter into judgments
of comparison, to say nothing of being compared infallibly.
Yet Protagoras, as we soon see, is driven to a position
where he must rely upon the possibility of judgments comparing these objects of perception. For there is no other way
in which Protagoras can explain, consistently with his claim
that each man is the measure of what appears, the sense in
which he is wiser than other men, or indeed the sense in
which any man is wiser than a pig or baboon. In response
to the insinuation that he is no wiser than any other sentient
creature, Protagoras' first protest is that remarks of this sort
"go entirely by what looks probable, without a word of argument or proof" (162E). This procedure would not be
allowed in any mathematical argument worth its salt, and
neither should we "allow questions of this importance to be
settled by plausible appeals to mere likelihood" (162E–163A).

Before considering how Protagoras might defend himself more fully, however, Socrates turns to a series of three
arguments obviously directed against Theaetetus' hypothesis
that knowledge is perception. Coming as they do immediately
after the suggestion that only cogent and serious argument
should be allowed in the discussion, these arguments at first
appear blatantly superficial. As suggested above, however,
each serves a serious purpose in the dialogue. Together they

distinguish several senses of the terms involved in which
knowledge obviously cannot be identified with perception.
Perhaps this in itself explains why they are entered into the
dialogue in a way which highlights their obvious inappro-
priateness as serious objections to Theaetetus' hypothesis.

The first of the "captious" arguments occurs at 163B. In
the case of a person seeing or hearing a language used which
he does not know, the assertion that knowledge is identical
with perception seems to require either (1) that he both perceives (because seeing or hearing) the language and does not
perceive it (since he does not know it), or (2) that he both
knows (since he perceives) and does not know the language.
Neither alternative is possible as stated. But the paradox is
so transparent that Theaetetus himself is allowed to disclose
what has gone wrong (163B–C). We need only distinguish
between the meanings, which we neither see nor (by hypothesis) know, and the symbols which we both see and (by hypothesis) know, and the paradox disappears. The constructive and
pertinent result of this little verbal exercise is to focus our
attention on one sense of the term ἐπιστήμη which obviously
is not equivalent in meaning to αἴσθησις. Knowledge of a
language is a skill, like knowledge of a musical instrument
or of a complex tool; and the Greeks used ἐπιστήμη for this
type of skill, just as we use 'knowledge'.[25] But the admission

[25] Runciman concludes, from a brief survey of those arguments
from 163D to 186E which are not obviously directed against the
extreme Heraclitean position, that "at the time of writing the
Theaetetus Plato had made no clear distinction" (*Plato's Later Epistemology*, p. 17) between "knowing that, knowing how, and knowing
by acquaintance" (*ibid.*, p. 13). (Unaccountably, Runciman reads all
these arguments as directed against Protagoras, whereas those at
163D–164B, 165B–C, and 184B–186E, by both content and context, may be seen clearly to be directed against Theaetetus' hypothesis.) The result is that he finds some of the arguments "obviously a
joke" (*ibid.*) or "not in fact . . . very good . . ." (*ibid.*, p. 14).
Runciman is made to suspect this lack of distinction between types
of knowledge by the fact that Theaetetus, in listing examples of
knowledge at 146C, names "crafts" as well as "sciences," and the fact
that in certain earlier dialogues Plato speaks as if skill is based on in-

that knowledge in this sense is not perception is one we are entirely ready to make, and one which reflects no lack of confidence in some more plausible interpretation of the hypothesis that knowledge is identical with perception.

The second "captious" argument occurs at 163D–164B. When a person remembers a thing he knows it, even if he is not presently perceiving it. But according to the identification of knowledge and perception in Theaetetus' hypothesis, a person in such a situation must admit either (1) to knowing (because remembering) and not knowing (because not perceiving) the thing, or (2) to both perceiving (because knowing) and not perceiving (by hypothesis) the same thing. Neither alternative is acceptable as it stands. But the argument, of course, relies upon "the methods of a professional contraversialist" (164C), and Protagoras' reply later on (166B) is right to the point. An object of perception is not the same as an object of memory, either singly or in general, so of course we shall say that the thing known in the sense of remembered is not known in the (alleged) sense of being perceived. Although Theaetetus felt that it would be "monstrous" (163D) to suppose that a thing with which one "has become acquainted" and which one still remembers was not thereby known in some sense of the term ἐπιστήμη,[26] this sense of the term, in which remembering entails knowing, is not germane to the consideration whether knowledge and perception are the same thing. Of course remembering is not perceiving, in the sense of αἴσθησις in question; but no one should feel that the intended claim of equivalence between

tellectual awareness of the Forms. None of this counts as evidence that Plato is not deliberately distinguishing various irrelevant senses of ἐπιστήμη in these arguments from 163A to 165D. And when there is no evidence against it, an interpretation which makes an argument both sensible and fitting to its context is to be preferred over one which accomplishes neither.

[26] See *Greek-English Lexicon*, rev. ed. (Oxford: Clarendon Press, 1925), in which the first meaning given for ἐπιστήμη is "acquainted with."

knowledge and perception is weakened by that observation.

The third "captious" argument occurs at 165B–D. There is in English a sense of the expression 'look at' in which it might be sensible to say that a person is looking at something he does not see. Indeed, it is perhaps more common than otherwise that a person thoroughly absorbed in thought, or in some manual task, does not see the better part of what is before his eyes. And even when someone tries to see something that he is looking at in this sense, it is not always an easy matter to succeed; for example, he may be looking right at a small object dropped on a multicolored floor, with the object directly before his eyes, yet continue for some time to be unable actually to see the object. A comparable sense of the term αἴσθησις existed in Attic Greek. It is the role of the third argument (which, although termed by Socrates "the most formidable poser of all" (165B), may strike the reader as the most captious argument in the entire dialogue) to remove this sense of αἴσθησις from consideration. Suppose, Socrates says to Theaetetus, that "you are trapped like a beast in a pit and an imperturbable gentleman puts his hand over one of your eyes and asks if you can see his coat with the eye that is covered" (165B–C). The answer must be that Theaetetus can see the coat with one eye but not with the other. Thus, in accord with a rigid interpretation of his hypothesis, he is driven to admit that he both knows and does not know the same object. In his subsequent "response" Protagoras is made to intimate, apropos of this outcome, that one should not "shrink from admitting that it is possible for the same person to know and not to know the same thing" (166B), but no explanation is offered there of what is behind this apparent breach of logic.

According to the theory of perception which has been constructed to stand behind both Theaetetus' and Protagoras' accounts, a unique object comes into existence with each instance of perception. But perception, in turn, involves awareness of the object, and is not accomplished merely by opening

the eyes. The difference between seeing and not seeing, in
other words, is not the same as the difference between having
one eye open and the other one shut, but rather is the difference
between being aware and not being aware of a perceptual
object. One can be aware of a single and, according to the
theory, of a unique object with either one or two eyes open. But
an act of awareness involving one eye is different from an act of
awareness involving the other eye alone or both eyes together,
and what the theory does not allow is that the same object can
be associated with different acts of awareness. Thus it would be
pointless to suggest that the same object seen with one open
eye might be seen by a closed eye as well, and necessarily
true to say that this could not be the case. This presumably
is what Protagoras would have answered if Plato had made
him elaborate on his suggestion that the same person might
know and not know the same thing. If 'knowing' meant 'perceiving' in the sense merely of "looking at," then this suggestion would be logically inadmissable; but insofar as the
sense is that of "being aware of," it is necessarily true. The
useful result of the "most formidable poser of all" is to point
out that just as certain senses of ἐπιστήμη are irrelevant to
Theaetetus' hypothesis, so too it is not relevant to observe
that merely looking at or failing to look at something, without actually perceiving it, is not the same as knowing or
failing to know that particular thing.

4 / Segregation of the Theses

After an eloquent appeal by Protagoras (as "originator" of
the "secret doctrine" [152C]) for an earnest response to his
theory, Socrates turns to the task of distinguishing the several
historically identifiable theses which have been merged indiscriminately in the theory of perception. Of ultimate interest
is Theaetetus' hypothesis that knowledge and perception are

identical. But accounts also have to be settled with the recon-
stituted Protagorean thesis that man is the measure of all
things, and with the extreme version of Heracliteanism
according to which, in some literal sense, all things are in
change. These three claims have been designated respectively
as follows:

(α) Knowledge is perception
(β) Man is the measure of all things
(γ) All things are in change

Plato's procedure in distinguishing these several theses is to
trace out necessary conditions of each which are not shared
by the others. Protagoras' thesis is the first to be separated
off in this fashion, after which (γ) (later at 179D attributed
to some extremist disciples of Heraclitus) finally is segregated
from (α). Thus Protagoras is met in the "candid spirit" he
requested, "without hostility or contentiousness," and we can
"honestly consider what we mean when we say that all things
are in motion and that what seems also is, to any individual
or community" (168B). And only thus can we finally consider the "further question whether knowledge is, or is not,
the same as perception" (168B) in light of its relationship to
these other hypotheses.

Hypotheses (α) and (β), as we have seen, share the necessary condition (σ) that each momentary perception is infallible with respect to its object. The point on which (β)
parts company with (α) and (γ) is in its implication regarding matters of judgment. For the claim that each man is the
measure of *all* things, as explicated by Plato and apparently
as intended by Protagoras himself, requires not only that each
man is the sole judge of what appears to him perceptually,
but requires that what each man believes *as a result of perception* is true for him as well. The phrase "as a result of
perception" (introduced at 161D where this further condition
is first explicitly mentioned in the dialogue) serves to facilitate

the transition from the claim merely that perception is infallible to the extended claim about the infallibility of judgment. Since it is part of the apparently genuine view of Protagoras which Plato is examining that all beliefs originate in perception, this qualifier achieves no distinction between types of belief. And at the beginning of the final criticism of (β) the qualifier is dropped, the thesis being made to read simply that "what seems true to anyone is true for him to whom it seems so" (170A). The later context indicates clearly that it is with the truth of judgments rather than of mere perceptions that we are now concerned. Thus Plato uncovers another necessary condition to be met if (β) is to be successfully maintained; namely

(τ) Every belief is true for the believer.

Since (α) has no direct implications regarding belief, and since (γ) will be seen shortly to rule out any application of the evaluative term 'true' whatsoever, (τ) provides a wedge whereby (β) is segregated from its companion theses. Condition (τ) then is turned against Protagoras in the argument beginning at 170E.

The terminal weakness in Protagoras' thesis, in fact, is displayed only in the second of the two arguments we are about to consider. The former argument (170E–171C), however, is more spectacular, involving what at least is claimed to be "a really exquisite conclusion" (171A) in which Plato "turns the tables" on his old opponent.[27] This argument is surely unsound, as Plato himself seems to realize (171D). Yet the argument is illusive in structure and its deficiencies are correspondingly difficult to analyze. At first reading, moreover, the argument might very well seem valid.[28] The argument is based on the factual premise that some people disbelieve Protagoras' thesis that every belief of each person is

[27] See Cornford, *Plato's Theory of Knowledge*, p. 79 n.
[28] As Aristotle apparently thought when writing *Metaphysics* 1009a 6–14.

true for the believer. Superficially read, it goes something
like this:

(1) Every belief of each person is true for the believer, and
(2) There exists a person who believes (1) is false.

Therefore, since Protagoras is committed to (1), and (1) and
(2)—it may appear—entail

(3) (1) is false,

it follows that Protagoras is committed both to the affirmation and the denial of the same proposition, which of course
is not permissible in rational discourse.

The formulation above, however, is simply incorrect. We
may presume statement (1) to be faithful to Protagoras' intention, emphasizing as it does that a belief is true *for the
believer*, and (2) expresses a fact which surely cannot be
denied. Statement (3), however, does not follow from (1)
and (2) at all. What follows instead would appear to be

(3′) (1) is false for the believer of (2)

and the believer of (2) certainly is someone other than Protagoras himself. What follows from (1) and (2) in conjunction, accordingly, would not contradict Protagoras' original
assertion that every belief is true for the believer. The result
of the argument in *this* rendition is simply that (1) is true
for Protagoras and false for someone else, which is neither
here nor there as far as the original thesis is concerned.

But this formulation will not do either. Given the argument as formulated above, save with (3′) in place of (3), we
may see directly that the alleged conclusion is on a different
level of reference from that of premise (1). The first premise
is a statement about the beliefs of individual persons, while
the conclusion is a statement about premise (1) itself. Since
(3′) refers to (1), (3′) is a meta-linguistic statement about
(1); hence there exists no direct logical relation between the

two, with or without an additional premise, apart from *another* meta-linguistic statement in the form of a semantic rule of correspondence permitting the inference of one from the other. An analogy might help make this clear. Although there is an obvious relation in sense between the object-language expression (i) 'snow is white' and the meta-language expression (ii) ' "snow is white" is true', neither statement implies the other by virtue of their propositional relationship alone. One statement is about snow while the other is about a statement, and since they are about different things they are logically unrelated. Given an easily admissible rule of inference, however, either statement can be deduced from the other. This rule is that a statement is true if and only if the statement that it is true itself is true in turn. The rule itself is meta-linguistic, involving as it does a meta-statement on the left and (relatively speaking) a meta-meta-statement on the right of the biconditional expression. The point to carry over from this example is that (i) is deducible from (ii), and vice versa, only if the rule of inference mentioned is admitted, and consequently that neither (i) nor (ii) is deducible from the other if the rule is denied. Let us formulate Socrates' argument against Protagoras' once again, this time with attention to level of discourse.

(1) Every belief of each person is true for the believer,
(2') Someone (Q) believes that not every belief of each person is true for the believer. Therefore
(3") The first statement in this argument is false for Q.

In this formulation the conclusion (3") is on the meta-linguistic level, while (1) and (2') are on the object level. Thus (3") can follow neither from (1) or (2') alone nor from (1) and (2') in conjunction, since a rule of inference bringing the two levels into logical contact is required before a consequence can be drawn on the meta-linguistic level from assertions on the level below. If (3") is to be an obtainable consequence from (2'), as Socrates intended in his argument, then (1) must function not as an additional premise but rather as a rule of inference more clearly formulated.

> (1') For all beliefs (B) and for all persons (P), P believes
> B if and only if B is true for P.

With the substitution of (1') for (1), which seems entirely in accord with the argument as it stands in the dialogue, the paradoxical nature of the argument begins to appear. Conclusion (3″) is derived with the help of (1'), but (3″) denies (1'). Therefore the conclusion (3″) is self-defeating, leading to the denial of the very rule of inference without which it cannot be deduced from (2'). This is certainly not a damaging result for Protagoras, for it shows merely that his own thesis cannot be used in conjunction with the disbelief of others in this thesis to achieve a valid deduction of its denial. We should carefully note, therefore, that Protagoras himself is not caught in the backlash of the paradox, since the falsehood of his thesis does not follow from its affirmation in conjunction with a statement of belief in the thesis as Protagoras maintains it for his own part.[29]

There is no immediate reason to think that Plato was aware of these various subtleties in his argument; nor, on the other hand, does there seem to be any absolutely compelling reason to think that he was not. At any rate, he most likely was aware of the inadequacy of the argument as it stands. And after an interlude in which Socrates with characteristic eloquence pleads the virtues of philosophy over mere rhetoric, we return to a second argument against Protagoras' thesis which is both perspicuous and conclusive.

As apparent from the first superficial criticism (at 161E), Protagoras' hypothesis (β) is in danger of compromise from his personal claim to be wiser than most men in matters of persuasion and litigation. This latter claim now is turned

---

[29] Theodorus accepts this argument as valid (179B). But he is depicted in the dialogue as an old man (about the age of Socrates, if the allusion to the indictment at 210D is relied upon) who prefers digressions to philosophic argument (177C).

against Protagoras by drawing consequences from it which
directly oppose consequences following from (β) itself. As
already established to the satisfaction of all parties in the discussion, (β) has as a necessary condition the claim (τ) that
every belief is true for the believer. But (τ) itself has relevant consequences which have yet to be unpacked. If *every*
belief of each man is true for him, then each of his beliefs
about his perceptions is true for him. In particular, not only
is each of his beliefs about his present perceptions true for him,
but so too is each of his beliefs about his past and about his
future perceptions. That is, the thesis that man is the measure
of *all* things entails that each man is his own best judge of
what *will* appear to him, as well as of what is appearing to
him in the present and of what has appeared to him in the
past. Let us formulate this consequence of (τ):

(τ') Each man's belief about what will appear to him is
         true for the believer.

The necessary condition (τ) has already been used to distinguish (β) from its companion theses. Its consequence (τ') is
now used to refute (β) by directly countering a consequence
of Protagoras' own belief that he is wiser than his students.

The final refutation (178B–179B) of Protagoras, following
as it does upon the fallacious "table-turning argument," is re-
freshingly uncomplicated. Just as the skill of the physician
lies in his ability to replace unsound with healthy appearances
in his patients, so the skill and superior wisdom of the sophist
lies in his ability to substitute sound for unsound thoughts and
beliefs. The basis for this skill, in either case, obviously is the
ability of the practitioner to anticipate what appearances will
occur under what conditions. Knowing this, the physician
undertakes to bring about healthy appearances by the use of
drugs (167A). The sophist, in his parallel wisdom about conditions under which sound beliefs can be produced, undertakes
to achieve those beliefs in his student by instruction or "discourse." Protagoras, among others with this skill, is wiser than

most men in his ability to anticipate the thoughts and beliefs
which will arise in his students as the result of his discourse,
for which people accordingly are willing to pay "huge sums
to talk with him" (179A). Protagoras' belief about what will
appear to the student thus is more often true *for* the student
than is the student's own corresponding belief about himself.
It follows that there are situations in which Protagoras, to say
nothing of other men, must admit that there are some beliefs
about what will appear to the believer which are not true for
the believer himself, whereas Protagoras' own belief in this
regard is true, both for himself and for the other man. Condition (τ') thus cannot be met as long as Protagoras persists
in his wisdom over other men in the fashion alleged. Thesis
(β) on that basis is refuted and drops from the argument.

It is a mark of Plato's dialectical skill that all facts brought
to bear in the final refutation of (β) would almost certainly
have to be admitted by Protagoras himself. Although (β) is
not shown *inconsistent* in itself (as Plato perhaps had aspired
to do through the "table-turning argument"), it is shown incompatible with other claims which the protagonist himself
would not deny. In the absence of a demonstration of internal
inconsistency, there is no sounder disproof of a disputed thesis.
Plato's disproof of Protagoras' hypothesis thus furnishes an
excellent example of the first stage in the procedure recommended at *Phaedo* 101D. When an hypothesis comes under
question the dialectician first must consider whether it is consistent, both in its immediate consequences and with other
theses which, in the context of the argument, cannot be
denied. Only if the hypothesis passes the test of consistency
should the question of its truth be allowed to arise. Protagoras'
claim has failed the test, and drops out of contention for the
remainder of the dialogue.

Plato's refutation (181B–183C) of the Heraclitean hypothesis (γ) is rich in metaphor and innuendo, just as presumably
was the verbal practice of the extreme Heracliteans of Ephesus
who are brought to task at this stage by a suddenly animated

Theodorus (179D–180D). It contains also the intimation of
some severe problems of a semantical nature with which Plato
himself comes to grapple in the *Sophist*. In view of the dialectical structure of the first section of the dialogue, however,
this refutation is almost as straightforward and undeniable
as the way in which Protagoras was ushered out of contention.
The reader should bear in mind that the school represented
by hypothesis (γ) apparently maintained a position comparable in its extremity to the diametrically opposed position of Parmenides. To remind us of this may be one reason Plato
introduces Parmenides onto the scene at this point, and then
refuses to deal with him. Just as Parmenides had maintained
that *nothing* is in motion, in any sense, so the proponents of
(γ) are construed as maintaining that nothing in any sense is
at rest. This radical claim of course cannot be attributed to
Heraclitus himself, with his emphasis on λόγος and on the
stability of moral as well as physical structure which is contributed by the involvement of λόγος in a universe of constant
change. The Ephesian followers of Heraclitus (179E), however, are in trouble from the beginning, for it soon appears to
be a consequence of what they say that meaningful discourse
itself is impossible. The untenability of this result is taken
for granted, and most of the argument against (γ) consists
in showing that this result is indeed among its consequences.

Given a literal construction of the claim that all is in motion, it follows that there is no fixity with respect either to position or to property of any object in the universe of change.
This being the case, no statement predicating a property of an
object will remain true from one moment to the next. Not only
would no term employed in the statement retain a fixed referent, but moreover any condition or state of affairs which
would make the statement true at the moment of utterance
would be nullified immediately thereafter. This consequence
for discourse about the material world, of course, was remarked earlier as a consequence of the theory of perception
(157B). But the implications for discourse in general are

drawn explicitly here for the first time. If thesis (γ) is correct, then meaningful discourse itself is impossible. If no statement, either affirmative or negative, can remain true for longer than the time taken in its utterance, then no statement can be treated as either true or false, and the cause of communicating with one's fellow beings must be given up as hopeless. This consequence, then, is a necessary condition of (γ), or of any point of view which accepts the theory of perception earlier developed as descriptive of entire reality: [30]

(v) Meaningful discourse is impossible.

As a necessary condition, however, (v) obviously cannot be met. Meaningful discourse obviously is possible as a simple matter of fact, and not even the advocates of (γ) can consistently maintain otherwise. For if the claim in (v) were assumed true, then by virtue of its very truth that claim would have to be deemed meaningless and hence not true, contrary to what was assumed.[31] The claim in (v) thus can only be maintained to be false or meaningless. But since (v) is a necessary condition of (γ), it follows directly that (γ) also cannot be consistently maintained as true. Plato does not draw out the consequences in just this fashion, although both he and the perceptive reader may be presumed to realize that a demonstration of inconsistency such as he sought against (β) is immediately in the offing against (γ), waiting only to be explicated.

What Plato does instead at this juncture is to point out that (a) itself cannot be maintained if (v) is the case. If terms have no fixed referent, and truth conditions never remain stable, then it is no more correct to say that knowledge is perception than to say the contrary (182E). Thus (v) entails the falsehood of (a), and (a) in turn entails the falsehood of (v).

---

[30] Cornford remarks that "Plato has now to point out that, if the objects of perception . . . are taken to be 'all things', there can be no such thing as knowledge at all, since no statement we make about these perpetually changing things can remain true for two moments together" (*Plato's Theory of Knowledge*, p. 97).

[31] Compare Aristotle, *Metaphysics*, IV, 4.

Whereas (γ) entails (v), (a) entails its negation. How could Plato have shown more convincingly that (a) and (γ) are doctrinely distinct?

It is worth emphasizing for future reference that (v) is a consequence of (γ) alone, and not of the theory of perception the constitution of which was the occasion for bringing (γ) into the discussion in the first place. A person might maintain this theory as an essentially correct description of the world of change, but deny that the world of change comprises the whole of reality. Such a person therefore would not be committed to the thesis that *everything* is in change, and would be free to seek grounds for the possibility of meaningful discourse on another level of reality.

The theses (a), (β), and (γ) have been cleanly separated. And the latter two have been conclusively refuted by the disclosure of consequences which conflict with other theses their defenders could not sensibly deny. It remains now "to deliver Theaetetus of his conceptions about knowledge" (184B), for which purpose the thesis (a) is subjected to serious and constructive criticism.

5 / Refutation of Theaetetus' Hypothesis

In Theaetetus' illustrative definition at the beginning of the dialogue, a property of the surds that distinguishes them as a class from the lengths is that there is no one unit by which each can be measured. The surds ($\delta v v \acute{a} \mu \epsilon \iota s$) in themselves are incommensurable, not admitting comparison in common terms. Closely parallel in this respect are the motions (characterized also only as $\delta v v \acute{a} \mu \epsilon \iota s$) in the theory of perception, providing the interpretation of Theaetetus' hypothesis which is about to be criticized at 184B.[32] Each perception is the re-

[32] The parallel is not exact, since no two "fast" perceptions are commensurable. The most to be said of the surds in this respect is that none is commensurable with any length and that as a class they have no common measure. See note 4 of this chapter.

sult of a particular interaction between an active and a passive motion, and each perception is associated during its brief period of activity with a unique perceptual object. The twin offspring of this intercourse are termed "fast" motions, and do not persist from moment to moment. But the active and passive motions themselves are "slow," and are capable of persisting to enter into various combinations of parenthood. Now the crucial features of this theory for the criticism about to begin are (1) that the "slow" motions themselves are never objects of perception, and (2) that each of the "fast" motions which is a perceptual object occurs in conjunction with one and only one perception. A consequence of this is that perception, which in Theaetetus' hypothesis is identified with knowledge, presents unique objects which are never repeated and which therefore in themselves can never be perceptually compared. This latter follows simply from the fact that any perceptual comparison of two distinct objects would require that both objects be present in a single perception, which is contrary to (2) above. Thus neither the "slow" motions (by (1)) nor the "fast" motions (by (2)) can be compared in perception. In short, there can be no perception in which objects of perception are directly compared.

A condition imposed upon the hypothesis that knowledge is perception thus is that there can be no knowledge about comparative relations among objects of perception. Let us formulate this condition:

(ϕ) Comparative knowledge about objects of perception is impossible.

As Socrates points out in a rather more direct argument than mine above,[33] no act of vision can compare colors and sounds,

---

[33] The value of drawing the consequence which proves fatal for Theaetetus' hypothesis directly from the theory of perception itself is that of showing that the very provisions which make possible the satisfaction of *one* necessary condition of the hypothesis, that perception be infallible, carry with them *another* necessary condition which is clearly contrary to fact.

nor could an act of hearing, for "the objects you perceive through one faculty cannot be perceived through another . . ." (184E–185A). This establishes only that objects of different senses cannot be compared in perception, a more limited claim than (ϕ), but the effect for Theaetetus' identification of knowledge and perception is equally devastating. If there can be no perceptual comparison of colors and sounds, and if knowledge and perception are the same, then there can be no knowledge of comparative relations between colors and sounds. But this consequence is clearly counterfactual. At the very least, we know "that each of the two is *different* from the other . . ." (185A, translator's emphasis), albeit the *same* as itself, from which it follows that there *is* comparative knowledge relating colors and sounds. Moreover, we can often know of two perceptions, whether of the same sense modality or not, "that they both exist" (185A), that they are *alike* or *unlike*, and that together they are *two* while apart they each are *one*. In each such case, again, we have comparative knowledge about objects of perception, which by (ϕ) would be impossible if knowledge indeed were identical to perception. The conclusion can only be that knowledge is *not* identical to perception, and that Theaetetus' hypothesis cannot be maintained.

The same result can be obtained by another consideration. One mark of knowledge, however defined, is infallibility (152C). This has led to the first necessary condition for the truth of Theaetetus' hypothetical identification of knowledge and perception, that perception be infallible itself. The theory of perception developed in token collaboration with Protagoras and Heraclitus provided a framework in which this condition could be met. A second mark of knowledge is that its objects exist (152C, 186E). This provides directly a further necessary condition for the truth of Theaetetus' hypothesis, which now is brought into play. This condition is that:

(χ) the objects of perception exist.

Having traced the consequences of the requirement of infallibility through the theory of perception, however, we are pre-

pared to see at once that condition (χ) cannot be met. The
price paid for infallible perception is that the objects of perception are in flux, along with the acts with which they are so
intimately associated. And no such object "*is* one thing just by
itself, but is always in process of becoming for someone, and
being is to be ruled out altogether . . ." (157A–B, translator's emphasis). But since the objects of perception themselves
do not have being, they do not in the requisite sense exist; and
condition (χ), being falsified, leads by another path to the rejection of the hypothesis that knowledge is identical with perception.

Socrates' argument in this connection again is somewhat less
direct,[34] but leads to the same conclusion. Observing that we do
indeed know that qualities like sound and color [35] (not *particular* instances of qualities, like the particular whites and blacks
that are objects of particular perceptions) exist (185A), Socrates points out that reflections about their existence come "if
they come at all, with difficulty through a long and trouble-
some process of education" (186C). Reference here, presumably, is to the education of the dialectician discussed in the
Republic, for only the dialectician or philosopher could appre-

[34] See note 33.

[35] A problem arises here since, in the theory of perception, the
quick motions *are* not in themselves but only become (157A). But
in 185A, color and sound are at least thought to *exist*. In Socrates'
"dream," again, the elements are denied the attribute of existence
(201E–202A). One way of reconciliation lies in the direction of taking the language literally. Socrates seems to say not that particular
perceptions (of color or sounds) or particular perceived objects
(colors or sounds) exist, but rather that color and sound exist. Reference at 185A thus seems to be to kinds, rather than to particulars.
E. W. Schipper seems to realize this when she says, in connection
with this passage, that "the nature of the existence of what is perceived is defined by the common attributes, which, although not explicitly called εἴδη, can only be the forms. . . ." This statement appears in "The Meaning of Existence in Plato's *Sophist*," *Phronesis*,
9, no. 1 (1964): 38–44, specifically, p. 39. See also J. Xenakis
"Plato's *Sophist:* A Defense of Negative Expressions and a Doctrine
of Sense and of Truth," *Phronesis*, 4, no. 1 (1959): 29–43, specifically p. 43.

hend the existence of color and sound as such. At any rate, the apprehension of existence requires training, while perception is a natural act for which no training whatsoever is required. This being the case, existence cannot be revealed through perception alone, and condition (χ) again leads to the falsification of Theaetetus' first hypothesis.

These final two arguments against (a) are distinct and produce somewhat different results. The first shows at most that there are some instances of knowledge that are not perception, but leaves open the possibility that some or even all acts of perception are knowledge. The second argument rules out perception from the field of knowledge entirely.[36] The first alone would have been adequate for Plato's immediate dialectical purpose of testing whether Theaetetus' hypothesis is consistent with other claims about knowledge which cannot be denied. But the second alone is consonant with the analysis of knowledge forthcoming in the *Sophist*, where knowledge is limited to the Forms and the realm of perception is left to those who deal in images and falsehood.

Each of the two final arguments, nonetheless, consists in drawing consequences which follow from the provisions which enabled Theaetetus' hypothesis to survive the test of the first necessary condition, that perception be infallible. The unalterable association between the twin offspring which makes each perception the sole measure of its own object requires in turn that perceptual objects cannot be perceptually compared and that the object of perception itself can properly be said only to *become* and not to *be*. But it is just this pair of consequences which falsify that hypothesis under its last two necessary conditions. Thus the very features of the theory of perception which enable it to pass through its first test lead to its downfall under the second, and Theaetetus' hypothesis is shown to suffer from an internal infirmity which calls for rejection rather than repair.

[36] Cornford points out this distinction, *Plato's Theory of Knowledge*, pp. 102, 106.

In the process of the final criticism of the first hypothesis, however, another hypothesis has begun to emerge. Since at least some knowledge is of comparative relations among perceptions, and since this knowledge is embodied in what we *think* about perceptions rather than in perception itself, perhaps it is typical of knowledge generally that it originates in thought and is manifest in judgment. Given these difficulties, Socrates suggests, it seems that "knowledge does not reside in the impressions, but in our reflection upon them" (186D), and Theaetetus himself has reached the point where it is clear to him "that the mind in itself is its own instrument for contemplating the common terms that apply to everything" (185D–E), including existence, the object of knowledge. Thus the step to the second hypothesis is almost automatic. Knowledge cannot be found in sense perception, but must be with "what goes on when the mind is occupied with things by itself" (187A), to which activity is given the name 'judgment'.

6 / The "New Way"

The injunction at *Phaedo* 101E for those who want to discover any part of what is true is to avoid muddling questions of necessary with questions of sufficient conditions.[37] This advice stands with respect to the method exercised in the *Theaetetus*. First in the concern of the dialectician must be the necessary consequences of his hypothesis. Only when these have been found consistent will he turn to search for a more general hypothesis from which his initial conjecture can be deduced, and which thereby provides a sufficient condition for its truth. Since Theaetetus' initial hypothesis, interpreted within the context of the theory of perception, has been shown inconsist-

[37] The consequences of an hypothesis are among the necessary conditions of its being true. Its sufficient conditions include further hypotheses of which it is a consequence in turn.

ent in its consequences, it is pointless to seek a more general
hypothesis from which it in turn might be deduced.

In tracing out the consequences of the first hypothesis, however, Socrates leads Theaetetus (and the reader) to a second
which has the advantage of being obviously consistent. We
know, as a matter of fact, that color is different from sound,
and that both color and sound exist (185A).[38] The faculty to
which this is revealed is the mind (185D–E), and the exercise
of this faculty is reflection (186D) or judgment (187A). Theaetetus' arrival at the second conjecture regarding the nature
of knowledge is a routine outcome of these observations. This
second hypothesis of Theaetetus is the fourth treated in the
dialogue thus far and may be formulated as follows:

(δ) Knowledge is identical with true judgment.[39]

The consistency of (δ) has been established by examples such
as those mentioned above, in which knowledge obviously includes true judgment at least among its parts. For if true judgment necessarily excluded knowledge, as has been shown in
the case of perception, then no examples of true judgment
could be given which are examples of knowledge as well.[40]

---

[38] See note 35.
[39] The term δόξα will be translated 'judgment' instead of 'belief'.
This is strongly suggested by Socrates' description of δόξα "as a statement pronounced, not aloud to someone else, but silently to oneself"
(190A). I cannot see, with Gulley, that the sense of 'belief' is intended by Plato instead (see *Plato's Theory of Knowledge* [London:
Methuen & Co., 1962] p. 162). Gulley's argument is based upon
the contention that the lawyer's skill, mentioned at 201B–C, is directed toward making people believe what he wants them to believe. But it would be no less apt to say that his skill is to make
them issue verdicts (judgments) favorable to his case.
[40] None of the judgments of existence, difference, or sameness,
and so forth, mentioned between 185A and 185D, are explicitly referred to as instances of ἐπιστήμη, but there is no way in which they
could be otherwise construed. At 186D, moreover, Socrates says that
ἐπιστήμη resides in our reflection upon impressions, and the examples
of such reflections which this remark must be intended to bring to
the reader's mind are those between 185A and 185D—thoughts of

Having disposed so easily of the question of consistency, we
might expect Plato to consider immediately whether (δ) can
be provided a set of sufficient conditions. But this is reserved
for the final moments in the discussion of this hypothesis. Plato's concern at the beginning, rather, is to examine the distinction between true and false judgment. The rationale behind
this is clear. Just as no meaning precise enough to be tested
could be assigned Theaetetus' first hypothesis without a prior
analysis of perception, so here it is necessary to understand
what is intended by 'true judgment' (ἀληθὴς δόξα) before one
can set about defending an hypothesis which identifies true
judgment with knowledge. That is, if the concept of true judgment is to serve in an explication of the concept of knowledge,
then what it is for a judgment to be true must be better understood initially than the concept to be explicated. To understand true judgment in the requisite sense would be to know
its necessary and sufficient conditions, for only if these are
known can it be determined if they are both necessary and sufficient for knowledge as well.

Under these circumstances, it is natural to wonder why
Plato addresses directly the problem of false judgment instead
of true. This apparently indirect approach to the concept of
truth is continued in the *Sophist* where, although the immediate problem is to account for the possibility of false impressions, a theory of true judgment is finally obtained. The
justification for this approach is that conditions which are both
necessary and sufficient for false judgment can be immediately
converted by negation into conditions which are both sufficient
and necessary for true judgment in turn. Thus, to find one set
of conditions is to find the conditions for the other as well. And
since the problem of the possibility of false judgments has already been raised in connection with Protagoras' thesis (β), it
is natural for Plato to continue this emphasis in the present
context.

---

existence, sameness and difference, on the part of color and sound,
and so forth.

All this presumably is behind Plato's decision to pursue the question of false judgment, "not as we did a while ago, but in a new way [ἄλλον τρόπον]" (187D). But a reason of considerably greater significance may lie in the background. What is this "new way?" What, for that matter, is the "old way" with which it is contrasted? And we might ask further, what is the point of referring so explicitly to another way at this stage in the dialogue? It would not be surprising if someone at this point were to recall the passage in the *Parmenides* where Socrates himself is being advised of a basic deficiency in his methodology. It is proper, Parmenides says, to extend one's search for truth "to those objects which are specially apprehended by discourse and can be regarded as forms" (135E).[41] Socrates has already shown his appreciation of this in his criticism of Zeno's treatise. But there is one thing more Socrates must do in preparation for his inquiry after truth. "If you want to be thoroughly exercised," advises Parmenides, "you must not merely make the supposition [ὑποτιθέμενον] that such and such a thing *is* and then consider the consequences; you must also take the supposition [ὑποτίθεσθαι] that that same thing *is not*" (135E–136A [translator's emphasis]).[42] It was his attempt to illustrate this approach, we recall, that led Parmenides into the dialectical exercise in the latter part of the dialogue which to this day numbers among the most puzzling sequences in the entire Platonic corpus.

Plato's approach to the problem of false judgment "a while ago" (187D), while examining Protagoras' thesis (β) that man is the measure of all things, was to show that this thesis is false precisely because false judgment *is* possible. As we have seen, it is a consequence of (β), which Protagoras himself was depicted as insisting upon, that no judgment (as no perception) is literally false. That is, if (β) were true, then the assertion that false judgment is possible would itself be

---

[41] The translator of the *Parmenides* quoted is Cornford.
[42] The term ὑποτίθημι occurring here should remind the reader of the discussion of method at *Phaedo* 101D.

false. If false judgment is possible, accordingly, then (β) must be false, and it was by exploiting this consequence that Socrates was able to refute the Protagorean thesis. The "old way" thus was to trace out the consequences of the fact that false judgment is possible.

Now the "new way" of 187D is just the opposite. Plato's concern at this stage is to isolate the conditions which, when met, will guarantee the consequence that false judgment is possible. Whereas before Plato was tracing out the necessary conditions for, or consequences of, the possibility of false judgment, now he is concerned to determine the sufficient conditions from which, when realized, the possibility of false judgment itself can be deduced. The difference between these two concerns is nothing more nor less than the difference between the two phases of the methodology described in *Phaedo* 101D.

Of considerable further interest, moreover, is the fact that the "old" and the "new way" of treating the possibility of false judgment correspond also to the two phases of the methodology which Parmenides recommends to Socrates in the passage reviewed above. To suppose "that such and such a thing *is* and then consider the consequences" (136A) is to test the consistency of the thing's necessary conditions, under which test Protagoras' thesis (β) was found untenable. To consider "the supposition that that same thing *is not*" (136A) and the consequences thereof, however, is to consider the sufficient conditions of the thing in question. If P, for example, is a consequence of the negation of Q, then Q is a consequence of the negation of P, and the negation of P thereby provides at least one sufficient condition for the truth of Q. Thus to seek the consequences of the negation of an hypothesis is to seek for its sufficient conditions in negative form. This is tantamount to the second phase of the methodology adumbrated in *Phaedo* 101D, and is the concern which is pursued throughout the second major section of the *Theaetetus* which we are about to examine.[43]

[43] There is therefore a close correlation between (a) the method recommended to Socrates by Parmenides, (b) the method described at

The specific approach from this stage forward in the dialogue is as follows. Judgment in general, Theaetetus and Socrates agree, can be divided into true and false judgments. But the concepts of being true and of being false are not well understood. To understand false judgment, in particular, we must seek to understand its sufficient conditions, and having achieved this we must determine whether these conditions are necessary as well. To seek sufficient conditions of false judgment is to seek a specification of judgment which can be expressed with the help of concepts less problematical than the concept of truth itself. Or to put it another way, we are to seek a type of judgment which is both clear and obviously possible, from which the possibility of false judgment follows as a consequence, and which therefore is such that its possibility (although obvious) would have to be denied if the possibility of false judgment itself were denied. Five possible divisions of judgment are tried before hypothesis (δ) is finally relinquished as indefensible. The first three are crude divisions which fail even to provide sufficient conditions for a judgment's being false. The fourth provides sufficient conditions for a limited type of false judgment, but then is easily seen not to supply the required necessary conditions. The final division of judgment shows the folly of attempting a general definition of false judg-

---

Phaedo 101D, and (c) the "old" and "new ways" practiced in the *Theaetetus*. A fourth parallel is added in the *Sophist* with the method of collection and division. The latter is a way of determining the necessary conditions for a thing's being what it is, and thus corresponds to tracing the consequences of the hypothesis that a thing *is* in (a), the first step in the test for consistency in (b), and the "old way" in (c). The method of collection, on the other hand, is one of determining sufficient conditions for a thing's being what it is, to which corresponds tracing the consequences of the hypothesis that a thing is *not* in (a), the step of justifying a challenged hypothesis in (b), and the "new way" in (c). These features of the method of collection and division are examined in detail in chapter IV. As we shall see there also, the argument in the *Theaetetus* from this stage onward begins to resemble more markedly that practiced in the *Sophist* itself. Thus Socrates' reference to the "new way" might also signal Plato's emerging emphasis on the "new" techniques of collection and division.

ment without reference to a *ground* for the distinction between true and false judgment, such as that provided in the *Sophist* according to "divisions among the kinds." After this, it is shown with remarkable ease that true judgment is not a sufficient condition for knowledge in the first place, and Theaetetus is led on to his third and final hypothesis. Let us trace these steps in detail.

7 / The Search for False Judgment

The task set for the major portion (187D–200D) of the second section of the dialogue is to find a subclass of judgment, membership in which will serve as a sufficient as well as a necessary condition for a judgment's being false. Should Plato succeed in this, a definition of true judgment likewise would be at hand, and he could proceed meaningfully to test the equivalence of true judgment and knowledge asserted by Theaetetus' second hypothesis. Of the five possible subdivisions of judgment examined in this section, all save the second involve what might be considered judgments of identification (as against, for example, judgments of property or characterization). The attempt in each case is to find a way in which misidentification could occur and count as false judgment. The implicit understanding is that true judgment would consist in correct identification.

Now for an object to be incorrectly identified it is necessary that the person performing the identification in some sense "have in mind" both the object incorrectly identified and another object for which this object has been mistaken. Misidentification thus involves a confusion between the "mental representations" of two objects, while correct identification involves a proper correlation between two "mental representations" of the same object. Crude as this may appear to the contemporary reader, it is adequate to sustain the two points Plato makes in this section: (1) that if knowledge is a true judgment of identification (which is all it could be if the theory of perception developed in the previous section is taken as a complete ontology), then there must be at least two distinct ways in which an object might be "present to the mind," and (2) that (given the theory of perception as a complete ontology) the distinction between correct and incorrect identification cannot be made *independently* of the distinction between knowledge and its opposite. The latter point, along with its consequences for hypothesis (δ), is established in the context of the aviary. The former comes out clearly with the first three possible subdivisions of judgment, in each of which only one way is provided in which an object can be "present to the mind."

It is proposed first that we consider merely the distinction between things known and things not known, without regard for the moment to "becoming acquainted with things and forgetting, considered as falling between the two" (188A). No further clarification is given of the sense of 'know' in question. It is apparent from the context, however, that to know an object is to have it present to the mind in a sense, ambiguous as it may be, requiring that if the object is not known then it is in no way present to the mind. To indicate that this sense of knowing (εἰδέναι) is crude, and not to be precisely related to other senses implicated in the dialogue, it will be distinguished henceforth by double quotes. The first subdivision of judgment can be represented as follows: [44]

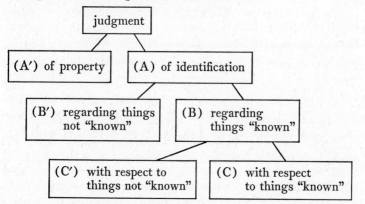

[44] The concept of knowing in the sense of εἰδέναι may be used without circularity in the definition of knowledge in the sense of

Bearing in mind that there is only one sense allowed here in which a thing can be "known," or "present to the mind," we can see at once that this subdivision leaves no room for false judgment. Subclass (B′) will not accommodate false judgment, since we cannot make any judgment of identification at all about things not known (188B). Neither, consequently, can things known be mistakenly identified with things not known, and (C′) also fails to be helpful. Subclass (C) finally can be seen to fail, because whether or not a person confuses two things he "knows," both are "present to his mind" in the same respect, and there is no ground for a distinction between true and false judgment.

The difficulty of not being able both to know (think about) and not to know (mistake) an object, if there is only one sense of the term 'know' allowed, pursues the argument throughout the remainder of the second part. The conclusion of this particular argument is that there is "no possibility of judging outside these alternatives, granted that everything is either known by us or not known; and inside them there seems to be no room for a false judgment" (188C).

It is proposed next, with no more anticipation of success, that falsehood be sought among judgments divided "by way of another alternative . . . 'being or not being'" (188C–D). This division concerns the objects of judgment rather than, as in the case above, the representation of objects in the mind. If there is a distinction here between false and true judgment, then of course the former must be caught within the class of judgments about what is not. The subdivision is as follows:

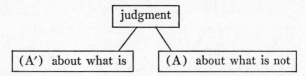

ἐπιστήμη. It would be "shameless," as Socrates playfully suggests at 196D, only if he attempted to define the latter in terms of that same sense itself. This is one of the weaknesses of the aviary account.

The difficulty brought against this possibility seems merely
verbal at first showing. But if we read this difficulty as pointing out that the only distinction between a thing's being and a
thing's not being "present to the mind" provided here is the
distinction simply between the thing's being and the thing's
not being, then the objection to this classification is quite overwhelming. To think a thing which is not is to think a thing
not "present to the mind," but this is to think nothing, and
hence "not to think at all" (189A). The only conclusion to be
drawn is that "thinking falsely must be something different
from thinking what is not" (189B). Another subdivision must
be made if falsehood is to be located somewhere under the
classification of judgment.

The advance of the third attempt over the two previous is
twofold. In this passage (189B–190E) for the first time (1)
an analysis of judgment is proposed and accepted and, in terms
of this analysis, (2) a more detailed breakdown of the judg-
mental act is used to provide a *second* sense in which an object
might be related to the mind beyond merely being "present" to
it. The analysis of judgment yields one of the most easily acquired definitions in the Platonic corpus. Since it is repeated
essentially unchanged at *Sophist* 263E–264A, one may conclude that Plato thought it adequate at least for his examination of the nature and grounds of knowledge. Judgment is
"caught" in the distinction between mental acts which are discursive (involving discourse) and those which are not, when
the former are further divided into those which do and those
which do not terminate in decision (190A). When judgments,
as discursive mental acts which are decisive, are further divided into those about objects which are thought only (as
against perceived) and those about objects which are not
thought (but only perceived), then false judgment might be
claimed to be those judgments of identification, about objects
which are only thought, which are in fact incorrect. The breakdown is as follows:

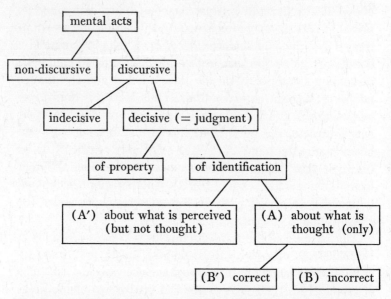

An object might be related to the mind by being the object of a decisive "silent discourse" of the agent within his own mind, or it might not be so related. Again, an object might be related to the mind by being or by not being present to the mind in thought alone, as against being present in perception. Thus there are two independent senses in which an object might be entertained by the mind, the necessity for which was evident in the fate of the former two attempts to define falsehood in judgment.

But this distinction is not yet powerful enough to accommodate false judgment. If falsehood in judgment is to be caught at all in this breakdown, it must fall under the category (B) of what is incorrectly present to the mind in thought only. But (B) turns out to be quite empty. As Socrates is made to put it, with convincing rhetoric, "Do you ever suppose anyone . . . mad or sane, ever goes so far as to talk himself over, in his own mind, into stating seriously that an ox must be a horse or that two must be one?" (190C) Given that a man is thinking of an ox, no amount of "inner dialogue" will ever convince him that he is instead thinking of a horse. To suggest otherwise is at best to suggest that he wasn't thinking of an ox in the first place. This is not to say, of course, that someone might not in confusion think that an ox has some of the *properties* of a horse, or that he might not mistakenly think that an animal he *sees* is a horse when in fact it is an ox. But insofar as he is merely thinking of an ox, regardless of what other judgments he is led to make about it, he will never think that the ox of which he is thinking is instead a horse. Thus again we have failed to provide a division of judgment under which the possibility of false judgment can be accounted for. If a person is merely thinking about two things, he will never judge that one is the other; nor could he confuse in this way things about which he is not thinking, if there is no other way in which he is entertaining these objects in his mind.

The fourth attempt to define false judgment relies upon the metaphor of the wax tablet. The main role of this model, for all its powerful imagery, is to provide two senses in which an object might be before the mind, sharp enough in their distinction to provide an account of how a thing can be thought about and at the same time misidentified. The distinction between memory and sense images permitted by the wax tablet imagery leads, for the first time in this series of attempts, to a set of sufficient conditions for false judgment. These conditions are easily shown not to be necessary, however, and hence are inadequate as a definition of false judgment in any general sense.

To facilitate discussion of the wax tablet, let us designate "knowledge" in the sense of memory 'M' and perception 'P'.[45] To "know" Theodorus, Socrates says, is to "have a memory in my mind of what he is like, and the same with Theaetetus" (192D). After a terse and enigmatic description of the cases in which error is not possible, Plato states quite clearly the cases in which false judgment can occur.[46] "Take things you

---

[45] The infinitive εἰδέναι bears the sense of "to know" involved in the discussion of the wax black. See note 44.

[46] Cornford declines to translate 192A–C, and the translation of Jowett is logically unintelligible.

know: you can suppose them to be other things which you both know and perceive; or to be things you do not know, but do perceive; or you can confuse two things which you both know and perceive." (192C) Four possibilities are schematized here. Two things, x and y, can be confused (1) when both are "known" and perceived (x is P and M, y is P and M). This possibility, the last mentioned above, is illustrated by the case in which Socrates, who knows both Theaetetus and Theodorus, and possesses imprints of both "like seal-impressions in the waxen block" (193C), sees both indistinctly at a distance and makes "the mistake of interchanging them, like a man who thrusts his feet into the wrong shoes . . ." (193C). Another possibility (2) is with things "known" (whether or not perceived) confused with other things "known" and perceived (x is either P or —P and M, y is P and M). Actually there are two possibilities here, one of which has already been mentioned. The new possibility is stated more fully as one "when a perception is present which belongs to one of the imprints, but none which belongs to the other, and the mind fits to the present perception the imprint belonging to the absent one . . ." (194A) and, alternatively, as "the case where I know both and perceive only one, and do not get the knowledge I have of that one to correspond with my perception" (193D). Also there are the possible cases when things "known," (3) whether perceived or (4) not perceived, are confused with other things not "known" but perceived ([3] x is P and M, y is P and —M; [4] x is —P and M, y is P and —M). These last two cases are not illustrated in the passages following. To grasp what the four possibilities have in common, let us symbolize them as follows:

	x	y
(1)	P and M	P and M
(2)	—P and M	P and M
(3)	P and M	P and —M
(4)	—P and M	P and —M

Now the common feature of all four cases is that in each at least one object is perceived and the other is remembered (alternatively, at least one object is remembered and the other is perceived). This suggests the following subclassification, in which for the first time a place can be found for false judgment.

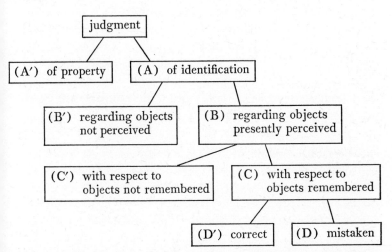

False judgment thus can be tentatively defined as the mistaken identification of objects which are perceived with respect to other objects which are remembered—that is, as an identification falling under subclass (D).

It is essential to note that the concept of mistaken identification can be explicated in the context of the wax block, whereas this turns out to be impossible in the context of the aviary immediately following. Correct judgment is the association of a memory image with a sense image originating with the same object, while mistaken judgment is the correlation of a sense image originating with one object with a memory image arising from another. This reference to objects independent of the "wax block" which can be both perceived and remembered, provides a ground for the distinction between correct and incorrect judgment, no parallel to which can be

found in the aviary where the objects represented to the mind
are abstract and thus never accessible to perception.

This division provides sufficient conditions for false judgment, which is to say that the judgments which fall within one
of its subclasses, namely (D), are exclusively false. It does not,
however, provide necessary conditions as well. To show this
is to show that there are some false judgments which do not
fall under (D). The demonstration that there are false judgments outside of (D) is immediate, and to the Platonist un-
questionable. People commonly make mistaken judgments
about numbers in the abstract, as when someone learning addition considers that $5 + 7 = 11$. But since numbers are never
perceived, these judgments fall neither under (B) nor consequently under (D). Thus our original difficulty recurs, for
again we have only one sense of "being present to the mind"
with which to account for this sort of false judgment. So we
seem pressed once again to the conclusion that "the same man
must at the same time know and not know the same thing"
(196C). The trouble, in short, is that false judgment also
crops up under (B'), which means that we have yet to find a
subdivision of judgment which will give both necessary and
sufficient conditions for a judgment's being false.

The aviary results, figuratively, from cutting the images
loose from the waxen block, and replacing the distinction between sense and memory with a distinction which can apply
in both parts to the representation of abstract objects within
the mind. A number might be known in the sense of having
it stored within one's so-called "long term" memory, or it
might be known by having it more immediately "on the tip of
one's tongue." [47] Knowledge of the number in the first sense
is called "possessing;" knowledge in the second "having."
Thus one "possesses" the phone number he learned some time
ago and is having difficulty recalling, while he "has" the number he is able to enunciate without pause. Knowledge "had"

---

[47] The term ἐπιστήμη for 'knowledge' comes back into play in the
context of the aviary. The birds represent "pieces" of ἐπιστήμη.

is likened to birds which the handler has actually within his grasp.

The reader will suspect at once that this image does not represent an adequate account of memory for Plato, when, at 198B, teaching and learning are described respectively as the passing over and the reception of birds into the aviary. Nothing could be more directly contrary to the theory of recollection of the *Meno* and the *Phaedo*. This, however, is not the feature of the aviary which leads to its final rejection as a workable image. Let us attempt to understand the difficulty by again providing a breakdown of the classification involved in the image.

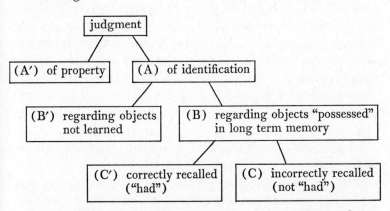

True judgment in this context is to be understood as "having," or grasping, the bird one intends to grasp, while false judgment is grasping the wrong bird. Each bird, figuratively, is a "piece of knowledge" (197E, 198A, 199B), and error in judgment is simply to grasp the wrong piece of knowledge. The awkwardness of this account is obvious at once, for it amounts to the claim that judgment which is false, and hence according to hypothesis not knowledge, is the result of knowing that about which we falsely judge. A precondition of error is that we know (have as a piece of knowledge) that about which we falsely judge and hence do not know. "On this showing," Socrates remarks, "the presence of ignorance might just as well make us know something, or the presence of blindness make us see—if knowledge can ever make us fail to know" (199D).

The basic difficulty, however, has yet to appear. Theaetetus suggests (199E), as a remedy to this apparent absurdity, that the aviary be amended to include "pieces of ignorance" as well. Cornford proposes yet another remedy in his commentary, suggesting that the aviary be conceived to contain complex items of knowledge, such as $5 + 7$, as well as simple items such as 5 and 7 themselves, and that false judgment be typified by the incorrect identification of the complex object $5 + 7$ with the simple object 11.[48] The difficulty with these two suggestions is just the same. There are simply no grounds, in the model of the aviary, on which the distinction between "pieces of ignorance" and "pieces of knowledge" can be accounted for, and no grounds on which the correctness of the identification $5 + 7 = 12$ can be distinguished from the incorrectness of $5 + 7 = 11$. In order to make either Theaetetus' or Cornford's suggestion work, it would be necessary to provide another ("meta-") aviary to account for this distinction (200B–C), and so on ad infinitum. Otherwise, we encounter the old problem of making knowledge the source of ignorance, which has plagued the analysis from the very first attempt to account for false judgment. The difficulty with the final subdivision of judgment is that it relies upon a prior understanding of the very distinction between knowledge and ignorance which it is supposed to elucidate.

The conclusion to be drawn from these difficulties is not that *any* attempt to analyze false judgment without relying upon the concept of knowledge is bound to be abortive. Such an analysis, in fact, has already been provided for the field which is limited to judgments of identification regarding perceptual objects. The lesson to be learned rather is that no distinction between true and false judgment can be adequately

48 *Plato's Theory of Knowledge,* pp. 137–38.

drawn without reference to a criterion or ground, external as it were to the judgment itself, which establishes the true judgment as true and the false judgment as false. In the model of the waxen block, the criterion is in the individual object which can stand as common source of both perceptual and memory images. And in Plato's answer to the problem of false judgment in the *Sophist*, as we shall see, the criterion is found in the "blending" of the Forms.

8 / Insufficiency of the Second Hypothesis

Although all attempts have failed to provide a general elucidation of the distinction between true and false judgment, the possibility nonetheless remains that all true judgment is knowledge as well.[49] The possibility remains, that is, that true judgment, however explicated, is a sufficient condition for knowledge. This possibility is removed with a final counterexample at 201A–C.[50]

When Theaetetus persists (200E) in maintaining his second hypothesis, Socrates brings to bear "a whole profession to

[49] What has failed explicitly is the attempt to extend to judgments about abstract objects the account in the wax block sequence that serves to distinguish false from true judgments of identity regarding perceptual objects. This latter account, however, covers all the illustrations of true judgment entering into the discussion of the third hypothesis. The elements of the "dream theory," spoken words, Hesiod's wagon, the written letters 'T', 'H', and 'E', and the Sun; all are perceptible objects within the range of judgment treated in analogy with the wax tablet. Thus Plato has solved enough of his problem in the second section to move on to the third without unaccounted assumptions.

[50] This counterexample could have been introduced immediately at 187C, thus settling the question of Theaetetus' second hypothesis in less than two pages. The main philosophic burden of the second section of the dialogue is an examination of the difficulties involved in accounting for the possibility of error in judgment, not an examination of the second hypothesis as such.

prove that true belief [judgment] is not knowledge" (201A).
This is the profession of the lawyers, who often are able to
elicit true opinions from jurymen about "facts which can be
known only by an eye-witness . . ." (201B). A necessary condition for the truth of the hypothesis identifying knowledge
and true judgment is that any person in a state of true judgment is in a state of knowledge as well. Since jurymen
therefore can have true opinion (δόξα: judgment) without
knowledge, however, the two mental states cannot be correctly
identified. Theaetetus' second hypothesis, like his first, thus
turns out to be a lifeless deliverance.

It may be pointed out that the issue of finding sufficient
conditions for the second hypothesis itself never arises explicitly throughout the second section of the dialogue, as one would
expect with the methodology discussed in the previous chapter
freshly in mind. What has been shown instead by the example
of the jurymen is that true judgment is not a sufficient condition for knowledge. This in itself, however, shows that no
sufficient conditions for the second hypothesis could ever be
reached. If true judgment (A) is identical to knowledge (B),
then it follows both that A is a sufficient condition for B and
that B is a sufficient condition for A. To show that A is not a
sufficient condition for B is to show conclusively that the identification of A and B is false, and hence that no sufficient
conditions for this identification itself can be found. It is worth
noting, however, that Theaetetus' second attempt to define
knowledge has not fared as badly as the first. The previous
hypothesis, against the background of Socrates' account of
perception as motion, was shown to engender inconsistencies
among its consequences, whereas the second is shown merely
not to hold for some true judgments about facts which can be
"known" only by an eyewitness.[51] In other words, while per-

_____

[51] The force of this counterexample is further diminished by the
fact that "eyewitness knowledge" is not ἐπιστήμη. The term used in this
connection is the now-familiar εἰδέναι, (201B) for which see footnote
44 and associated text. Runciman is unjustified in commenting that

ception, in its failure to grasp existence (186D), is represented
as *never* commensurate with knowledge, nothing Plato says
in the *Theaetetus* rules out the possibility that in some cases
true judgment is at least an integral part of knowledge.

The results of the second section, indeed, are not entirely
negative. Plato has isolated several sets of conditions under
which the distinction can be drawn between true and false
judgment (192C–194B), thus leaving open the question
whether knowledge of objects, in whatever sense obtainable,
might not be identical with judgments truly identifying
memory and sense impressions deriving from the same individual. And apart from the question whether judgment of this
sort amounts to knowledge, the fact that such judgments are
shown possible completes the analogy between the two types
of δύναμις described earlier in the dialogue. Whereas the
"roots" in Theaetetus' illustration are incommensurable on
their own level, they become commensurable in their squares.
And whereas the motions in the theory of perception are incommensurable merely as objects of perception, they become
comparable as true or false on the level of judgment.

The possibility of comparing perceptions in judgment, however, is not a sufficient condition for knowledge in general,
since there are objects such as numbers which we correctly
claim to know but which are never presented in sense experience. The major negative conclusion of the second section of
the dialogue is that the distinction between true and false
judgment regarding abstract objects cannot be based on sense
experience alone, but requires a prior understanding of the
sense in which a person might be said to know such objects.

"if eye-witness knowledge is not knowledge but 'knowledge', then the
argument has only proved that true opinion is not 'knowledge'; and
this will hardly do" (*Plato's Later Epistemology*, pp. 37–38). The
counterexample is used to show that there are cases in which true
judgment is *neither* "knowledge" nor knowledge, for Socrates at 201C
elicits Theaetetus' agreement that the true opinion of the juryman,
admittedly not knowledge in the sense of the eyewitness, is not
ἐπιστήμη either.

What the difficulty with the aviary has shown, Socrates suggests, is "that we were wrong to leave knowledge on one side and look first for an explanation of false judgment. That cannot be understood until we have a satisfactory account of the nature of knowledge." (200C–D) With this, Plato drops the problem of truth and falsehood, subsequently to reappear in the *Sophist*, and turns in the final section of the dialogue to examine the hypothesis that knowledge is true judgment accompanied by λόγος.

9 / The Mysterious "Dream Theory"

Although true judgment is not a sufficient condition for knowledge, there are passages roughly contemporary with the *Theaetetus* which indicate clearly that Plato considered knowledge to be a sufficient condition for true judgment, and a sufficient condition as well for the capacity of rendering some appropriate form of λόγος.[52] And in the present dialogue Socrates expresses an initial satisfaction with Theaetetus' third hypothesis, identifying knowledge with true judgment accompanied by an account, by remarking "how can there ever be knowledge without an account and right belief?" (202D) Thus knowledge is thought at least to coexist with the combination of true δόξα and λόγος, neither necessarily excluding the other. This being the case, the hypothesis that knowledge is identical with true judgment accompanied by an account obviously is accepted as consistent.

Plato's problem in the remainder of the *Theaetetus* is to provide an appropriate sense of λόγος in terms of which this final hypothesis can meaningfully be brought to an account.[53]

[52] *Symposium* 202A; *Timaeus* 51E.

[53] Prior to testing the first hypothesis, the theory of perception was developed to specify an appropriate sense of αἴσθησις, and one of the first moves in the serious analysis of the problem of false judgment was to provide an explicit definition of δόξα (190A). Similarly, a suitable sense of λόγος would have to be isolated before the third

The dialogue ends after failure to find the needed sense of
λόγος in three initially unpromising candidates. It is most significant that Plato does not provide a disproof of this final
hypothesis by the end of the dialogue. Although Socrates does
remark, for Theaetetus' benefit, that "neither perception, nor
true belief, nor the addition of an 'account' to true belief can be
knowledge" (210A–B), there is no counterexample or demonstration to show that the final hypothesis is false. There is no
argument that true belief accompanied by an account is not
sufficient for knowledge, and no reason displayed why anyone
should consider this hypothesis unworthy of belief if only an
adequate sense of λόγος could be provided. Thus, whereas the
first hypothesis is shown to be self-defeating and the second
counterfactual, the third hypothesis is never brought to a final
accounting, and certainly is never shown false.[54]

The major portion of the dialogue following the introduction of the final hypothesis, instead, is divided between a discussion of one sense of λόγος which would make knowledge
impossible and three other senses which would render the hypothesis false for other reasons. The first, and by far the more
sophisticated, sense of λόγος is introduced in a strange theory
which Theaetetus remembers vaguely from an unknown
source and which Socrates claims to have heard in a dream.
This "dream theory" has intrigued philosophers recently beyond any other passage in the *Theaetetus*. Wittgenstein found
in it an anticipation of his logical atomism in the *Tractatus*.[55]

---

hypothesis could meaningfully be subjected to analysis. Since this is
never accomplished in the dialogue, the hypothesis identifying knowledge with true judgment accompanied by an account is never
seriously criticized.

[54] Plato's failure to find three or four out of many possible senses
of λόγος suitable in no way constitutes grounds for rejecting this
final hypothesis. The fact that so many commentators have thought
otherwise attests to the strength of the mistaken tradition that the
Theaetetus ends in genuine doubt about the nature of knowledge.

[55] L. Wittgenstein, *Philosophical Investigations* (New York:
MacMillan Co., 1953), p. 21, section 46.

Ryle discerns in Plato's criticism of the "dream theory" an implicit criticism of the doctrine of Forms.[56] Others more recently read Plato's discussion of the theory as an indication of his confusion between, or bewilderment caused by, the distinction between propositional knowledge and knowledge by acquaintance.[57] Apart from such questions relating to supposed Platonic doctrine, however, there is the tantalizing question why Plato introduced the "dream theory" into the dialogue in the first

[56] The difficulty for the doctrine of the Forms which Ryle finds in the criticism of the "dream theory" is discussed in R. C. Cross "Logos and Forms in Plato," and R. S. Bluck "Logos and Forms in Plato: A Reply to Professor Cross," both reprinted in R. E. Allen, *Studies in Plato's Metaphysics* (New York: Humanities Press, 1965). Ryle argued, in a privately circulated paper, that "if the doctrine of Forms was the view that these verbs, adjectives and common nouns are themselves the names of simple, if lofty, nameables, then Socrates's criticism is, *per accidens*, a criticism of the doctrine of Forms, whether Plato realized this or not" (Cross, in Allen, *ibid.*, p. 14). Among attempts to evade this incipient difficulty for the theory of Forms which Plato was supposed to hold at some earlier time, Cross lists the suggestions (1) that the arguments from 203A to 206B hold only with respect to *perceptible* elements, (2) that Plato in fact had abandoned the theory of Forms by this time, (3) that Plato continued to hold the doctrine despite being unable to meet his own objection, and (Cross's own) (4) that the Forms were not simple substantial entities at all but rather verbal formulations that give the essences of things. Bluck adds a fifth, that for Plato knowledge of the Forms was not of the sort that can be given in a λόγος, but is rather having an understanding of the teleological purpose of a thing (Allen, *ibid.*, p. 40). I will argue shortly, contrary to all this, that we have no reason whatsoever to think that Plato ever thought of the Forms as simple in the sense of admitting no connections between themselves, and that connections of this sort are an adequate basis for giving λόγοι about the Forms themselves.

[57] Runciman, *Plato's Later Epistemology*, p. 45, decides that Plato confuses propositional knowledge with "the sense in which a dog knows its master or a baby knows its mother. . . ." And W. Hicken, in "Knowledge and Forms in Plato's *Theaetetus*" (reprinted in R. E. Allen, *Studies in Plato's Metaphysics*), argues that Plato is in a quandary. Being convinced that knowledge really is a direct intuition of reality, he is able to distinguish between knowledge and true belief only by treating knowledge as if it were discursive and capable of being given an account.

place.[58] It is sufficiently clear that the theory presents one
possible interpretation of the third hypothesis, but nothing is
said explicitly in the dialogue to prepare the reader for those
details of the theory which go far beyond anything required
for the interpretation of the hypothesis itself. The theory apparently is one which Plato feels he must take into account.
Yet the theory as such does not admit positive identification
on the basis of what we know about the state of philosophy at
Plato's time,[59] and Plato himself offers no clue regarding its
sponsorship, or why he is particularly concerned to refute it.
This theory, in short, seems at first to be without connecting
links, either historical or systematic, to any other theory or
philosophic viewpoint treated in the dialogue. And if so, one
can only wonder what Plato's reasons were for introducing it
at this crucial point, and why he takes such great care to show
that the theory is internally self-defeating. Despite the inherent
interest of such doctrinal problems as those mentioned above,
it is this latter problem of methodological tactics with which
I shall be primarily concerned.

Socrates' description of his "dream" may be divided into

[58] H. Meyerhoff, in "Socrates' 'Dream' in the Theaetetus," *Classical
Quarterly*, n.s. 8, no. 3 (November, 1958): 131–38, remarks that
"it is perfectly clear why the 'dream' occurs to Socrates at this point
in the dialogue. It is suggested by the third definition according to
which knowledge is true belief 'with logos' . . ." (p. 131). The
dramatic connections are clear enough, of course. What is not clear
is why Plato depicted Socrates as being reminded of this theory at
all, and why at this particular stage in the dialogue.

[59] As Meyerhoff points out, *ibid.*, the "dream theory" is tradi-
tionally ascribed to Antisthenes, who, according to Aristotle, "showed
his simplicity by his contention that nothing should be spoken of
except by its proper verbal expression (λόγος), one expression for
one thing" (*Metaphysics*, 1024b 32) (Cornford's translation, p.
254). There is an undeniable resemblance here. The main difficulty
with the ascription of this theory to Antisthenes is that Plato had no
particular reason to refute his theory in the *Theaetetus*, and particularly had no reason to allude to such a minor figure at this stage
of the dialogue. Another consideration is that Plato's description
expressly denies λόγοι to elements, directly contrary to that of
Antisthenes quoted above.

three parts, each seemingly with a different purpose. (1) The
major portion presents the theory itself, which in origin seems
to have no necessary relevance to Theaetetus' third hypothesis.
All things, including people, are composed of basic elements,
which admit only names but no λόγοι. The composite things,
however, are given λόγοι, or descriptions, by combining the
names of their elements. Since each element has a unique
name, the combination of names gives a unique λόγος for each
thing. A composite object, accordingly, can be the subject of
true judgment, as when we think of its composition correctly,
and this judgment can be augmented with a λόγος which is
unique to the thing concerned. But an element itself is beyond
judgment and λόγος, being nameable only. This conception of
objects, elements, and names thus provides one possible interpretation of the third hypothesis that knowledge is true judgment with an account. (2) A second portion of Socrates' speech
then makes this interpretation explicit.

> So when a man gets hold of the true notion of something
> without an account, his mind does think truly of it, but he
> does not know it; for if one cannot give and receive an
> account of a thing, one has no knowledge of that thing.
> But when he has also got hold of an account, all this be-
> comes possible to him and he is fully equipped with knowl-
> edge. (202B–C) [60]

This interpretation provides the first sense of λόγος, which is
then criticized and found indefensible by the argument from
202D to 206B. (3) Beyond this, there are a number of details which seem to be inessential to the description of the
theory itself, and which do not enter directly into the subse-

---

[60] As Runciman suggests, "the last six lines are not really a part of
the exposition of the theory of the 'dream'. Read in isolation, they
are merely a summary of the general suggestion that true opinion
accompanied by an account is equivalent to knowledge" (*Plato's Later
Epistemology*, p. 43).

quent criticism. For one thing, the elements are described, almost as an afterthought, as perceptible (202B); yet this particular feature has no part in the *reductio ad absurdum* argument ending at 205E.[61] Moreover, an element cannot be said either to exist or not to exist, for such could not be said of it uniquely. Socrates then goes on to list other expressions that cannot be assigned to the elements, such as " 'just' or 'it' or 'each' or 'alone' or 'this', or any other of a host of such terms" (202A). Although it is true that the elements cannot share terms like these with other elements if they are to be totally uncomposite and unique, these *particular* expressions are totally irrelevant to the criticism following.

Now since these particular details are not essential to the "dream theory" as it appears in the final section of the dialogue, it is reasonable to speculate that if Plato had any reason at all for including them in the theory then this reason is connected with his reasons for introducing the theory in the first place. Since it is a priori unlikely that Plato would have entered into such detail purposelessly, the fact that the elements are perceptible, and the fact that they admit neither attributions of exist-

[61] Some of the letters are described as noises at 203B, but this is gratuitous as far as the argument is concerned. And in the counter-example at 206A the letters are learned "by sight and hearing." But there is no necessity for employing this counterexample at all; another could have been chosen in which the senses do not play such a direct role, such as one involving numbers rather than letters. It might be suggested further that the perceptibility of the elements is a necessary condition of anyone's making true judgments without λόγος about the assemblages composed of them; for if true thinking is distinct from naming the elements, it must be merely thinking *that* such and such elements are there to be named, and this could be determined only by perception. This suggestion assumes a close connection between the "dream theory" and the earlier theory of perception, in which latter perception alone provides a possible way of gaining knowledge about things. I propose shortly, in fact, that the purpose of the "dream theory" is to be understood in connection with the theory of perception. But, apart from this connection, there seems to be no necessity for Plato to assume that perception alone reveals the composition of things. No such assumption, for example, finds a place with the image of the aviary.

ence nor ascriptions which suggest that they are permanent or
stable, may serve as clues to the significance of this theory in
its particular context. And what these features suggest to us,
of course, is the theory of perception developed as part of the
examination of Theaetetus' first hypothesis.

The parallels between the two theories are considerable. In
both there are elements and things composed of elements, to
which in the former theory are given "the name of 'man' or
'stone' or of any living creature or kind" (157C). In both, the
elements are perceptible, but not properly said to exist. In
both, moreover, terms that suggest fixity are not to be assigned
to the elements—such terms for example as 'this' (τόδε, 157B;
τοῦτο, 202A) and 'it' or 'that' (ἐκεῖνο, 157B, 202A).[62] And
since an element in the theory of perception admits no fixed
description, it too, like an element in the "dream theory," is
incapable of being provided a λόγος which would designate it
uniquely.[63]

Yet it would appear that the analogy between the two theories is not complete. Perhaps the most striking difference at
first glance between the fast motions of the earlier theory and
the elements of the latter is that the elements are denied even
the description of being in a state of becoming, whereas in the

---

[62] See Cornford's discussion of τοῦτο, *Plato's Theory of Knowledge*, p. 143 n.

[63] Meyerhoff ("Socrates 'Dream' in the *Theaetetus*," p. 133) draws
attention to certain parallels between the two theories, and remarks
that it "is hard to escape the conclusion that there is a closer con-
nexion between these two parts of the *Theaetetus* than has previously been noticed." Since his list of similarities is somewhat
overdrawn, this conclusion may be less inescapable than he suggests.
It is a valuable suggestion nonetheless. Meyerhoff's final conclusion,
on the other hand, is unduly conservative, namely the conclusion that
Plato's analysis of the "dream-theory" was intended "to show the
inadequacy of constructing a theory of knowledge (as outlined in
the 'dream') in which the primitive terms designate simple, unan-
alysable perceptual data" (*ibid.*, p. 136). This conclusion can be
reached without regard to the parallels between the two theories.

theory of perception we are admonished to speak "in accord-
ance with nature, of what is 'becoming', 'being produced', 'perishing', 'changing' " (157B). Neither the elements nor the fast
motions may be described as existing (or not existing); but it
seems that the fast motions are properly describable in terms
of becoming, while the elements are not describable at all.
Along with this apparent difference goes the even more obvious distinction between the fast motions which *are* motions and
the elements which apparently are neither motions nor otherwise, insofar at least as no descriptive adjective can properly
be attached to them.

These differences are certainly suggested by the texts and,
on the basis of the texts, do not seem to admit "explaining
away" in any definitive manner. Yet it does appear on a very
close reading of the relevant passages that the descriptions of
the elements (which after all *are* described by Plato himself)
and the descriptions of the fast motions are not *necessarily* incompatible. Although it is said at 157B that we should speak,
in connection with particulars and assemblages alike, only of
what is becoming or being produced, it is not the suggestion
of this passage surely that the terms 'becoming', 'changing',
and so forth, *name* particular motions. Moreover, although
these terms, and 'motion' itself, *describe* the motions, they do
not attribute to them properties the motions have in themselves.
The point of saying that motions are entirely in change and
becoming, to the contrary, is just that no properties *can* right-
fully be ascribed to them in themselves. With the assemblages it is different, for although their components are continually changing, certain overall features remain constant
enough for us to apply the names 'man', 'stone', and so forth.
But if the motions themselves cannot properly be said even to
exist, then they cannot be said to have properties in and by
themselves. Strictly speaking, they cannot even be said *themselves* to be changing. What we should say instead is that
there is a constant change *in the flow* of fast motions, which in

perceptual experience is a flow which never stands still, and which is always such as to warrant the descriptive phrases 'becoming', 'being produced', 'perishing', 'changing', and the like. It is hard admittedly to square this suggestion with the passage at 156D, where the fast motions, or "generated off-spring", are described as "quicker, inasmuch as they move from place to place and their motion consists in change of place." [64] Maintaining the interpretation suggested above, one could only say that it is not the *individual* offspring which here are said to move from place to place but rather series of individuals generated afresh at each successive place along the path of apparent motion. There is the further possibility, of course, that *if* Plato intended a close analogy between the two theories, he overlooked this particular point of apparent dissimilarity, and would have remedied it (as he rather easily could have done, if the suggestions above are intelligible) to remove the discord.

Thus there is indeed a slight strain in this merging of the two theories, and it would be pointless to push the matter further if the merging itself did not help remove the mystery from the "dream theory" intruded with such emphasis at this critical juncture of the dialogue. Such a desirable result, however, seems forthcoming when we recall that the score between Plato and the philosophers of flux remains unsettled at the end of the first part of the dialogue. The sophisticated philosopher of flux, who was bound to defend as a complete ontology the theory of the perceptual world presented along with the theory of perception, would not rest with Socrates' proof against Theaetetus that knowledge is not perception. Such a person would not be impressed by Plato's lightly veiled intrusion of the Forms Existence, Sameness, and Difference into the discussion, or by his claim that any act of mind which falls

---

[64] Cornford expresses doubt about this translation, *Plato's Theory of Knowledge*, p. 47 n.

short of these falls short of knowledge as well.[65] The material-
ist instead would be likely to stand his ground, and claim that
knowledge amounts to the ability to *enumerate* the elements
going into such objects as man and stone. And he would be
likely further to recount how one set of elements regularly re-
places another under certain common circumstances, the
awareness of which regularities counts as wisdom and knowledge in the eyes of those unskilled in these descriptions and
predictions. This is, in fact, just what wisdom was considered
to be among the prisoners chained in the lower depths of the
cave (*Republic* 516 C, D), an image which we might do well
to bear in mind while attempting to understand the "dream
theory," regardless of its relationship with the earlier theory of
perception.

It may be suggested, therefore, that Plato is now turning to
the final issue remaining in his refutation of the theory of
knowledge associated with the sophisticated form of material-
ism he is combating in the *Theaetetus*. Granted that the flux
philosopher might be clever enough to laugh off Socrates'
refutation of the thesis that knowledge is perception, and
might go on to maintain the rather more plausible thesis that
knowledge is the ability to enumerate the parts of the series of
elements that go into the make-up of men, stones, and so forth,
how should this further thesis be countered? It is at least possible to read Socrates' very detailed and careful refutation of
the "dream theory" as directed against this quarter. After all,
as we shall see, this refutation shows that the "dream theory"
in fact is inconsistent, in that its necessary conditions lead ultimately to self-defeat. Apart from the arguments against the
various hypotheses based on the theory of perception in the
first part of the dialogue, this is the only other instance of this
mode of argumentation in the *Theaetetus*. This fact in itself

[65] These, of course, are the very Forms that figure so prominently
in the *Sophist*.

suggests a close association in Plato's mind between the earlier
theory of perception and the mysterious "dream theory" of the
final section.

10 / Refutation of the "Dream Theory"

The hypothesis that knowledge is identical with true judgment
accompanied by λόγος does not collapse with the "dream theory." It would stand with this theory, however, if the latter
could be satisfactorily defended, for that hypothesis expresses
just the account that would have to be given of knowledge if
the "dream theory" were true. Truth of the "dream theory"
thus amounts to a sufficient condition for the truth of the final
hypothesis, but one which Plato takes great pains to show cannot be met. In the refutation of this theory, the syllable is considered as a whole and the letters constituting the syllable as
elements or parts. The argument applies quite generally to the
relationship of part to whole, however, without respect to this
particular interpretation.[66] The argument may be schematized
as follows.

The whole (syllable) is either (1) the sum of its parts (letters) or (2) a whole different from the sum of its parts (203C).
If (1) then, according to the theory, all the parts (the sum)
can be known, since the whole can be known and the whole is
the sum of the parts. But also according to the theory, the parts
cannot be known. Thus, all the parts can be known, but none
of the parts can be known, and since this is a "monstrous ab-

[66] This is one of the earlier occurrences of the letter and syllable
imagery in Plato's writings. Meyerhoff, "Socrates 'Dream' in the
Theaetetus," *Classical Quarterly*, p. 132 n, has listed the following
additional occurrences: *Cratylus* 422 ff, 425 ff; *Phaedrus* 244 ff;
Philebus 17 ff; *Politicus* 278 ff; *Timaeus* 48 ff; *Sophist* 253 ff; *Seventh
Letter* (if pertinent) 342 ff. Plato's use of this imagery is discussed
in Ryle's "Letters and Syllables in Plato," *Philosophical Review*, 69,
no. 4 (October, 1960): 431–51.

surdity" (203D) (a contradiction), alternative (1) must be relinquished. If (2), however, then either (a) the whole has no parts or (b) the whole has parts. Consider (a): "Then, on the present showing, a syllable will be a thing that is absolutely one and cannot be divided into parts of any sort." (205C) But if the whole is indivisible, then according to the theory no account can be given of it, whereas the theory has stated explicitly that the whole is knowable but not the parts.[67] Thus, according to the theory, the whole is both knowable and unknowable, which is inconsistent. Alternative (a) therefore must be relinquished. Now consider (b), wherein it must be the case either (i) that the whole is the same as the sum, or (ii) that the whole is different from the sum. The first alternative has already been examined: if (i) the whole is the same as the sum, then the inconsistent consequences of (1) above follow. This leaves only alternative (ii). But it is also the case that " 'sum' and 'all the things' denote the same thing (204D)," and the case that "anything that has parts consists of parts (204E)." The former quotation may be read as a statement of identity between the sum and all the parts, while the latter may be read as a statement of identity between the thing which has

[67] It is at this point that the danger Ryle has indicated for the doctrine of Forms arises (see footnote 56). The doctrine in question, insofar as it relates to the present issue, is that Forms are incomposite and that they are known by some sort of direct intuition. The argument against the "dream theory," however, leads to the conclusion that nothing incomposite can ever be known. The whole problem vanishes when we recall that the characteristic of incomposite things, which leads to the refutation of the "dream theory," is that nothing whatsoever can be said of them apart from their names. Of each Form, however, many things can be said, among which is that it is not any other Form, and so forth. The very dialogue which suggests the incomposite nature of the Forms most explicitly (*Phaedo* 78C–D), in fact, also states explicitly that the Forms are capable of relationships of "entailment" and "incompatibility"—as Three and Five, for example, are invariably Odd (*Phaedo* 104A). As the *Sophist* shows, these relationships are all that is required for giving λόγοι pertaining to the Forms, regardless of any other sense in which the Forms are "incomposite."

parts and all the parts.[68] From these two identities and (ii), it is readily deducible that the whole is not a thing with parts.[69] But this case has already been examined, with the inconsistent consequences of (a). It is the case, moreover, that (ii) cannot be maintained in the first place, since the sum and the whole are "exactly the same thing—that from which nothing whatever is missing" (205A). And this leads back to the inconsistency of (1). Thus, on any account, we must conclude either that the part as well as the whole is knowable (205D), or that the whole as well as the part is unknowable (205E), neither of which possibilities is consistent with the "dream theory."

Like the consequences of the theory of perception drawn out in the first section of the dialogue, the consequences of this "dream theory" also have been shown inconsistent. This particular interpretation of the final hypothesis, therefore, cannot be defended.

11 / The Meanings of 'Logos'

The "dream theory" provides one possible interpretation for the hypothesis that knowledge is true judgment accompanied by λόγος. Refutation of this interpretation, however, does not refute the hypothesis itself, for there are other senses of the term λόγος which might fare more favorably under examina-

---

[68] The assertion that a thing with parts consists of parts does not amount, in general, to an assertion that such a thing is identical with its parts, since it is conceivable that a thing (e.g., a national group) might consist of its parts (the individuals involved) in addition to something else (e.g., their language and customs). In a context established by the presuppositions of the "dream theory," however, there is nothing other than the parts of which a thing might be constituted.

[69] If (1) sum = all the parts
    (2) all the parts = thing with (those) parts
    (3) whole ≠ sum,
then (4) whole ≠ thing with parts.

tion.[70] The remainder of the dialogue discusses the inadequacies of three of these senses. They are (1) *delivered speech*, (2) *sum* or *enumeration*, and (3) *description* or *definition*.[71] With these three senses, none of which is particularly promising in the present application, Plato drops his search and pronounces the hypothesis a false birth along with its two predecessors.

There is a quite common use of the term λόγος which Plato does not permit himself to consider in the *Theaetetus*. This is the use according to which λόγος means (4) *ground*. And there are shades of meaning within this use, several of which would be highly suggestive in a serious attempt to make the third hypothesis work as an analysis of knowledge. There is the use of λόγος to convey the sense of reason or *justification*, as with its occurrence in *Gorgias* 512C. There is the use to convey the sense of *hypothesis, argument*, or *tentative ground*, as occurs in *Protagoras* 344B. Even more promising is the sense of *principle, explanation, cause*, or *reason*, as in *Gorgias* 465A. Plato's procedure in ignoring these uses most certainly was deliberate. Yet if he had considered these senses the dialogue could not have ended on the entirely negative note for which it has been famous during generations of commentators.

Disposal of the three meanings Plato does consider is a relatively routine task. If λόγος means merely (1) delivered speech ("giving overt expression to one's thought by means of vocal sound with names and verbs . . ." [206D]), then it is clear that knowledge is not true judgment with λόγος , for any

---

[70] The term had a wide variety of senses at the time of Plato's writing, most of which have no relevance to the present context (such as natural law, speech to oneself, concise saying, etc.). A summary listing of prima facie relevant senses is given in a footnote by Cornford, *Plato's Theory of Knowledge*, p. 142. Of the several uses mentioned there, Plato fails even to consider the most plausible, that expressing the sense of explanation or ground.

[71] The sense of *definition* suggests giving the essence of a thing. This, in itself, is an appropriate sense for the context, but Plato's example obviously falls short of giving the "essence" of the Sun.

man "not born deaf and dumb" (*ibid.*) can express his thoughts
on any subject, whether or not he has knowledge of what he is
talking about.

Given that λόγος is used to designate (2) a summing or
enumeration of the parts of the thing known, then we are dealing with the hypothesis that judgment can be subdivided in
the following way to produce a definition of knowledge: [72]

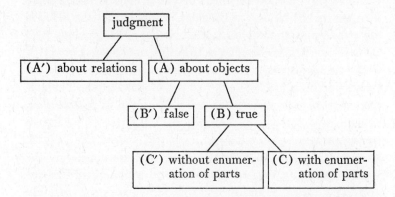

Thus to know a wagon might be to think truly about its construction, and to be able to provide a λόγος in the sense of item-
izing all its parts. To take a more contemporary example, a
mechanic who can identify all the parts of an automobile
surely *knows* the machine in a sense beyond the claim of any
person who has only a general, albeit correct, notion about
how an automobile is constituted.

But this will not do either, for there are some true judgments
about things accompanied by enumeration of their parts which

[72] Refutation of the "dream theory" has shown only that this particular conception of what can meaningfully be said about parts and
wholes cannot be relied upon to give a viable interpretation of
Theaetetus' third hypothesis. It does not serve as a refutation of this
hypothesis under the present interpretation. This refutation is
achieved by a counterexample which shares none of the presuppositions of the theory previously refuted. There is no suggestion, for
example, that the parts of the wagon can be named only, and in no
sense described.

nevertheless are not instances of knowledge. The example
given by Plato again employs the distinction between a syllable and its constituent letters. When a child just learning to
write undertakes to spell the name 'Theaetetus', and both
thinks that the first syllable is the sequence T, H, E, and
itemizes the letters in that order, then he has made a true judgment about the syllable and has produced an enumeration of
its parts. But he may still lack knowledge about the syllable,
as would be shown if he wrote or spelled the same syllable in
the name 'Theodorus' leaving out the H. In short, although a
person might judge correctly about a thing and be able to
enumerate its parts on one occasion, there is nothing in this
performance to prevent his judging incorrectly about the same
thing at another time. If and only if he had knowledge of the
thing would we be justified in being assured that he would not
be wrong on another occasion. Since we are not justified in
this assurance on the basis of his doing it right on one occasion, knowledge cannot be the same thing as true belief accompanied by an enumeration of the parts. This division thus
fails to provide even sufficient conditions for the identification
of knowledge with true judgment accompanied by λόγος.

A third sense of λόγος, Socrates then suggests, is the "meaning most people would give: being able to name some mark by
which the thing one is asked about differs from everything
else" (208C). Λόγος in this sense signifies (3) a definition or
formula giving the characteristics which make the thing defined different from all other things. The illustration of such a
definition following this suggestion is provocative: "Take the
sun as an example. I dare say you will be satisfied with the
account of it as the brightest of the heavenly bodies that go
round the earth." (208D) What is suggestive here is not the
definition, giving a distinguishing mark which although
unique is quite accidental, but rather the fact that the sun, of
all physical objects, is chosen to supply the example. The
reader of the *Republic* or the *Timaeus* will recall that for
Plato the sun is the most exalted of physical objects, serving as

a visible analogue to the Good in the realm of the Forms. One may sense here that Plato is reaching as close to the Forms as he can without bringing in a sense of λόγος which would yield an hypothesis concerning the nature of knowledge which he would not choose to take sides against. The sun, after all, symbolizes the highest level in the realm of the Forms, where all statements representing knowledge are supposed, in some sense, to find their ultimate ground among formal structures which themselves require no further accounting.[73]

Plato's argument against this third proposal begins with the observation that one's true judgment about a particular object in some sense already includes a grasp of what distinguishes that object from others similar to it. If the judgment provides a grasp only of characteristics shared by several objects, then it is about all these objects indifferently and not about one in particular. Only if the judgment includes a grasp of the distinguishing features of a particular object can it be considered a judgment about that object and no other. Thus, in some sense, "the correct notion of anything must itself include the differentness of that thing" (209D). But if so, what is left for the λόγος to add to the true judgment? The λόγος cannot add mere true opinion about the object's distinguishing characteristics, for that is part of the true judgment itself. Nor can the λόγος add knowledge of the distinguishing features, since the suggestion that knowledge is true judgment accompanied by knowledge is circular in the worst sort of way. But no further alternative seems to be available, and this final sense of λόγος proposed in explication of the third hypothesis also is rejected as unhelpful.

At this juncture (210A–B) the attempt to find a workable sense of λόγος is dropped, and Plato quite prematurely rejects the final hypothesis along with its two predecessors. The hy-

[73] Whether or not Plato thought of the Good as the ground of knowledge at the time of writing the *Theaetetus*, he must surely have anticipated that the term would carry this imagery for the reader of the *Republic*.

pothesis that knowledge is perception has been shown literally self-defeating, and the hypothesis identifying knowledge with true belief has been shown incapable of being provided a sufficient condition. This final hypothesis, however, which already has been accepted as self-consistent, is never subjected to any analysis which would put its sufficiency to the test. This leaves entirely open the possibility that Plato felt there was more to say about the third hypothesis, and that it could be said better in a context more conducive to an explicit discussion of relationships among the Forms.[74] Let us examine the *Sophist* with this possibility in mind.

[74] Gulley rightly remarks, in *Plato's Theory of Knowledge*, p. 101, that "it is clear that, though the difficulty remains here unresolved, this last attempt to specify 'account' gives a significant pointer to the solution which Plato offers in later dialogues. It is clear in the first place that by the end of the dialogue Plato is very near to thinking of 'account' in terms of definition. Moreover . . . his specification of 'account' in terms of the method of division . . . in the later dialogues is the final result of the inquiry in the *Theaetetus* and closely linked with the final part of that inquiry."

I I I

The *Sophist*

1 / Prior Debts

The *Theaetetus* not only has failed to produce an explicit definition of knowledge, but moreover has broached without resolution several related problems which Plato himself must have considered to be of top priority. For one, there is the problem of accounting in general for the possibility of false judgment, assumed soluble in the formulation of Theaetetus' third hypothesis, but with no hint in that dialogue of how to begin an adequate solution.[1] Another is the problem of explicating a sense of λόγος which will sustain the thesis, explicit in the *Theaetetus* and elsewhere, that knowledge, if not the *same* as true judgment with λόγος (an identification not yet disproven), at least is divided from true judgment by its ability to provide a λόγος or account.

The problems of false judgment and of λόγος are important problems in their own right, apart from their involvement in the problem of defining knowledge. But they are all the more important for being so intimately involved in this latter problem. Insofar as knowledge includes both true judgment and

[1] In this regard, see note 49, chapter II.

λόγος, no definition of knowledge will be adequate which does not provide an account of these two components as well. We should recall, moreover, that Socrates (prematurely) had relinquished the hypothesis identifying knowledge with true judgment accompanied by λόγος precisely because no adequate sense of λόγος had emerged from the inquiry at the end of the *Theaetetus*. If false judgment in general were given an adequate account, and if a sense of λόγος were isolated which might plausibly be considered a part of knowledge, then Theaetetus' third hypothesis could be taken off the shelf and put back in the running. This indeed appears to be one among other things the *Sophist* is intended to accomplish.

Thus, although the problems of false judgment and of λόγος are interesting in themselves, Plato has a particular reason for raising them again in this subsequent dialogue. No one who reads the *Theaetetus* carefully can fail to sense Plato's sympathy with the third hypothesis, and the fact that this hypothesis is never refuted should not be underestimated. The *Theaetetus*, indeed, is inconclusive, but not in the sense of leading into a blind alley. It is inconclusive in the sense of being open-ended, suggesting but not pursuing a possible definition of knowledge which is not prey to any of the difficulties which proved so devastating against the two previous definitions. Plato's intention in writing the *Sophist*, it is plausible to conjecture, was at least in part to provide answers to the problems of false judgment and of λόγος which will answer the central problem of the *Theaetetus* as well.

There are other debts of considerable importance left over from the *Theaetetus* which are discharged in the present dialogue. Although both extreme Heracliteanism and the diametrically opposed thesis of Parmenides are challenged in the *Theaetetus*, only the former is there brought to an accounting. Serious criticism of Parmenides is left for the *Sophist*, where it is absorbed into Plato's more general program of accounting for the possibility of false judgment. As part of the same inquiry, finally, the downright scandalous conclusion of *Theae-*

tetus 157B, that the perceptible world does not exist, is softened considerably by a detailed and skillfully woven account of an entirely obvious sense in which *that which is not* also, by that very token, in another sense *is*.

Perhaps the most striking thing about the *Sophist* as a sequel to the *Theaetetus*, however, is the way in which it exemplifies the sort of knowledge a definition of which was unsuccessfully pursued in the other dialogue. Not only are there three distinct examples of definitions which for Plato would count as knowledge, but, moreover, there is both an illustration and a description of the kind of procedure by which such knowledge can be achieved. The *Sophist*, in a word, not only completes the definition of knowledge left dangling at the end of the *Theaetetus*, but also illustrates knowledge and shows how it is to be accomplished. Whereas the *Theaetetus* serves as a δύναμις to produce true judgment about knowledge in the mind of the tenacious reader, the *Sophist* provides on a higher level the λόγος which would change that judgment into knowledge about knowledge itself. To sustain these claims is the purpose of the present chapter.

2 / A False Start

"At present," says the Stranger, "all that you and I possess in common is the name" (218C) of the Sophist.[2] The thing to which the name is given "we may perhaps have privately before our minds; but it is always desirable to have reached an agreement about the thing itself by means of explicit statements, rather than be content to use the same word without formulating what it means" (ibid.). The term translated 'statement' in this passage is λόγος. Thus, while at present each of us has only his own opinion as to what the Sophist is, and per-

[2] Cornford is the translator of the *Sophist* quoted, save between 218D and 230E where Jowett's translation is used.

haps this opinion is true, to define the Sophist and thereby to *know* what he is requires bringing "his nature to light in a clear formula [ἐμφανίζοντι λόγῳ τί ποτ' ἔστι]" (218C). To achieve this knowledge of the Sophist is the goal which binds the dialogue into a dramatic whole. The dialogue begins, however, with a number of unsuccessful definitions which may appear at first to contribute nothing in particular to the definition of the Sophist finally achieved by the end of the dialogue. The apparent irrelevance of these six "falsely defined" Sophists poses a problem which we must consider.

Before approaching the problem of the Sophist, however, the Stranger advises carrying through a practice definition on "something comparatively small and easy" (218D), for which purpose the lowly Angler is chosen. The definition of the Angler is short, untroublesome, and the first among three successful definitions accomplished within the dialogue. Like its companion dialogue, the *Sophist* begins with a λόγος citing necessary and sufficient conditions. Its role here is not only to illustrate the task the Stranger is about to undertake, but also to exhibit the features of a successful definition in contrast with the several faulty definitions which follow. Let us examine this preliminary definition in detail.

The Stranger begins at 219A by subdividing art (τέχνη) into the productive and the acquisitive, each subclassification being supplied with a collection of examples which exhibit its essential feature. The art of angling is grouped on this level with the arts involving learning and cognition (219C), along with those of trade, fighting, and hunting, which are involved in the control of things existing prior to the exercise of the art. The acquisitive class then is further subdivided into voluntary exchange and forceful conquests, which separates the angler at least from the merchant. These and subsequent divisions within the definition are diagrammed on the following page. Although scarcely exciting in its detail, this definition illustrates the method to be used in tracking down the Sophist. The Sophist, indeed, is first to be sought within the same general class of acquisitive artisans where the Angler has been successfully enclosed.

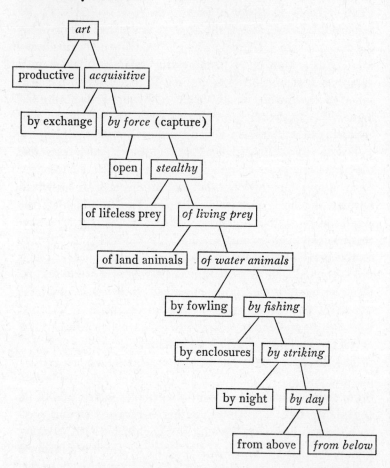

= Angling
(219A–221C)

The important feature of this definition is that it captures both necessary and sufficient conditions for angling within the same chain of division. The characterization of each level is *necessary* to angling, on the one hand, in that no activity which cannot be characterized in each of these ways could properly be called angling. It is essential to specify that the angler *strikes* his prey from *below*, for example, to distinguish him from the net—or spear—fisherman; and if we assume angling without bait, *daylight* appears essential to enable the angler to see the fish he is attempting to hook.[3] It is essential to say that he seeks to *capture* his prey to distinguish him from the servant buying fish at the market, that he does so by *stealth* to distinguish him from the child who blunders after fish while wading offshore, that what he seeks by stealth is *living* prey to distinguish him from the thief of another's catch, and that the water animals he seeks are *fish* to separate him from the hunter of ducks and geese. And his art obviously is *acquisitive* overall, for he is not the creator of the objects with which he deals. This is not to say, of course, that true anglers never hunt geese, nor buy fish, nor steal from another's creel, and so forth. The point rather is that insofar as he warrants the title 'angler' any sportsman must at least try to catch fish stealthily with a hook driven home with force from below. These features are not the only aspects of the angler's activity, but they are essential to it.

The multileveled characterization, on the other hand, provides as well a description of conditions which in themselves are *sufficient* for being an angler. Any person who is engaged in the acquisitive art of stealthy capture of living fish by striking in daylight from below, that is to say, is an angler by virtue merely of being correctly describable in this fashion. Given this as a true description, no further information is needed to assure the correct application of the name 'angler' to the person so described. Other descriptions might be possible, of course, which justify application of the name in an

---

[3] As described, in angling "a hook is used, and the fish is not struck in any chance part of his body, as he is with the spear, but only about the head and mouth . . ." (220E–221A). This suggests that Plato is thinking of a mode of fishing in which the prey is not induced to take the hook *within* its mouth.

equally definitive way; but these might mention characteristics which are not necessary as well. Since the present description specifies both necessary and sufficient conditions, it provides an adequate definition of what it is to be an angler.[4] In the terminology of the *Phaedrus*, we may say that this definition reflects a division according to the "objective articulation" (265E) among the Forms.[5]

Now, says the Stranger, "following this pattern, let us endeavour to find out what a Sophist is" (221C). In at least one important respect just reviewed, however, the first five definitions of the Sophist which immediately ensue (from 221D to 226A) do not follow this pattern at all. None of them gives necessary conditions for being a sophist.[6] This is indicated by the fact itself that five competing definitions of the Sophist are given. Although each of these is sufficient, in the sense that there are people called 'sophists' who meet each description, none mentions features which, either separately or in combination, are *necessary* to being a sophist. The practitioners specified by these five definitions will be called 'Sophist I', 'Sophist II', and so forth. Following these five, there is a sixth definition of an art which the Stranger quite explicitly refuses to consider on a level with the others, but which is described with reservation as the "Sophistry that is of noble lineage" (231B). The practitioner of this art accordingly will be designated (with quotation marks) as "Sophist VI." The definition of "Sophist VI" then is followed by a proper definition of the Sophist, which we will call 'Sophist VII', problems in the definition of which occupy the remainder of the dialogue. Let us consider

---

[4] It may be noted that the definition could be shortened without sacrifice of either its necessity or its sufficiency. Although capture of water animals is essential to being an angler, this is entailed by the capture of fish. Thus the distinction between land and water animals could be dropped from the definition without effect. This is discussed further in the first section of chapter IV.

[5] Hackforth is the translator of the *Phaedrus* in the passages quoted.

[6] I shall write 'a sophist' when referring to individual sophists, and 'the Sophist' when reference is intended to what the Stranger is trying to define.

Sophists I–V, first in their relation to the Angler, and then in their relation to "Sophist VI" and Sophist VII.

Sophists I (221D–223B) and V (225A–226A) are defined through divisions of the art of acquisition by capture already introduced as part of the definition of the Angler. We may pick up the classificatory scheme at this juncture.[7]

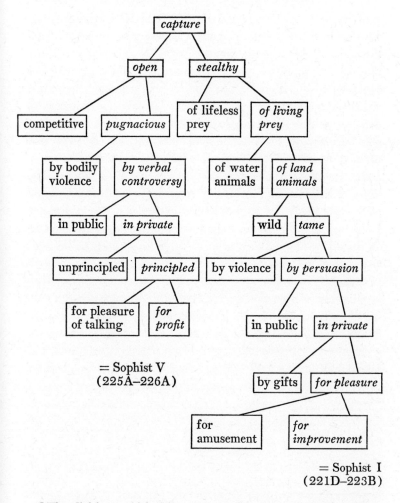

[7] The divisions which follow are of the *practices* of the various Sophists rather than of the practitioners themselves. This is for ease

None of the features in either definition is necessary. Since the art of capture itself is not essential to the Sophist, as is evident shortly in the fact that three more types of sophistry are to be found under the subclassification of acquisition by exchange, none of the particular ways in which capture might be achieved itself can be counted as necessary. In particular, there are (were, or might be) sophists who are not controversialists (but well-intended teachers), who are not interested in profits, and who are not interested even in persuading their listeners for the purpose of winning them over. Although the definitions may be presumed to be sufficient, in that each captures some sophistic type within its mesh, neither can be said to contain only necessary features. A definition with only one unnecessary category within its structure is inadequate, judged against the standard set by the definition of the Angler, and one with many unnecessary features is defective all the more.

No less defective in this respect are the remaining definitions, of Sophists II, III, and IV, which constitute subdivisions of the arts involving acquisition by exchange.[8] Whereas Sophists I and V are hunters, their three comrades are now shown as members of the mercantile class. The differences between Sophists of this middle range are slight. Sophist II sells goods produced by another man in commerce between cities, while Sophist III is engaged in local retail. Sophist IV, finally, sells his own products on the local market. A further and quite common appearance of the flesh-and-blood sophist would be the man who peddles his own wares from city to city. Sophists II, III, and IV are illustrated diagrammatically on the facing page. Since there are other sophists who are not engaged in ex-

---

of representation only. Plato vacillates between the two sorts of description. The distinction, however, is of no particular importance for what Plato is trying to do.

[8] As we shall see, Sophists III and IV are only barely distinguishable, which may account for the fact that Sophist V is referred to as the Sophist reappearing "for the fourth time" (225E). At 231D–E, however, six distinct Sophists are named, numbered as in the present text.

change at all, however, no specification of this particular form of acquisition can be a necessary feature of the Sophist in general. Each of the five definitions shows a sufficient condition for being a sophist, but none shows conditions with any legitimate claim to being necessary. Each definition thereby fails

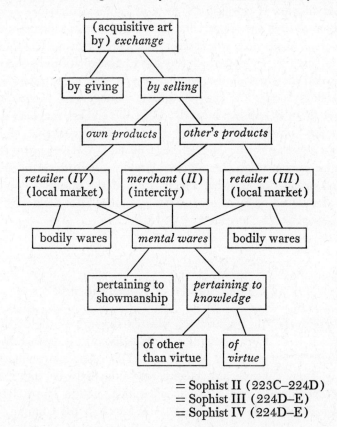

= Sophist II (223C–224D)
= Sophist III (224D–E)
= Sophist IV (224D–E)

to disclose the nature of the Sophist which the Stranger is out to capture.

A careful examination of the five definitions, however, shows at least one feature in common, which has only to be described in a common term to be seen as present in each manifestation of the Sophist's art. Each Sophist (in person) produces, or purports to produce, some sort of improvement, either to himself or in the person upon whom the art is exercised. Sophist I persuades by producing the sort of pleasure that goes with the apparent acquisition of virtue, Sophist V produces controversial discourse which in turn produces profit, and Sophist II through IV have in common that they bring about at least the appearance of knowledge about virtue in the souls of those with whom their wares are exchanged.

Thus the Sophist which has been pursued fruitlessly along several divisions of the acquisitive arts shows up rather surprisingly under the entirely different category of production. Yet there is nothing inconsistent in the sudden reappearance of the Sophist under a category competing with that of his first appearance; for as Sophists I through V have shown, the same person might be engaged simultaneously in acquisition and production. Further specification of the essential Sophist under the category of production is pursued after the definition of "Sophist VI," to which we now turn.

3 / The "Sophist of Noble Lineage"

As with the Angler, unlike Sophists I through V, the division which leads to the definition of "Sophist VI" is preceded directly with a collection of instances. This collection produces a division of the arts, not yet explored in the dialogue, into those of combination and those of separation, within which latter classification the "sixth Sophist" is found in the company of such menial servants as the threshers, the winnowers, and those whose concern is to effect a proper separation of wool in one or another of its various forms. Of particular note relative to the other Sophists, then, is that "Sophist VI" is engaged in neither acquisition nor production, but rather works with material which has been produced and acquired prior to the exercise of his art. Of particular note further, with reference to the subsequent "chance discovery" of the Philosopher and the "free man's knowledge" (253C), is the fact that the practice of "Sophist VI" is a matter of art (τέχνη, [230E], ff.) and not, as with the Philosopher, the exercise of a science or knowledge.[9] A further caution, if one is needed, against reading the description of the practice of "Sophist VI" as a definition of the Philosopher's "division according to Kinds" is that the former's task is elaborated as one of separating better from worse (226D), while the function of the Philosopher falls out under the opposite subdivision covering the separation of like from like (Form from Form) (253C).[10]

After identification of "Sophist VI" as one who separates better from worse, the analogy shifts from that of the menial to that of the physician. Whereas the physician is concerned with the purification of bodies, the practice of "Sophist VI" is to effect the purification of souls.[11] But there is an important parallel between types of impurity in body and soul which leads to an interesting further subdivision of this "Sophist's" art. Among maladies of the body are disease, which is the subject of the physician's purge, and lack of symmetry due to deformity which is more the concern of the gymnast or trainer (229A). Correspondingly, there is the difference among maladies of the soul between vice (moral asymmetry) and ignorance, the former being properly subject to chastisement as

[9] The practice of the grammarian (253A) and of the musician (253B) also is τέχνη, while that of the philosopher is ἐπιστήμη (253C).

[10] This poses a severe problem for any attempt to read this part of the *Sophist* along with the *Statesman* as describing respectively the Philosopher's functions of division and collection, as if the Philosopher were just "Sophist VI" and the Statesman rolled into one. The function of "Sophist VI" is *analogous* to the Philosopher's function of division into Kinds, just as the task of the Statesman is analogous to the Philosopher's task of collection. But in each case also there are several important differences, not the least of which is the relationship each to each of what is divided and collected.

[11] Jowett's translation of λόγων μεθόδῳ (227A) as 'dialectic art' is misleading. "Sophist VI" is not a dialectician, but rather a practitioner of the art of disputation. The translation "dialectic process" for λόγοις at 230B also is misleading in this respect.

corrective (229A) and the latter to education. Education then is divided into that which corrects stupidity, the weakness of the person who thinks he knows but does not, and an unnamed remainder (229C), the former being divided finally into admonition and dialectic. Our "Sophist of noble lineage" has as his task, thus defined, the purely negative one of purifying the soul of stupidity by the technique of cross-examination. The definition of "Sophist VI" may be graphically represented as follows.

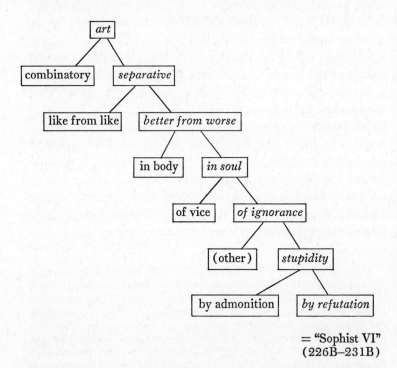

= "Sophist VI"
(226B–231B)

Plato's subsequent description of this art can scarcely fail to remind one of Socrates' negative elenchus, or method of refutation. The dialectician cross-examines his subject's words with the intent of exhibiting inconsistencies in his beliefs born of over-confident ignorance. This is accomplished by marshalling his beliefs within the critique [12] and, placing them side by side, by showing "that they contradict one another about the same things, in relation to the same things, and in the same respect" (230B). The result is that the patient is delivered from his prejudices, becomes more gentle with others, and presumably is prepared for a more constructive form of education aimed at producing knowledge or true belief where previously there was only pride and ignorance.

One of the most intriguing problems arising out of the definition of "Sophist VI" is that of his relation to Socrates of the earlier dialogues. That Socrates was (or was depicted to be) a master of refutation there can be no doubt, and the role which Socrates described for himself in the *Apology* is parallel to that of "Sophist VI" in essential respects. Both involve the discovery of ignorance in the souls of pretentious men by verbal controversy, and both aim to impart an awareness of ignorance where ignorance is indeed present. More important, however, is that neither Socrates of the *Apology* nor "Sophist VI" is depicted as having any particular ability to *produce* true belief or knowledge in the soul purified of falsehood. It is hard to resist Taylor's identification of "Sophist VI" with Socrates,[13] and it seems likely that Plato intended to make the identification irresistible.

[12] See note 11.

[13] A. E. Taylor, *Plato: The Man and His Work* (London: Methuen & Co., 1926), pp. 380–81. Cornford also identifies the practice of "Sophist VI" as Socrates' cathartic method, but qualifies by saying that "Plato has been careful to analyse only the negative side of Socrates' practice—the side on which the resemblance lies" (F. M. Cornford, *Plato's Theory of Knowledge* [London: Routledge and Kegan Paul, 1935], p. 182). The "positive side" of this practice, as Cornford sees it, is "a series of suggestions criticised and amended by bringing in fresh considerations. The end should be the correct definition of the meaning or 'Form' which has all along been coming more clearly into view." (p. 184) Perhaps Socrates *aimed* at a result such as this, but none of the early "Socratic" dialogues indicate much success in this direction. The Socratic *practice* shown for the most part in the dialogues, apart from any Socratic goal, is just the method practiced by the "Sophist of Noble Lineage."

Yet if it was Plato's intention to portray the Socratic art in this description of "Sophist VI," it must also have been his intention to chide it, gently perhaps but also emphatically. For arising as it does in the context of the *Sophist*, the art ($\tau\acute{\epsilon}\chi\nu\eta$) of refutation stands in sharp contrast with the science of the Philosopher. Not only is "Sophist VI" devoid of the Philosopher's concern with Division "according to Kinds," which lies along the opposite path (separation of like from like), but he is incapable, moreover, of the practice of Collection which seeks out the common element among diversified Forms. More accurately, perhaps, we should say that "Sophist VI" is capable of only part, and the least creative part, of the method of Collection. He is an expert at refutation, insofar as this consists in uncovering inconsistencies among the beliefs of unknowing men, and this is the first step in the process of Collection. But "Sophist VI," as such, is not one particularly qualified to pursue the common Form which might be exhibited as a result of the negative elenchus. At very least, he is not an *expert* at this matter. He possesses no *method* by which this is to be achieved. This correlates perhaps in a more than accidental way with the fact that the results of most of the Socratic dialogues are often disappointingly inconclusive. As we shall see, on the other hand, the Philosopher, in his search for "the free man's knowledge," not only has a method for seeking the common Form, but moreover has a criterion by which he can tell whether the common Form has been located in a particular case.

Of more immediate dramatic interest, however, is the fact that the Socratic method will not tell us where to go from this point in the dialogue, in order eventually to reach an adequate definition of the Sophist. Up to this point, the Sophist has been inexpertly misplaced in a jumble of conflicting definitions. It would be too strong to say that the definitions are strictly inconsistent, for none of the five contains a direct negation of anything asserted in any other. But when any one is taken as a proper definition, and taken in this to display the necessary

conditions for being a sophist, then refutation may be found
in one of the other Sophists the special characteristics of which
do not meet these conditions. Sophist I, for example, is a
hunter, but any claim that this feature is necessary for being a
sophist must be incorrect, because Sophists II through IV are
merchants, and so forth. In this sense, then, the very fact that
the Sophist has been dispersed through several subclasses,
rather than being finally caught in one, renders it logically
improper to read any one of these descriptions as the definition the Stranger and company have set out to discover.

Now either a practitioner of the Socratic method or "Sophist
VI," if these remain different characters, could discover this
conflict among the five descriptions in a most effective and
entertaining (230C) way. But having exposed the logical difficulty, neither would have the discipline needed to work these
abortive descriptions into one definition displaying both necessary and sufficient conditions. This latter is a job for the
"philosophic science" which has yet to be described. What,
then, is the role of the definition of "Sophist VI," occurring as
it does at this place in the dialogue? It cannot *tell* us how to
work the five Sophists into one. But it can do the next best
thing. It can *show* us how to look upon what has gone before,
and what accordingly to do next in pursuit of the essential
Sophist. Just as the definition of "Sophist VI" began with a
collection over the various separative arts, and proceeded from
there to trace out the features which are peculiar to this "noble
variety" of Sophistry, so we in effect are instructed to treat the
first five descriptions of Sophistry as themselves providing a
collection over a particular type of activity, and hence to trace
out the features which mark out the true Sophist from others
of similar pursuits. As the Stranger remarks, after reviewing
the five appearances of the Sophist and the dubious (231E)
sixth, "when one who is known by the name of a single art
appears to be master of many, there is something wrong with
this appearance" (232A). When someone has that impression
of any art, as we have thus far of Sophistry, surely it is be-

cause he "cannot see clearly that feature of it in which all these forms of skill converge . . ." (232A). Collecting the several appearances of the Sophist together, we must seek in them the common feature, which then can be taken at least as one of the necessary conditions of being a practitioner of that art.

At this stage, then, Socrates is left behind. Never cleanly separated from the Sophists proper in the dialogue, Socrates remains essentially a specialist in the art of refutation, whereas what is needed now is a specific skill for tracing out "*one* Form connected in a unity through many wholes" (253D [translator's emphasis]), which the Stranger alone among the company seems to possess. This very likely is the reason why Socrates has been upstaged in the *Sophist* (as in the *Statesman*). At any rate, there is no place in the corpus where Plato indicates more clearly his departure from Socratic methodology than in this passage, where Socrates is left behind with the Sophists and the dialogue given over without reservation to a Stranger with a "new method," [14] and a new approach to the Forms.

But this is not *quite* right; for Socrates is not left with the Sophists in the sense of sharing the essentials of their calling. This is why Cornford is wrong in suggesting that the first *six* Sophists serve as a collection for the last and finally adequate definition.[15] What is essential to all six is that all are controversialists. But the five part company from the sixth with regard to the purpose of their controversy. Whereas "Sophist VI" disputes to purify his partners of false belief and conceit, I through V show up essentially as producers of the very con-

[14] I argue in chapter IV that this "new method" is that adumbrated in *Phaedo* 100A–101D. Socrates' isolation from this "new method" is not complete, since elements of it appear in the final proof of immortality in the *Phaedo*, and a description of it is put in Socrates' mouth in *Phaedrus* 265D–266A. But Socrates is never pictured in the dialogues as successfully practicing this more powerful method in its fully developed form, the first clear illustration of which appears in the present dialogue.

[15] Cornford, *Plato's Theory of Knowledge*, p. 187.

ceit the other strives to purge. What appears to be the case
instead is that the first *five* Sophists serve as a collection for the
seventh, and that the definition of "Sophist VI" illustrates the
way in which a common property is to be sought among the
disparate Sophists thus far brought to light.

With the discovery of productiveness as a common property
among sophists, something divisions I through V failed to produce, the hunt for the essential Sophist starts afresh along an
entirely different branch of the arts. The five Sophists which
appeared dispersed through various arts of acquisition will
now be unified in sharing a particular form of productive art,
the description of which requires the remainder of the dialogue to complete.

Now there may appear at first glance to be an inconsistency
in the suggestion that the five Sophists, all involving *acquisi-*
tion of one sort or another, now turn up together under the
general category of *production*. The original division of art into
acquisitive and productive at 219A was intended to be in
some sense exclusive. This, of course, is never presented as the
only way of separating the arts, for in "Sophist VI" an entirely
different division is introduced. But the subclassifications "acquisitive" and "productive" are at least in opposition. As Socrates remarks, none of those who acquire through learning,
trading, fighting, or hunting "produces anything, but is only
engaged in conquering by word or deed, or in preventing
others from conquering, things which exist and have been already produced" (219C). This being the case, how could the
same five Sophists discovered under the acquisitive branch of
the arts now be expected to show up as productive?

The appearance of a problem here is illusory. Even though
two characteristics, A and B, are exclusive, in the sense even
of each entailing the other's negation, there is nothing in this
alone to prevent a given thing from having both properties, as
long as the two properties are not possessed in the same respect. A man might have black hair and blue eyes, or be
strong of limb but weak in mind, and so forth. Similarly, a

given sophist might be acquisitive in one respect and productive in another; and this is just what the Stranger at this stage
purports to have discovered. To give up the search for the
genuine Sophist under the acquisitive arts thus is not to relin-
quish the claim that all sophists in some way or another are
acquisitive. The difficulty is that they have been found to be
acquisitive in different ways. Indeed, the very fact that this
diversity appears under the category of *acquisition* suggests
that being acquisitive is not essential to being a sophist. To
put it another way, the fact that the several Sophists share
only acquisitiveness among their features, but share none of its
more specific forms, suggests that this was the wrong branch
along which to pursue the essential Sophist in the first place.[16]
It is natural, accordingly, that the next attempt to find what
is shared by all types of Sophistry will begin with the opposite
division of the arts. Under this line of specification it will be
found, in due time, not only that all sophists are productive,
but moreover that all are productive in the same respect.

Like Divinity, a sophist is in a sense productive of all
things, but unlike Divinity his productions are images and his
material is discourse. Moreover, the images he produces are
not truly proportioned (like a photograph), but are distorted to
appear attractive from the point of view of the beholder
(235E–236A). The division "according to Kinds" of the
Sophist is now under way. But at this point an obstacle appears, the overcoming of which permits Plato to fulfill one by
one each of the debts left unpaid by the *Theaetetus*. The
Sophist, if he exists at all, is necessarily a creator of false discourse. But we have been unable to understand what this is
that he creates and, unless a better explication of falsehood can

---

[16] The appearance of the several Sophists under opposing Forms
has the same effect in thought as those experiences, mentioned in
Book VII of the *Republic*, which yield "a contradictory impression"
(523C), and thus "provoke thought to reflect upon them" (523B),
tending thereby to "convert the soul and lead it to the con-
templation of reality" (525A).

be provided than in the *Theaetetus*, the present attempt to define the Sophist is bound to be abortive in turn. The next major task of the dialogue, accordingly, is to define falsehood in appearance and in speech, in the course of which Plato manages also to explore the problems of "defining" the Real, to refute Parmenides, to describe the function of the Philosopher, and to explain the sense in which "that which is not" nonetheless is.

4 / The Refutation of Parmenides

Having exhibited two examples of division properly executed and having embarked upon a third, Plato now proceeds most ambitiously to examine a concept which cannot be defined by this method, that of the Real (τὸ ὄν).[17] The occasion is his need to explain the sense in which "that which is not" (τὸ μὴ ὄν) *is*, and his first result in this direction is to show that "that which is not" cannot be defined by dividing the Real into itself and what is not itself.

Since what is not Real is not something, to speak of what is not Real is to speak of nothing and hence to say nothing at all (237E). Indeed, what *is not* in the sense of not Real cannot even be spoken of, for any term we might attempt to use for this purpose will implicitly or explicitly attribute either unity or plurality to what is not Real, which is not permissible since what is cannot be attributed to what is not (238C). Moreover, the existence of what is not Real cannot even be denied,

---

[17] J. M. E. Moravcsik points out (p. 41), in "Being and Meaning in the *Sophist*," *Acta Philosophica Fennica*, 14 (1962): 23–78, that Plato in the passages following seems to be dealing with existence and its opposite, rather than with what is real and what is not real (e.g., fictitious), which latter is not necessarily nonexistent. Since my quotations are from Cornford's translation, however, I shall follow his rendition of τὸ ὄν as 'the Real' or 'Existence' according to context.

since any attempt to mention it (as for example *this* attempt) will attribute to what is not Real properties (in this case singularity, with the use of 'it') which contradict the intended reference (239A). The mistake here, of course, is in the attempt to "dovetail" (240C) the Real and what is not Real as if together they were subdivisions of some other Form, and could be characterized as such in terms of opposing specific properties. But this is a senseless undertaking, since the Real cannot itself be a subdivision of anything else.

Some other way must be found of catching the Sophist who deals with what is not Real in discourse, whereby we can "define his art without contradicting ourselves" (240C). Parmenides has warned: "Never shall this be proved—that things that are not are; but do thou, in thy inquiry, hold back thy thought from this way" (237A). And Plato has just demonstrated some of the hazards against which this barrier was erected. But the problem of false statement can be pursued no further without trespassing upon Parmenides' forbidden grounds. Whatever else a false statement may be, at very least it is one "stating that things that are, are not, and [or] that things that are not, are" (241A); and to account for the possibility of such statements it will have to be shown "by main force that what is not, in some respect has being, and conversely that what is, in a way is not" (241D). The Sophist thus has his staunchest ally in Parmenides himself, but for reasons upon which the two parties could not agree. While the Sophist will maintain, with Protagoras, that there are no false statements since all appearances are equally true, Parmenides reaches the same conclusion on the entirely different grounds that there are no appearances.

The approach now to be attempted towards an understanding of "that which is not" thus must include explication of some sense of the term 'Real' and its cognates which will enable the Stranger to say meaningfully of "that which is not" that it is, and this requires in turn becoming more clear about what is meant by the 'the Real' itself. In short, if one is to understand what it is *not* to be Real, then one must understand no

less what it is to be Real, a problem which in the estimation of
the Stranger is "the chief and most important of them all"
(243D). This sounds like a call for a definition of the Real itself. Although it will become clear later that concept of the
Real *cannot* be defined like that of the Angler or that of the
"noble Sophist," the Stranger begins his examination of this
concept as before with a collection, this time in the form of
various (faulty) "definitions" of the Real taken from Plato's
predecessors. First it is shown that the Real cannot be defined
by identifying it with a particular number of "principles."
Then it is shown that it cannot be explicated by identifying it
with a particular property which all things might share. In his
criticism of the first faulty division by number of "principles,"
Plato finally takes his stand against the awesome Parmenides,
and in criticising the second he distinguishes his position from
that of his more immediate intellectual forebear, Socrates.

The upshot of these faulty "definitions," however, is not as
before to disclose a common feature which can be taken as a
subdivision of a more general concept, and hence to lead eventually to a definition by division "according to Kinds." The
result rather is to show that the Real cannot be defined at all.
What can be done, at best, is to disclose a feature which is
commensurately general with the Real itself and which thus
can be taken as a "mark" or invariable sign of what is. The
mark of the Real thus disclosed is *power* (δύναμις), and in
particular the power of *being known*. What is Real, in short,
cannot be *defined* by division "according to Kinds," but it can
be *characterized* as that which can be known by this method.
The Real thus is nothing more nor less than the Forms themselves. Let us examine the several arguments which together
lead to these results.

The Stranger considers first, at 242C, those philosophers
who have made the distinction between unity and plurality,
and have located the Real under either of these while denying it
of the other. There is no need to determine whether Plato intended to single out for criticism particular persons who had

maintained a plurality of things to be real, for the objection against such a position is entirely general and does not depend upon the specific number of things in question.

Let us examine the contradictions involved in claiming that the Real is any number of things greater than one, say n. If n things (a, b, . . . , n) are real, then either (1) one of them distinct from the others is the same as the Real, in which case the others are not Real, or (2) all of them together are the Real, in which case the Real will be the same as those n things only insofar as the n things are one (the collection a, b, . . . , n). (243E–244A) In either case the Real turns out to be one, and not n. The only other alternative is that (3) the Real is not the same as the n things either separately or in combination but is distinct from them, in which case if there are these n things then there must be n + 1 things, since there is also the Real. Thus it cannot be consistently maintained that the Real is any particular number of things greater than one.

Plato's refutation of Parmenides (244B–245E) is more complicated but equally succinct. Those who say that the Real is one, first, cannot admit that the name 'Real' and the name 'One' refer to the same thing, because then there would be at least two things, namely those two names. Nor can they even admit that the name 'Real' applies to something different than itself, for then again there would be two things, the thing and its name. Such a claim thus leads to the admission either that the name 'Real' is not a name of anything, or that 'Real' names only a name and hence that the Real is nothing whatsoever beyond a name (244D). This is not in itself a demonstration of inconsistency, but it shows at least that Parmenides' doctrine that the Real is one leads to consequences which he would not willingly have accepted.

An examination of the relationship of the Real to the Whole, on the other hand, draws out consequences of the Parmenidean doctrine which are simply in contradiction with the doctrine itself. It must be the case first that the Real either (1) is a whole divisible into parts or (2) is not a whole (is either a unity without parts or a plurality not constituting a whole). If (1), then the Real has parts, which as part of what is a real must themselves be real, and the consequence follows that what is real is not one (245A–B). With alternative (2) there are the further exhaustive alternatives that either (a) the Whole (τὸ ὅλον) (245C) exists or (b) the Whole does not exist. If (a), given (2), then either (i) the Real is not, or (ii) both the Whole and the Real are, with the consequence that there are more things than one.[18] Both (i) and (ii) contradict the doctrine that there is only one real thing, and (a) thereby is untenable by Parmenides. Plato's argument under alternative (b) is distressingly obscure, but may be reconstructed as follows without deviating far from Plato's likely intentions. One interpretation of (2) is that the Real is one, not in the sense of having the property of unity (245B), but in the sense of being one indivisible. This interpretation cannot be true under (b), since if the Whole does not exist there are no whole things, and "what is not a whole cannot have any definite number" (245D); specifically, nothing can be numbered one. The only other interpretation of (2) is that the Real is of many elements but does not thereof constitute a unified whole.[19] But this is incompatible with the Parmenidean doctrine in itself. In neither interpretation, then, can (2) and (b) be maintained together in a way compatible with the Parmenidean doctrine. But since (a) and (b) exhaust the possibilities left open under (2), and since (a) is untenable itself by Parmenides, (2) itself is untenable. Since Parmenides therefore can maintain

[18] Possibility (ii) obtains only if possibility (i) is denied. Thus (i) and (ii) must be taken as alternative, not as conjunctive consequences of (a). This is contrary to Cornford's schematization of the argument, *Plato's Theory of Knowledge*, p. 223.

[19] The pairs of consequences (i′) that the Real is not one and (ii′) that the Real is many, following from the two interpretations of (2), may be close enough to (i) and (ii) under (a) to make sense out of Plato's remark (245C) that the same things are true of the Real under the second hypothesis (that the whole does not exist) as under the first (that it does).

neither (1) nor (2), one of which must be the case, his position
is shown self-contradictory. With the downfall of Parmenides,
whose shadow has hung over the proceedings thus far, Plato
is free to inquire further into the nature of "that which is not."

5 / The Mark of the Real

The approach of those who attempt to "give an exact account
of what is real or unreal" (245E) by specifying how many
things there are, has led to contradiction both for those who
claim the Real is many and those who claim it is one. The so-
called "Battle of Gods and Giants" to which Plato next turns
depicts another false start, but of an essentially different sort.[20]
Whereas the others had attempted (fruitlessly) to provide an
exact λόγos, or definition, of the Real by attributing to it properties (unity, plurality) which were not necessarily confined to
the Real itself, the Gods and Giants attempt to explicate (but
not to define) the Real with single terms whose referents are
claimed to be coextensive with it. For "the Giants" the Real
is that and only that to which the term 'tangible' applies, while
for "the Gods" the Real is all and only that which can correctly
and without qualification be called "changeless." These latter
contenders, then, "put the matter in a different way" (245E),
in the sense of suggesting a *mark* of everything that is, as

---

[20] The suggestion by Cornford, *Plato's Theory of Knowledge*,
pp. 218 ff., that the philosophers who attempt an "exact definition" of
the Real are "ancestors" of the "Gods" and "Giants" has little in its
favor. As we shall see, these two groups approach the problem of
characterizing the Real in essentially different ways, the one seeking a *definition*, the other a *mark* of what is. Further, the issues
which separate the champions of the one from those of the many
have nothing to do with tangibility or their attitude toward the
Forms, while the differences between the "Gods" and the "Giants"
has nothing to do with the number of "principles" each admits as
real.

against the former who attempted (vainly) a *definition* of the Real.[21]

Neither tangibility nor changelessness prove adequate to mark off the Real from "that which is not." "The Giants" are constrained by other admissions to recognize some intangible things as real, and "the Gods" must admit some sense in which the Forms submit to change. These results are shown in the negative parts of the passages from 245E to 251A. No less important in these passages, however, is the positive result of disclosing a feature which is at least a more promising candidate than the other two for the title "the mark of the Real." The contention between the materialists and the Friends of the Forms thus serves two central purposes in the dialogue: it functions as a collection out of which power ($\delta\acute{\upsilon}\nu\alpha\mu\iota\varsigma$) as the mark of the Real emerges and it illustrates the difference from Plato's point of view between a definition and a mark, which latter alone can be provided for the Real. Let us examine more closely the difference between these two types of explication.

Although Parmenides had maintained that there is *one* real thing, he had not maintained that 'One' and 'Being' ($\check{\epsilon}\sigma\tau\iota\nu$) have the same reference. He at least did not maintain this explicitly in any remaining fragments and it has been shown already (244B–C) that he could not maintain it consistently on pain of admitting more than one real thing. 'One' rather designates a property of Being, which apparently however can be shared by others among the unreal realm of appearances.[22] Similarly, those who maintained that the real principles are

[21] I concur with Ryle's belief ("Plato's Parmenides," reprinted in R. E. Allen, *Studies in Plato's Metaphysics* [New York: Humanities Press, 1965]) that Plato was aware that the Real and "that which is not" are not "co-ordinate species of a genus" (p. 119), without approving however of the use of 'species' and 'genus' in this connection (see below). As Ryle points out, these concepts "require a very different sort of elucidation" (p. 142) than that afforded by the method of division.

[22] See the first few sentences in "The Way of Seeming," G. S. Kirk and J. E. Raven, *The Presocratic Philosophers* (Cambridge: Cambridge University Press, 1957), p. 278.

two or three in number surely had not meant to suggest that
the Real is the same as the numbers two or three. Their point
rather, as it might be put today, was that the principles which
are real fall under the class of pairs or of triples, either of
which classes certainly has other members as well. To attempt
to characterize the Real by numbering it, therefore, is to call in
features which do not belong to the Real uniquely, but which
include "other things" from which it must be distinguished by
further characteristics. This approach is obviously nonsensical,
and Plato has shown that it leads to utter contradiction no matter how pursued. But this is just the approach one would have
to employ in attempting to define the Real along lines already
successfully pursued with the Angler and the "Sophist of noble
lineage."

The procedure of the "Giants" or materialists, on the other
hand, does not involve an attempt to find a λόγος of the Real by
dividing it off from everything else by appropriate classification and subclassification in terms of general properties.[23]
The materialists, in a word, do not attempt to *define* the Real.
Their claim, rather, is that the Real is the *same thing* as body,
or what can be touched (246B). Body, or tangibility, is the
property which all real things possess, and which moreover is
not possessed by anything unreal. Thus tangibility is conceived
as the *mark* of the Real which distinguishes it from all pre-
tenders.[24] To say that the Real is body, or what is tangible, is

[23] This is the second appearance of the crude materialists in the
pair of dialogues we have been examining. First they were represented at *Theaetetus* 155E as the uninitiate "who believe that nothing
is real save what they can grasp with their hands and do not admit
that actions or processes or anything invisible can count as real."
They were depicted there as unsympathetic to the theory of perception based upon the presence of δύναμις within the material world.
(See also fn. 28 below) In the present context, they will be constrained to admit δύναμις among what is Real. Their dilemma overall
is either that δύναμις must be accepted within the material world or
that part of the Real is not material.

[24] Cornford (*Plato's Theory of Knowledge*, p. 230) translates the
passage at the beginning of 246B as "They define reality as the
same thing as body. . . ." The term translated as 'define' is ὁριζόμενοι,

not to define the Real after the fashion employed with the Angler and with "Sophist VI," for there is no matter here of subdividing properties or Kinds to discover a unique characterization of the type of thing in question. Tangibility, as the mark of the Real, does not require subdivision, for it is claimed by the materialists to be a property in itself coextensive with the Real. Nor, on the other hand, can tangibility be considered a specification of some other property, for no property can be claimed to be more general than the property common to all that is real. But since tangibility is neither subdivided to provide a unique description of what is real nor is itself a subdivision of some other category, to say that the Real is the same as what is tangible is not to provide a λόγος of the Real by division "according to Kinds." It is not, in short, to provide a definition of the Real.

The "Gods" agree with their adversaries at least in not seeking a definition of the Real. They differ in proposing that, instead of tangibility, unchangeability is the characteristic possessed uniquely by all real things. Hence they are called also "Friends of the Forms" (248A).[25] It is interesting to note, in

---

meaning in the infinitive "to bound or to mark out." The noun form (ὁρίζειν) is used at 247E to say of power (δύναμις) that it is the mark to distinguish real things. When Plato refers in the Sophist to definition by division, to the contrary, the key word is λόγος. Thus, for example, at the beginning of the dialogue the Stranger announces his intention to bring the "nature [of the Sophist] to light in a clear formula" (ἐμφανίζοντι λόγῳ τί ποτ᾽ ἔστι) (218C); at 218E the Angler is claimed to be as susceptible of definition (λόγον) as any more important thing; and at 245E those who number the Real are referred to as giving an exact account (διακριβολογουμένους).

[25] The most conspicuous "Friend of the Forms" is Socrates as depicted in the Phaedo. These philosophers (1) maintain a distinction between Being and Becoming (as in Phaedo 78C–E), (2) distinguish between modes of apprehending these two realms (Phaedo 79A), and (3) consider unchangeability as a mark of the absolutely existing Forms in contrast with the constantly changing world of the senses (Phaedo 80B). The Pythagoreans in the Phaedo would also be included, and Parmenides is the champion of the One mentioned at Sophist 249D. These common doctrines of the "Friends of the Forms" are discussed more fully by Cornford (Plato's Theory of

this connection, that the mark proposed by the Friends of the Forms is not the opposite (in the sense of denial or contrary) of the mark proposed by the materialists. The opposite of tangibility is intangibility, which in no sense is the same as unchangeability, while the opposite of unchangeability is variability, which again is not the same as tangibility. Thus again we see that "the battle of Gods and Giants" is not a conflict between two groups who follow opposite branches in an exhaustive dichotomous subdivision of a common Kind. Their conflict arises rather in proposing different features as coextensive with the Real. Neither feature as such, however, is either a subdivision of some other feature or is itself subjected to further subdivision.

The difficulty encountered by both the materialists and the Friends of the Forms is that each is led to admit, as real, things which do not share the required distinguishing characteristic. Materialists, at least those who can find a distinction between the just and the unjust or the wise and the foolish soul (247A), must admit that justice or wisdom in some sense is real, but cannot maintain that justice or wisdom is a tangible body. Thus tangibility fails as an exhaustive mark of the real, not for reasons of self-contradiction but by reason simply of not accommodating all admitted facts (247B–C).

Similarly, the Friends of the Forms cannot avoid admitting some change among things that are real. Just as things in the

Knowledge, pp. 242–48). As in the discussion of the materialists, however, Plato's reference seems to be primarily to a philosophic outlook rather than to one or more specific philosophers. Plato's criticism of both outlooks is that they are too narrow to encompass the whole of what exists. An interesting point is that this is the second time in only a few pages that Socrates' thought and method are being shown in a rather unfavorable light (the first was in the discussion of "Sophist VI"). The full significance of this will not come clear until we examine the philosopher's "science" of collection and division in the passages close ahead. At least there can be no puzzle at this point why Plato put the narration in the _Sophist_, as it were, into the mouth of a "Stranger" instead of leaving it to Socrates as in the earlier dialogues. The _Sophist_ appears to be Plato's manifesto of independence, both from Parmenides and from Socrates himself.

realm of Becoming are revealed "by means of the body through sense," they maintain that "we have intercourse with Real being by means of the soul through reflection" (248A). But to discern or to know (γιγνώσκω) (248D) what is real is to act upon it, and for what is real to be known is for it to be acted upon. But either to act or to be acted upon in some sense is to undergo change (248E). Thus if these philosophers are to maintain consistently that only the changeless is real, they will have to retract their admission that what is real can be known. At first showing, at least, the Friends of the Forms cannot admit δύναμις, or the power to act or to be acted upon, as the mark of the Real. As the Stranger is quick to point out, however, this conclusion is intolerable, for it rules out not only the possibility of the Real being known but also the possibility that intelligence, along with soul and life, is real (248E). And "all the force of reasoning must be enlisted to oppose anyone who tries to maintain any assertion about anything at the same time that he suppresses knowledge or understanding or intelligence" (249C). To reject the identification of the Real with the changeless, however, is not to open the door wide to all changeable things indiscriminately. If we were to say that the Real includes "all that is unchangeable and all that is in change" (249D) alike, then the old problem of the Real as two things would again emerge: either the Real is one but not the other, or both as a pair, or else it is some third thing not yet named (250A–C).[26]

---

[26] Plato's point here seems to be as follows. Although the arguments preceding have shown that some changeable things and some changeless things must be admitted among what is real, we cannot take change to be the mark of reality of the former nor changelessness that of the latter. If we take both change and changelessness as marks of the Real, we encounter the same difficulty expressed previously (243D ff.) in connection with those who say that two or more "principles" comprise the Real. Moravscik, "Being and Meaning in the *Sophist*," p. 37, apparently reads 249D 1–5 as a characterization of Existence, and finds it faulty for being tautologous. I read the passage instead as claiming that both what changes and what is unchangeable are included among what exists, but that neither change nor changelessness is a mark of Existence.

The examination of the conflict between the materialists and the Friends of the Forms, like all previous attempts to account for the Real in the dialogue, thus ends inconclusively. If neither rest nor movement is a mark of the Real, which must yet lie outside either alternative (250D), then we must admit to being as puzzled about the Real as about "that which is not." Yet there is some consolation, for we may take it that our difficulty with both "is now completely stated" (250E); and "since reality and unreality are equally puzzling, there is henceforward some hope that any light . . . thrown upon the one will illuminate the other to an equal degree . . ." (250E–251A). Thus, although no positive conclusions are yet in hand, Plato apparently considers that the stage has been set for a solution of the several problems accumulated thus far in the dialogue. It should be noted also that Plato has carefully prepared us to give up the search for a *definition* of the Real, in the sense of finding a λόγος, and to be content instead in our desire to understand the Real with a mark which is coextensive with all that is.

It is particularly noteworthy in this regard that the Stranger's suggestion that δύναμις is the mark of the Real is never refuted in the dialogue. When the materialists are deprived of tangibility as a common feature of all that is real and are unable to provide a further feature covering both bodily existence and traits of character, the Stranger proposes for their acceptance that anything is real which "is so constituted as to possess any sort of power [δύναμιν] either to affect anything else or to be affected, in however small a degree, by the most insignificant agent, though it be only once. I am proposing as a mark to distinguish real things, that they are nothing but power" (247E).[27] Lacking a better suggestion, the materialists are

[27] See note 24 regarding the use of ὀρίζειν = mark. Moravscik, "Being and Meaning in the *Sophist*," p. 37, declines to read this passage as asserting that δύναμις is a mark of all that exists, on the grounds apparently that the "complete characterization" of what exists is given in 247D9–E3, where Plato says "that what exists has to

depicted as at least tentatively (248A) agreeing with the Stranger's proposal.[28] And although the Friends of the Forms initially reject this proposal (248C), this rejection is brushed aside, and the Stranger goes on to show that the Forms themselves must possess the mark of δύναμις if they are to be known, and that the same must be said of any mind capable of knowing them. Thus all three parties in the discussion—the "Gods," the "Giants," and the Stranger himself—come to agree that δύναμις is characteristic of the Real.

In the discussion ensuing, however, the strong hint that δύναμις is the *mark* for which they are seeking is overlooked, and the Stranger leads Theaetetus into an expression of perplexity (250E) which terminates the review of what Plato's predecessors have had to say about the nature of the Real. There are at least two reasons why the Stranger's proposal cannot be pursued further at this particular stage in the dialogue. First, if δύναμις is coextensive with the Real, then the illusory perceptions and their objects characterized essentially as δυνάμεις at *Theaetetus* 156A–C, and as nonexistent at 157A–B, must be admitted to exist in some sense; but the sense in which "that which is not" *is* has not yet been clarified. Further, although the *Theaetetus* has provided an account of the intercourse between sense organs and material bodies, the

---

some degree, however small, the ability to affect or to be affected," and that "to affect" (ποιεῖν) and "to be affected" (παθεῖν) mean merely to be "a subject or a predicate in a genuine assertion. . . ." This argument seems to amount to the claim that δύναμις is not represented as the mark of what exists, because being subject or predicate of a genuine assertion is given that role by Plato instead. But the statement at 247D9–E3 is literally that anything exists that has the *power* (δύναμις) to affect or to be affected by something else. Interpreting the mode of "affecting" in question as grammatical does not counter the claim that power (of some, perhaps any, sort) is represented by Plato here as the mark of what exists.

[28] In the theory of perception developed in the *Theaetetus*, both objects of perception (including tangible objects) and perceptual acts were conceived as δυνάμεις. In a fine bit of irony, Plato here makes the materialists accept the theory based upon the same concept as that which they alone were depicted as rejecting at *Theaetetus* 155E.

sort of δύναμις possessed by the Forms is still obscure. Not only must the suggestion that the Forms possess δύναμις have appeared as a considerable innovation to the first readers of the *Sophist*, but moreover it has not yet been explained in what sense the Forms can admit of "intercourse" with the mind. Both deficiencies are remedied before the end of the dialogue. Yet the Stranger never returns to consider further the proposal that δύναμις is the mark of what is. Instead he turns to take up one by one the various problems that have been accumulating since the middle of the *Theaetetus*. If Plato intended the reader to consider more fully the suggestion that δύναμις is what is real, it is clear that this consideration is to be under the impetus of the reader's own dialectical power. To lead a reader to grasp a truth under his own initiative, of course, is a role already made familiar by the *Meno* and, I have contended, by the *Theaetetus* as well. It seems reasonable to conjecture that Plato intended the *Sophist* to serve a similar role in reminding the reader that one sure sign that a thing exists is that it is capable, in one way or another, of influencing other things.[29]

6 / The Free Man's Knowledge

The difficulty of explicating what is real and what is not has been "completely stated" (250E), and takes its place in line with other problems still awaiting solution. Among these is the recurring problem of the possibility of false judgment, left over from the *Theaetetus* and due for solution only in the final passages of the *Sophist*. Coupled with this in the present context is the problem of understanding semblance-making, which stalled the definition of the Sophist at 237A. Also remaining from the *Theaetetus* is the matter of explicating a sense of

[29] I suggest that the *Sophist* itself is intended to serve as a δύναμις leading the reader to understand that δύναμις is the mark of the Real.

λόγος which would complete the definition of knowledge as
true judgment accompanied by an account. This latter is the
first of the several remaining difficulties to be resolved. It is
the function of the philosopher to guide our discourse, according to the natural blendings and separations among the Forms,
by the dialectical processes of collection and division. In these
divisions "according to Kinds," which is "the business of the
science of Dialectic" (253D), we finally stumble "unawares
upon the free man's knowledge" (253C), for division of this
sort provides the λόγος which distinguishes the knowledge of
the philosopher from the true opinion of another man.

The role of dialectic is to disclose the ways in which the
Forms can and cannot combine.[30] For Plato, the fact that the
Forms combine in some but not in all ways is evident in the
fact that we often call things by several but never by all possible different names. To explain how the Forms combine,
then, is to explain "how it is that we call the same thing . . .
by several names" (251A). The passages which follow are
addressed, not only to those "enthusiasts . . . poorly endowed
with intelligence" (251C) who think that only one name can
properly be attributed to any one thing, but also to the other
groups of thinkers "whom we have been conversing with earlier" (251D). And the first thing of which all concerned with
questions about existence must be persuaded is that some
Forms combine but also that some are incapable of combination with each other.

Now it must be the case with a given number of Forms,
that either (1) all combine with all others, (2) none combine,
or (3) some combine with some or with all others (251D,
252E). In his argument for the elimination of (1) and (2),
Plato considers three of the Forms that have figured prominently in the "Battle of Gods and Giants"—Existence, Motion
and Rest. Plato's argument here is *ad hominem*, in the sense

[30] Cornford translates both εἶδος and ἰδέα 'Form'. At 253B–C and
elsewhere, γένη is used as synonymous with εἴδη. See Cornford, *Plato's
Theory of Knowledge*, p. 261 n.

of being directed towards the several philosophic contenders
he has been criticizing since 242B: the pluralists, Parmenides,
the materialists, the Friends of the Forms, and finally those
who will attribute only one name to one thing. The result of
the argument is to assure that none of these, including "all
alike who have ever had anything to say about existence"
(251D), can oppose him in the claim that some forms combine
but not all Forms combine with all others.[31]

The admission, first, that no Form combines with any other
allows neither Rest nor Motion to exist, nor will it allow that
anything can be predicated of anything else. Hence this admission is fatal alike for "those who have a universe in motion
[the materialists], and those who make it a motionless unity
[Parmenides], and all who say their realities exist in Forms
that are always the same in all respects [The Friends of the
Forms] . . ." (252A). Further, it is fatal for "those who
make all things come together at one time and separate at
another" (252B) (the pluralists) and for those unnamed persons "who will not allow one thing to share in the quality of
another and so be called by its name" (252B).[32] Thus no one

[31] The nature of this combining is discussed in the following section. Other expressions sometimes used to refer to this relationship
are 'partake of', 'participate in', and 'share'. See note 45.

[32] J. L. Ackrill argues, in "Plato and the Copula: *Sophist* 251–259"
(reprinted in R. E. Allen, *Studies in Plato's Metaphysics*, pp. 207–18),
that Plato at 256A–B distinguished the 'is' of predication (copula)
from the 'is' of identity as a means of refuting the "paradoxes" posed
by these "late learners" (p. 211). The paradox, in general, consists
in the claim (251B–C) that since no two things are the same, nothing can be called by the name of another thing. Although in fact we
truthfully say that a man is good, and so forth, this would appear
to be impossible, since man and good are not the same thing. Behind this "paradox," of course, is the confusion between the two
senses of 'is' in question. It is false to say 'man is good', meaning
man is identical with good; but it may be true to say 'man is good',
meaning this is a good man. Thus, if Plato *does* distinguish these
two senses of 'is' at 256A–B, then Ackrill is right in saying that
the distinction rebuts the "late learners." The primary purpose of
Ackrill's argument, however, is to establish that Plato does in fact
make the distinction, and the claim that he uses this distinction to

can maintain alternative (2) above. Alternative (1), moreover, is equally unacceptable, for if all Forms combine with all others, then Motion would be at rest, Rest would be in motion, and generally all things would be what they are not, which "is to the last degree impossible . . ." (252D).

The only remaining possibility is that some Forms combine with others, but not all with all other Forms. As just indicated, for example, Rest and Motion will not combine, for nothing is at rest insofar as it is in motion, nor in motion insofar as it is at rest. Existence, on the other hand, combines with both, "for surely they both exist" (254D). That is, what is either at rest

rebut the "late learners" is part of Ackrill's evidence that this distinction is made. Other facets of Ackrill's argument will be examined below. It is enough for the moment to see that the fact that the "late learners" would be refuted by the distinction, if it were made, is not an argument in favor of the claim that the distinction in fact is made. The "late learners" have been refuted already at 252B–C. As Ackrill himself puts it, Plato's reply to the "late learners" here regards their claim that "only identity-statements can be true; but this statement—'only identity-statements can be true'—is not an identity-statement; so on your own theory your theory is false" (p. 212). Since Plato has already refuted the "late learners" there is no need for a further refutation at a later point in his dialogue. Surprisingly enough, however, although Ackrill *admits* (p. 212) that Plato's argument at 252B–C is valid against the paradoxical thesis of the "late learners," he still holds that Plato had to distinguish the 'is' of predication from the 'is' of identity to "dispose satisfactorily" of this thesis. His argument is that there were other "serious thinkers" (unnamed by either Ackrill or Plato) who embraced the same paradox, and that *these* thinkers would be satisfied only with an explanation of the confusion which leads to the "paradox" in the first place. Hence, Ackrill decides, Plato had to distinguish the two senses in question, and does so at 256A–B. But the argument has none of the effect Ackrill desires. The fact that some unnamed person, however serious, *might* (or even did) raise a question about the "paradox" of the "late learners" which is not answered at 252B–C, but which would be answered by the distinction in question if it were made, in no way supports Ackrill's claim that Plato in fact ever made the distinction. It should be added that *if* Plato made the distinction in question at 256A–B, and if his reason for making it was to answer philosophers he never in any way names or mentions, who held a thesis he has already refuted, then the distinction at best is of minimal importance in the interpretation of the dialogue.

or at motion thereby exists, and Existence accordingly is compatible with Rest and Motion as with all other Forms. Thus two of the "very important" (254D) Forms under discussion will not combine with one another, and one will combine with the rest.

Now since some of the Forms combine and some do not, "they might be said to be in the same case with the letters of the alphabet" (253A). The vowels, for example, like the Form Existence, are "specially good at combination—[serving as] a sort of bond pervading them all, so that without a vowel the others cannot be fitted together" (253A). And the task of discerning which letters combine and which do not, to be rightly done, requires the art of grammar. The use of the analogy of alphabetical symbolism at this crucial spot in the dialogue is probably more than fortuitous. The reader will recall that the last time Plato used imagery involving letters and syllables, in the last section of the *Theaetetus*,[33] his concern was to specify a sense of λόγος with which the identification of knowledge with true judgment accompanied by an account might be made plausible. The "dream theory," in which the elements were unknowable while the complexes composed of them as such could be known, was refuted by showing its unacceptable consequences when applied to the case of the syllable and its constituent letters. The sense of λόγος suggesting merely the expression of thought in speech was discredited in light of the fact that any judgment whatsoever could be expressed by vocal sounds. And the sense suggesting enumeration of parts was eliminated by observing that one could correctly enumerate the parts of the first syllable in 'Theaetetus' without knowing the syllable, as evident in a subsequent listing of 'T' and 'E' only in spelling 'Theodorus'. This extensive use of letter imagery in the earlier context suggests an association of this imagery with the problem of defining a sense of λόγος appropri-

---

[33] Assuming no other writing than the *Parmenides* has intervened between the *Theaetetus* and the *Sophist*.

ate in the explication of knowledge. Whether this was intentional with Plato is a question we need not pause to examine. The fact of the matter is that the next time Plato uses this imagery after the *Theaetetus* is also the next time he returns to the problem of explicating knowledge. This time a sense of λόγος is displayed which sustains the burden of the alphabetical analogy.

Just as the art (τέχνη) of grammar is needed to deal with the correct combination of alphabetical symbols, the Stranger suggests, so is a special competence required to distinguish which of the Forms combine and which do not.[34] A special science is required, moreover, to tell "whether there are certain Kinds that pervade them all and connect them so that they can blend, and again, where there are divisions (separations), whether there are certain others that traverse wholes and are responsible for the division" (253C). This special competence is that of the philosopher, and the result of its exercise is termed "knowledge" (ἐπιστήμη). As the Stranger remarks with disingenuous surprise, "good gracious, Theaetetus, have we stumbled unawares upon the free man's knowledge and, in seeking for the Sophist, chanced to find the Philosopher first?" (253C) By the same knack of the "side wind" (231B) which brought the art of Socratic refutation under examination earlier in the dialogue, the science of the philosopher has now been brought into focus. And his science is such that its exercise provides just the λόγος needed to account for the difference between true judgment and knowledge. This λόγος is that of definition, illustrated in proper form twice previously in the dialogue, and now explicitly described. The function of the philosopher is to divide "according to Kinds,

[34] When first mentioned at *Sophist* 253B–C, the science of dialectic is described as being directed to "pointing out which Kinds are consonant, and which are incompatible with one another. . . ." The term translated 'consonant' is συμφωνεῖ. Thus the reader might be reminded of the description of the method of hypothesis at *Phaedo* 101D. Yet Plato is about to embark upon a discussion of the method of collection and division.

not taking the same Form for a different one or a different one
for the same" (253D), and the task of doing this belongs to
the science of dialectic.[35]

Now there are two aspects of the philosopher's function,
both of which must be properly fulfilled if he is to avoid "taking the same Form for a different one or a different one for the
same. . . ." Both have been amply illustrated in connection
with the definitions of the several Sophists already attempted.
Each of these, whether or not successful in the sense of exhibiting the *necessary* properties of being a sophist, formulates a
combination of characteristics which are possessed by at least
some sophists. Each, that is to say, formulates a set of *sufficient* characteristics for being a sophist. The method by which
this was done in each case was to divide general classifications
into more and more specific subclassifications, until finally a
combination of properties is reached which can be attributed
only to an individual of the sort in question. To classify in this
fashion is "[d]ividing according to Kinds [τὸ κατὰ γένη
διαιρεῖσθαι]" (253D), and to provide adequate divisions of this
type is the business of philosophy. For a division to be adequate, however, and not to involve a mistaking of Kinds, it
must show not only sufficient characteristics of the thing defined but the necessary characteristics as well. It is one thing
to formulate a particular combination of properties which attach only to sophists, but another thing again to formulate a
set of properties which attach to all sophists indifferently. The
adequate division is one which divides Kinds to display not
only features which *only* sophists possess but features which
are possessed by *all* sophists as well. And the task of assuring
that a division shows the *necessary* features of the thing to be
defined goes by the name 'collection' (συναγωγή).[36] Each of the
divisions of Sophist I through V gave sufficient conditions for

[35] The term here is διαλεκτικῆς, which was not used in description
of the practice of "Sophist VI."
[36] See *Phaedrus*, 266B.

being a sophist, but since there were five separate divisions no one of them gave conditions which could be considered in any sense necessary. By the end of the dialogue, however, Sophist VII will be defined in terms so combined as to show both necessary and sufficient characteristics, and this definition will join those of the Angler and of "Sophist VI" as proper illustrations of the dialectical method of collection and division.

These two aspects of the science of dialectic are described rather cryptically in the passages at hand as the things involved in dividing according to Kinds without mistaking one for another (253D). First, "the man who can do that discerns clearly *one* Form everywhere extended throughout many, where each one lies apart, and *many* Forms, different from one another, embraced from without by one Form . . ." (253D [translator's emphasis]). This is a description of the process of collection, the end result of which is to disclose a feature or features possessed in common by all things of the sort being defined.[37] This feature might be one which appears explicitly as being shared by each of several different kinds of the thing being classified; for example, the characteristic of *production* was seen at 219A–B to be common among the arts of agriculture, construction, herd tending, vessel molding, and imitation. Or the common feature might show up in the process of examining what has gone wrong in a series of unsuccessful divisions, as when the Stranger points out subsequently that each of the Sophists I through V is productive in some phase of his activity. By whatever process, however, an examination of several Kinds with a property in common serves as a collection if it exhibits that property as shared among the several Kinds. Thus the philosopher, in the process of collection, discerns the *one* Form (e.g. Production) extended

[37] An interesting geometrical interpretation of the two aspects of method described at 253D is given by A. C. Lloyd, "Plato's Description of Division" (reprinted in R. E. Allen, *Studies in Plato's Metaphysics*, pp. 219–30), esp. p. 228.

throughout the many (the Sophists I through V) originally
lying apart, and thereby comes to see the latter now as unified
by the single common Form in question.[38]

Having discerned a Form shared by each of the several
manifestations of the thing he is to define, and being assured
thereby that his definition will display what is necessary to the
thing in question, the philosopher turns next (perhaps again)
to the process of *division*. He then attempts, that is, to discern
"*one* Form connected in a unity through many wholes, and
many Forms, entirely marked off apart" (253D [translator's
italics]). The many Forms here are not, contrary to what
Cornford suggests,[39] the same as the many serving the process of collection. The many Forms here, rather, are the many
subclassifications which result from combining together the
several Forms, the proper combination of which finally produces an adequate definition of the single Form in question.
Each time a class is further subdivided by distinguishing

[38] The several initially disparate Forms are "embraced from without" by the single unifying Form in the sense that a description of
the former would not initially mention the latter, as Production was
not mentioned in the definitions of Sophists I through V.

[39] *Plato's Theory of Knowledge*, p. 267. Cornford states that the
"many Forms, which after Collection were seen to be embraced by a
single generic Form, are now seen 'entirely marked off apart'." It
seems correct to say that the Forms "embraced from without by one
Form," as seen in the collection of the Sophists I through V, are the
several Forms each of which is sufficient to mark off a type of sophist, but none of which is necessary. But the Forms now "entirely
marked off apart" are the several subclassifications, one of which
contains all and only sophists within its bounds. So the "many Forms"
are not the same in the two cases. This, of course, is a minor mistake. Perhaps less so is Cornford's suggestion (*ibid.*) that the structure of Forms is conceived by Plato "as a hierarchy of genera and
species. . . ." In the final and adequate division of Sophist VII, for
example, the property "dealing in ignorance" is no less generic, and
no more so, than "dealing in illusion," and yet the latter occurs
"higher" in the tree of division than the former. As will be argued
in the following section, it is misleading to think of the tree of division either as one according to the relation of genus to species or
as one in which there is a "higher" and a "lower" level.

within it a further pair of exclusive Forms, the thing to be
defined is more closely approached. But other Forms are also
explicitly added to the resulting tree of division. At each stage
in the development of the tree, therefore, there are new
"wholes" clearly marked off. These are the "many wholes"
through which the one Form is "connected in a unity," the
unity being that of a continuously developing line of division
along one side of the tree. The one Form therein connected,
finally, is that which is seen at the end to provide the necessary and sufficient formulation of the thing to be defined. The
one Form, in short, is the λόγος of the thing to be defined,
which the philosopher can then rightly claim to know by virtue of a successful exercise of the science of dialectic.

If, by characterizing the "free man's knowledge," Plato intends to characterize that knowledge which posed the problem
in the *Theaetetus*,[40] then the definition unsuccessfully pursued
throughout that earlier dialogue can now be supplied. To
know a (Kind of) thing is to display its necessary and sufficient characteristics by the processes of collection and division.
This provides a definition or λόγος of the (Kind of) thing in
question, and induces a true judgment about what the thing
is.[41] Knowledge thus defined, however, is not about particular

---

[40] There are no apparent reasons to reject this supposition, and
several for accepting it have been mentioned above. For an additional
reason, we may recall that the philosopher was characterized as a
"free man" in *Theaetetus* 172D.

[41] R. Robinson says that Plato "argued elaborately and energeti-
cally that knowledge would not be true opinion even if that opinion
could give an account of itself" (*Plato's Earlier Dialectic* [Oxford:
Clarendon Press, 1953], p. 146). Many others share the opinion
that for Plato knowledge is something essentially different from true
judgment. If understood as the claim that true judgment does not
become knowledge merely by having an account added to it, there
is no necessary conflict between this and the statement above. The
temporal priority here appears important. One does not start with
true judgment and end with knowledge merely by acquiring λόγος to
go with the judgment. Nonetheless, as I read Plato, when one obtains knowledge, true thought or judgment necessarily goes along
with it. Knowledge is true judgment accompanied by an account in

objects. It is of the Forms which, in some way or another, particular objects manifest. This is why the *Theaetetus*, proceeding as it does on the level of the particular thing, cannot arrive at an account of knowledge. But the *Sophist*, to this point, has proceeded entirely on the level of the Forms. On this level, the *Sophist* has both described the sense of λόγος needed to complete the account of knowledge begun in the *Theaetetus* and illustrated this λόγος in its definition of the Angler and of "Sophist VI." A further illustration is provided at the end of the dialogue with the definition of the authentic Sophist.[42]

Now it is important to urge again, in the light of what has transpired in the dialogue to this point, that the philosopher whose function is depicted in these few passages is not the same as "Sophist VI" defined previously. Whether or not the "Sophist of noble lineage" is intended to be Socrates, he cannot at any rate be the philosopher in possession of the "free man's knowledge." "Sophist VI," for one thing, is a practitioner of τέχνη. His practice falls, with that of the carder and the winnower, under the category of the separative arts. This practice, moreover, is never referred to in the dialogue as διαλεκτική.[43] The practice of the Philosopher, on the other hand, is called both διαλεκτική (253D) and ἐπιστήμη (253B, C). The ability to divide according to Kinds is the source of the knowledge which was sought throughout the *Theaetetus*, and there is no hint of this ability in the description of "Sophist VI" as a specialist in the detection of inconsistencies. The

the sense that true judgment invariably accompanies the account which is a necessary condition of knowledge. Thus true judgment itself is a necessary condition of knowledge.

[42] These definitions are not examples of knowledge themselves, for they do not in themselves include true judgment. For Plato, it would be nonsense to speak of imparting knowledge upon a written page. Plato represents the *achievement* of knowledge, rather, in the persons of Theaetetus and the Stranger, for their having worked out the Forms in question.

[43] "Method of accounting" would seem to be more faithful rendition of λόγων μεθόδῳ (227a). See note 11 of this chapter.

most notable thing about the "Sophist of noble lineage," in fact, is that as such he is capable only of refutation and not of constructive investigation *by a specific method*. He has nothing like the philosopher's method of collection to discern the common Form in diversity. Neither is he necessarily concerned to provide formulations (λόγοι) which would serve adequately or otherwise as definitions of the things he is dealing with. He might indeed, like Socrates, be committed to finding the general characters of the various virtues, but he has no method for doing so which leads him to a systematic and procedurally controlled examination of the relationships among Forms. In a word, although he perhaps shares with the philosopher a concern with finding common properties, he knows nothing of the method of collection which is the latter's instrument for this purpose, and he does not share with the philosopher any interest or competency in the matter of tracing out the connections and discontinuities holding among the Forms in themselves.

If any further evidence is needed that the "Sophist of noble lineage" is not a philosopher, one need only recall that the former is involved in the separation of better from worse. The only sense, however, in which the philosopher is involved in separation is that of finding divisions among the Kinds. This can be conceived only as a matter of separating like from like, which is claimed at 226D to have no generic name corresponding to 'purification' which names the other type of separation.

Finally, although there may be no conclusive reason at hand for identifying Socrates with "Sophist VI," there are yet other grounds for denying that Socrates can be classed with the philosophers of 253C. If only we allow that Socrates is among the Friends of the Forms, it is quite clear that he cannot be one who is concerned to point out "which Kinds are consonant, and which are incompatible with one another" (253B–C), nor in general can he study which Forms combine and which do not. One who maintains that the Forms are changeless and incapable of relations, and that in general the Forms lack δύναμις, could not have any part of the free man's knowledge.

7 / The Mingling of the Forms

Although neither the Real nor "that which is not" can be defined after the fashion of the Angler or "Sophist VI," we may come as close to giving an account (λόγος) of them "as we can under the conditions of our present inquiry" (254C) by examining the way in which a limited number of Forms combine with and exclude each other.[44] In this way we may discover how it is possible to "assert that what is not, *really is* what is not, and to escape unscathed" (254D [translator's emphasis]). This will clear the path finally for an explanation of the possibility of false judgment in the following section of the dialogue, and thus provide for the completion of the definition of the Sophist interrupted at 237A.

Solutions to these remaining problems, however, seem anticlimactic after the unusually exciting passages dealing with the free man's knowledge and the combination of the Forms. The former passage has described the science of dialectic, providing thereby a sense of λόγος which marks the distinction between true judgment and knowledge. The present passage dealing with the combination of Forms now explains the sense in which Forms are able to combine with each other, thereby exhibiting the δύναμις which in some sense is the mark of the Real.[45]

---

[44] I take it that the "conditions of the present inquiry" are set by the fact that the Forms under examination are τὸ ὄν and τὸ μὴ ὄν themselves, which Plato has already shown beyond comprehension in a λόγος, or definition.

[45] Several terms are used to speak of combination among the Forms, notably μετέχω, meaning 'to share in' or 'to partake of', συμμίγνυμι, meaning 'to mix with' or 'to mingle with', and κοινωνέω meaning 'to share with', 'to have intercourse with' or 'to communicate with'. The

Five Forms are selected for the exhibition: Rest, Motion and Existence, from the discussion of the "Battle of Gods and Giants," and Sameness and Difference, prominent in the *Timaeus*. Existence excludes no other Kind, but combines with all. Rest and Motion exclude each other, but together are co-extensive with Existence. Sameness and Difference are seen to be other than Rest and Motion for this reason, since neither excludes Rest or Motion (255A–B).[46] Sameness is shown different from Existence, on the basis that Motion and Rest as a pair mingle with Existence but not Sameness (255B–C). And Difference, finally, is shown other than Existence, in that some things are (share in Existence) without reference to other things, whereas "whatever is different . . . is what it is with reference to another." (255D) Plato seems to be saying here that things that *are* "in and by themselves," without reference to other things, partake of Existence through Sameness, while 'that which is not' will be seen to partake of Existence through Difference. It is through Difference also, apparently, that knowledge and the objects of knowledge as such find their part

---

sense of 'to mingle with' ('combine with') seems central, and more apt than that of 'to share' or 'to communicate with', which suggest a mediated relationship, and that of 'to have intercourse with', which suggests an interaction of parts. 'Partaking of' is also in line with Plato's sense, suggesting *partitioning* or *having part in*, as Rest would be said to have part in Sameness. The latter expression will frequently be relied upon in the discussion which follows, since it is favored by Cornford from whose translation the quoted passages are taken. For the same reason, I shall render τὸ ὄν 'Existence'. Although from some points of view 'Being' might seem a preferable rendition, nothing in the present analysis hangs upon this issue.

[46] This is a key passage in the debate whether Plato in the *Sophist* distinguished the copula from other senses of the verb 'to be'. Interesting as this debate may be in itself, it is not directly germane to the present study of Plato's methodology. A fair sampling of the issues may be had from Cornford, *Plato's Theory of Knowledge*, pp. 256–79; J. L. Ackrill, "Plato and the Copula: *Sophist* 251–259" (*Bulletin of the Institute of Classical Studies in the University of London*, no. 2, 1955), pp. 31–35, reprinted in R. E. Allen, *Studies in Plato's Metaphysics*); and W. G. Runciman, *Plato's Later Epistemology* (Cambridge: Cambridge University Press, 1962), pp. 84–98.

in Existence (257C); [47] and such, moreover, would be the entry (if any) into Existence of those fast and slow motions of the theory of perception in the *Theaetetus* which are what they are *only* in relation to each other.

Given that each Form mingles with Sameness and Difference, a number of things can be said both about what they are and about what they are not. First, Motion is not Rest. Being "altogether different from Rest" (255E), there is something Motion unqualifiedly *is not*. As sharing in Existence, on the other hand, Motion unqualifiedly *is*. Thus there are senses beyond dispute both in which Motion *is not* and *is*.

Motion, further, is not Sameness, but is the same as itself because it mingles with Sameness (256A). [48] Thus Motion both is the same and not the Same, but the senses in which this is so are not unqualified. "For when we say it is 'the same' and 'not the Same' we are not using the expression in the same sense" (256A–B), the first applying rather because of its part in Sameness, the second because of its part in Difference.

Motion moreover is not Difference, but rather is different from Difference. Thus Motion is both different and not (the) Different, but in senses which are no longer mysterious. Finally, although Motion *is*, since it partakes of Existence, it is not Existence (256D); and so it goes with any other Form. "That which is not," then, includes in its reference any Form which is different from Existence, or from any other Form; but at the same time all Forms included in the reference of "that which is not" *are* by virtue of their sharing in Existence

---

[47] Although this feature is not elaborated, Plato seems to suggest here, perhaps in response to the misgivings of the Friends of the Forms, that the Forms in themselves are immutable, partaking in Existence through Sameness, but that the same Forms nonetheless are knowable through sharing in Difference.

[48] Motion is the same as itself *because* (διά) everything (including motion) partakes of the Same. That is, participation in the Same is the reason for identity.

(256E). This must be true even of Existence itself, which *is not* an "indefinite number of other things" (257A). The sense in which "that which is not" *is*, long under search, now is close at hand.

It is the mistake of conceiving "that which is not" as contrary to Existence which led to the excesses of Parmenides, and which accounts for the apparent elusiveness of the Sophist. "[T]hat which is not," however, signifies not "something contrary to what exists but only something that is different" (257B). What is not, in this sense, partakes of Existence no less than *what is*, but through Difference rather than through Sameness. Partaking of Difference are the opposites of every Form, the not-Beautiful, the not-Tall and the not-Just (257E–258A) among the others, each of which is what it is with reference to that of which it is the opposite, and the negation or opposition is "as much a reality as Existence itself . . ." (258B). Thus, concludes the Stranger, we may "now be bold to say that 'that which is not' unquestionably *is* a thing that has a nature of its own," and is "a single Form to be reckoned among the many realities" (258B–C [translator's italics]).

As a result of this deliberate and well-considered violation of Parmenides' instructions to refrain from inquiry concerning what is not, Plato not only has shown that "that which is not" *is*, but has also "brought to light the real character of 'not-being' " (258D). With the concept of the Different in his conceptual arsenal, Plato now can move on to explicate the sense in which a true negative statement or a false affirmative one can state "what is not," and can explain finally how it is possible for the mind to terminate an "interior discourse" in agreement with itself about "that which is not," which we call by the name 'false judgment'. Before picking up the thread of these problems again, however, let us trace out the consequences of the mingling of the Forms for the practice of dialectic.

Now very little insight into the philosopher's business is

afforded by a discussion of the various relations among Existence, Rest, Motion, Sameness and Difference.[49] We know that the philosopher is one "whose thoughts constantly dwell upon the nature of reality" (254A), and that he is concerned to make divisions among the Forms without "taking the same Form for a different one or a different one for the same . . ." (253D). From the *Phaedrus*, which is a bit more specific about this matter, we learn that dialectical division follows "the objective articulations [κατ' ἄρθρα ᾗ πέφυκεν]" (265E) among the Forms like the skilled butcher dissects an animal with a knowledge of its joints. But what, with respect to the Forms, would correspond to the dissection of an animal according to the natural articulation of its joints and sinews? Cornford's answer [50] is that the division according to Kinds, which for Plato results in the free man's knowledge, is the division of generic Forms into specific differences. Thus, for example, the generic Form Animal might stand at the top of a division, and be further subdivided "down through the subordinate differences" [51] into Bipedal Animals and Bipedal Animals that are Rational, at which juncture Man (or, with another set of dif-

---

[49] Runciman remarks that the examination of these relationships among the μέγιστα γένη cannot be regarded "as an exercise on a higher level of the same kind as the search for the Sophist and Statesman" (*Plato's Later Epistemology*, p. 61). But his reasons are not convincing. It is true as he points out that the relations among the "very important Kinds" are not those of genus and species; but neither, I argue below, are those in the definition of the Sophist and the Angler. On the other hand, it is wrong to say that none of the μέγιστα γένη is "logically or otherwise superior to any or all of the others" (*ibid.*), since Existence but not Rest and Motion blends with all Forms. The reason the dialectic method is not illustrated in this passage is simply that none of the Forms discussed is *defined* in terms of the others. As H. Cherniss points out in *The Riddle of the Early Academy* (Los Angeles: University of California Press, 1945), Being, Identity, and Difference are equally extensive, and although Rest and Motion are less extensive than these, they "are not natural divisions of any, nor does Plato reach them by division. . . ." (p. 55)

[50] *Plato's Theory of Knowledge*, p. 269.

[51] *Ibid.*

ferences, another class of animal) would be defined. Thus, says Cornford, when we divide Animal in this way we are dividing, not "the class of all individual animals, but a single complex Form or nature, of which the subordinate Forms are called 'parts' (μόρια, μέρη)." [52] It is this generic Form Animal "that we divide, as the *Phaedrus* says, 'according to its natural articulations'. . . ." [53]

Now there is nothing in this description that is flatly contrary to Plato's practice, and Cornford is surely right in insisting that the dialectical divisions of the philosopher have nothing to do necessarily with the *individuals* in the classes corresponding to the Forms with which he is concerned.[54] But the use of the expressions 'generic Form', 'subordinate difference,' and 'indivisible species' is downright misleading (as is the example of Animal divided into Man, Ox, Lion, and so forth) as an illustration of Plato's method of division. Cornford himself is properly insistent that "no satisfactory account of the relations of Platonic Forms can be given in terms of Aristotelian logic;" [55] and he shows conclusively that the ontology of substance and accident which is behind Aristotle's methodology has no place within the Platonic framework. For Plato, the individual spatial and temporal substances of Aristotle are not real in any primary sense, for they are indefinite, constantly in change, and as such unknowable. The goal of philosophy therefore cannot be to establish truths about the natures of Aristotelian substances, but has to do rather with exhibiting relations among properties which for Aristotle might be entirely accidental in their attribution to individual things. But Cornford does not go far enough in dissociating Plato's from Aristotle's conceptual scheme. For, having remarked that the goal of dialectic is not to establish truths about the natures of substances, Cornford goes on to say that

[52] *Ibid.*
[53] *Ibid.*
[54] *Ibid.*
[55] *Ibid.*, p. 268.

the objective of dialectic "is the definition of an indivisible species—a Form—by genus and specific differences." [56] And this will not do at all as a description of the philosopher's practice, at least not if the terms 'genus', 'specific difference', and 'indivisible species' are allowed to carry certain familiar connotations.

The sense for Plato, as Cornford rightly remarks, in which the so-called "*infimae species*" are indivisible, is that the process of division at that stage cannot be carried any further. And this is not to say that the species, being indivisible, is simple and unanalyzable, for "if it were, it could not be defined;" and, according to Cornford, "the object of the whole procedure is to define it in terms of the generic Form and all the differences that occur in its ancestry." [57] But Cornford goes on to speak of the Forms Animal, Biped and Rational, for example, as general "parts or constituents of the complex specific Form, Man." [58] Thus both the higher and the lower Forms are complex, although in different ways. "The generic Form contains all the species and its nature pervades them all," while the "lowest species contains the nature of the genus and all the relevant differences." [59] Thus Animal (for Aristotle, the secondary, not the primary substance [*Categories* 2 a 16–18]) is said to contain Man, marked off by the differences Bipedal and Rational. The class of Animal can be broken up, as it were, into the subclasses of Man, Ox, and so forth, and the differences which mark off Man from the other species are particular to that species itself. As Aristotle says, "if genera are different and co-ordinate, their differentiae are themselves different in kind," with the exception that when "one genus is subordinate to another, there is nothing to prevent their having the same differentiae: for the greater class is predicated of the lesser, so that all the differentiae of the predicate will be

[56] *Ibid.*, p. 269.
[57] *Ibid.*, p. 270.
[58] *Ibid.*
[59] *Ibid.*

differentiae also of the subject." [60] Thus, to take Aristotle's own example, the genus Animal can be differentiated by the features Two-footed, Winged, and Aquatic, but not so the genus Knowledge.

But all this is entirely foreign to Plato's procedure of division according to natural articulations among the Forms.[61] Consider the definition of the Angler, as one plying the art of stealthy acquisition, by capture, of fish struck from below by day instead of night. The Forms going into this definition, in the first place, do not invite division into genera, species and subordinate differences. Although Angler, thereby defined, might be considered a secondary substance in Aristotle's sense, there is no "higher substance" or genus of which Angler thereby is exhibited as a part. The Form Art is not genus to Angler, for Art is a Form of activity of which the angler is at best a practitioner and in no sense a part. Art by acquisition is a kind of art, indeed, and in that sense subordinate to Art in general, but the Angler is neither Art nor Art by acquisition, as Man in the analogy is properly said to be Animal, and in particular Animal that is Rational.

Not to be lost in grammatical quibbles, however, one might point out that Plato's intention is to divide not Art but rather *Artisan* into its subordinate species, including Angler, and that 'acquisitive', 'by capture', and so forth, are differentiations among others which mark off the Angler from other artisans, just as 'rational' and 'bipedal' mark off Man from other animals. The response must be that if Plato *were* dividing a genus into species by subordinate differences in his definition of the Angler, then Artisan is as likely a candidate as any for the genus thereby divided. It would indeed be the case, ac-

[60] *Categories* 1b 16–24; Oxford translation, edited by W. D. Ross. In this connection see also *Posterior Analytics* 97a 22 ff.

[61] N. Gulley remarks correctly that the method of division "is introduced . . . as a method of classification, not of definition in terms of genus and specific differences (*Plato's Theory of Knowledge* [London: Methuen and Co., 1962] p. 114)."

cording to the dictum that "if the genus is predicable of the species then it is predicable of that of which the species is predicable," [62] that Artisan is predicable both of Angler ("Angler is part of Artisan") and of individual anglers (if X is an angler then X is an Artisan). And it would be the case also that Artisan in some sense would be more universal than Angler, since there are many artisans who are not anglers, but (if Plato's definition is right) no anglers who are not artisans. But here compliance with the rules of definition according to genus and species ceases. For as we shall see, not only is the choice of Artisan as genus arbitrary, but also the relation among the properties *art*, *acquisition*, *by capture*, and so forth, simply is not like that between a genus and its subordinate differences.

There is no reason why, in the first place, if a genus must be found in Plato's definition of the Angler, that genus might not be either Acquirer or Captor instead of Artisan. It is as appropriate to say of an angler that he is an acquirer or that he is a captor as to say that he is an artisan.[63] An angler, among other artisans, is acquisitive, hence an acquisitive artisan; but an angler is no less an artisan among acquirers, hence an artful acquirer. In the same sense he is no less an artisan who captures than a captor who employs artful means.

Related to this is a more forceful reason why we should not attempt to conceive Plato's definitions after an Aristotelian model. This is that there is no relationship of subordination necessary among the properties contributing to the definition. Apart from the question whether any of the properties going

[62] Paraphrase of *Categories* 1b 10–15.

[63] In response to the possible objection that neither Acquirer nor Captor is a substance, it need only be said that either is as much a substance as Artisan. In point of fact, it would seem much more appropriate, given the framework of Aristotelian predication, to locate these properties in adjectival form under the category of quality. To be skilled in an art is on a par with being grammatical (see *Categories* 1 b 29), which is one of Aristotle's examples of quality, and the same may be said of the property of being acquisitive. Being a captor, on the other hand, seems comparable with being armed and other attributes of state.

into the definition of Angler ought to be construed as a genus, we should realize that it is only *incidental* when one property in the definition turns out to be a further specification of another in a nonreciprocal fashion. In the Aristotelian definition of Man as rational Animal, indeed, it would be wrong-headed to think of animality as a specification of rationality; rationality, rather, distinguishes one from other kinds of animal. So, analogously, in Plato's definition of the Angler, we have 'captor of fish' specifying 'captor of water animal', where it would be senseless to think conversely of the latter as specifying the former. But this nonreciprocity is not a general feature of the various levels in the definition. Although 'acquisitive' does in a sense specify 'art', there is no reason why 'artful' in the same sense should not be conceived as specifying 'acquisition'. Just as there are some arts which are not acquisitive, so that to speak of acquisitive arts is more specific than to speak merely of arts (unqualified), so too there are forms of acquisition which are not artful (being instead scientific or fortuitous, as by inheritance), so that to speak of artful acquisition also is more specific than to speak merely of acquisition (unqualified). And so with 'forceful', where we could as well have 'acquisitive forcefulness', and with 'force involving stealth', where we could have as well 'stealth involving force'. The point here is that there are forms of acquisition which are not arts, forms of forceful exercise which are not acquisitive, forms of stealth which are not forceful, and so on down the line. The upshot is that there is no relationship of decreasing generality built into the ordering of the properties in Plato's division leading to the Angler. To put the point another way, we may say that 'acquisitive' is not a differentia belonging under 'art' exclusively, but rather can qualify various other attributions as well (such as 'science' or 'personality' or 'tendency'), nor is 'forceful' a differentia belonging specifically either to 'art' or 'acquisition', and so forth. This is quite contrary to the rule of Aristotelian definition that if genera are different and coordinate, their differentiae are themselves different in kind.

We should note, in passing, that this reciprocity of order among levels in definition applies to the other definitions given in the *Sophist* as well. In the definition of "Sophist VI" as an artisan concerned with the separation of better from worse in matters of the soul, and so forth, there is no reason why the definition could not have been put, rather, as an artisan concerned with matters of the soul who separates better from worse, and so forth. And the "true Sophist," when finally defined, is no more accurately said to be an artisan dealing in the production, by human means, of illusion, and so forth, than to be a human engaged in production of an artful sort of illusion, and so forth. For Plato, we may say in general, the order in which the various attributes of a thing are built into its definition has nothing to do essentially with the dialectician's division according to the natural articulation among the Forms.[64]

Now this contention that the Forms are not hierarchically arranged in division may appear to presuppose that Plato is not dealing with *predication* in his discussion of the communication among the Forms. Predication in general is a nonsymmetrical relation. If B is correctly predicated of A, then in general A cannot be correctly predicated of B; if this latter were possible, the relation between B and A would not be predication but rather identity. This being the case, however, A is subordinate to B in a way in which B is not subordinate to A, and this amounts to a hierarchical ordering between A and B. For example, it is true to say that Justice is Virtue in a way in which it is not true to say that Virtue is Justice; Justice, being only one form of Virtue, is therefore subordinate to Virtue. Thus it might appear that in maintaining the

[64] Cherniss argues convincingly that "Plato could not . . . have intended by the use of diaeresis to produce an ontological hierarchy of the world of ideas." Nor, further, "does Plato anywhere make the distinction of genus and species among the ideas . . ." (*The Riddle of the Early Academy*, p. 54.)

absence of hierarchical ordering in a proper definition I am
committed to denying that Plato distinguished predication
from other relations among the Forms. In view of the vigor-
ous debate [65] on the latter issue in recent years, this would be
a risky commitment.

No such commitment, however, is involved. Perhaps showing why this is the case will clarify further the sense in which
combination among the Forms as depicted in the *Sophist* is a
symmetrical relationship. Now apart from the question
whether Plato intended to *distinguish* predication explicitly in
his discussion of the "very important Kinds" it is entirely clear
that he *employed* the relation in developing the definition of
the Angler and of the Sophist, and in other contexts as well. At
222C, for example, Theaetetus admits that man is a tame
animal who is hunted; and at 235A the Sophist is called a
wizard and an imitator of what is real. Even if Plato had not
explicitly employed the relation of predication in his discussion, it would be totally incredible to suggest that he was not
aware that things had properties which could be attributed to
them in statements of the form (rendered in English) 'A is B'.

But all of this is incidental to what Plato is doing in his discussion of combination among the "very important Kinds."
What he is doing there is not discussing various types of statements we make about things, but rather exhibiting the relation
among Kinds which makes *possible* statements about things
of any type whatsoever. The relation of combination which
holds between Motion and Sameness (256A), for example,
but not between Motion and Rest (255E), is not the relation of
predication, nor is it the relation of identity or any other rela-

---

[65] See F. M. Cornford, *Plato's Theory of Knowledge*, pp. 256–79;
R. Robinson, "Plato's *Parmenides* II," *Classical Philology*, 37, no. 2
(April, 1942); J. L. Ackrill, "Plato and the Copula: *Sophist* 251–59,"
R. E. Allen, *Studies in Plato's Metaphysics;* and W. G. Runciman,
Plato's Later Epistemology, pp. 84–98. Some of the main points in
the debate are reviewed in footnote 74 below.

tion reflected in use of the verb 'to be'. Combination, rather, is the relation of compatibility.[66] When the Stranger says at 254D that Existence combines with both Motion and Rest, for example, he is not saying that Motion or Rest is identical with Existence, nor that any of these is an attribute of any other. Nor is he saying merely that Motion and Rest exist. Again, when he says at 254E that Sameness and Difference combine with Motion, Rest, and Existence, he is not saying that any of these are predicated of the others, or identical with another, or even (strictly, in *this* statement) that any of the Forms involved exist. And surely when he says at 255D that Existence partakes of both τὸ καθ' αὑτό and τὸ πρὸς ἄλλο, this is not to say anything about what can be predicated of Existence, nor anything about the identity of Existence itself.

It is *because* the Forms combine, rather, that we are able to make statements about them, attributing identity to them, and saying of various Kinds that they exist or that they are different from other things. Motion *is* because (διὰ [256A]) it partakes of Existence. Again, Motion is the *same* as itself because (διὰ [256A]) everything partakes of the Same.[67] Each Form

---

[66] As Cherniss says in *The Riddle of the Early Academy*, the relations among the Forms, however expressed, are "really those of implication and compatibility" (p. 54). The sense in which Forms "imply" each other is discussed below.

[67] As combination with Existence is the ground on which it is correct to say a thing *is*, so combination with Sameness is the ground for saying a thing is identical to itself. It is strange to find Ackrill ("Plato and the Copula," R. E. Allen, *Studies in Plato's Metaphysics*, p. 209) using "Motion is the Same" and "Motion is not the same" to illustrate respectively predication (the copula) and identity. Presumably Sameness here is conceived as a property attributed to motion, and denied to be identical with it. But surely sameness is a relation and not a property. It is not even a relative property, like large, for it is a relation a thing bears only with respect to itself. At best we can say that to the extent that sameness is a property at all it is an entirely atypical property, and not at all suited for an illustration of predication. It is equally unsatisfactory to find identity illustrated by a statement that asserts lack of identity. Cornford's reading (*Plato's Theory of Knowledge*, p. 287) of "Motion is the same"

is *different*, moreover, because (διὰ [255E]) all partake of Difference; and in general all things *are* because they all partake of Existence (256E).

Thus even if predication is involved in some of the things Plato is saying about the relation of the "very important Kinds," this in no way suggests that the relation of combination itself is nonsymmetrical. Combination, to the contrary, necessarily is a symmetrical relation, for if A "goes with" B, then B "goes with" A as well. Combination is the relationship between compatible Forms.[68] Retaining view of the fact that compatibility is a symmetrical relationship, we may admit (what is obvious anyway) that some Forms are more comprehensive than others. Existence blends with all Forms, Rest only with some; thus Existence is more comprehensive than Rest. But the relation of combination between them is one which Existence bears to Rest in the same sense that Rest bears it to Existence. For two Forms to combine is for them to share in each other, in the sense of mingling compatibly. And the fact that Forms combine is the reason we are able to

---

as a statement of identity surely is preferable. If Ackrill's reading is a mistake, then the same mistake is committed by Runciman (*Plato's Later Epistemology*, p. 89). The present discussion, however, does not depend upon the correctness or incorrectness of either reading.

[68] Combination between Forms is not strictly analogous either to logical consistency between propositions or to compatibility between physical properties. Two propositions may be consistent without both being true, and two properties may be compatible without both characterizing the same physical object. Thus consistency, in a sense, is potentiality for mutual truth, and compatibility between physical properties is potentiality for mutual inherence in actual objects. Combination between Forms, however, is not a potentiality, but a relation which is as changeless as the Forms themselves. Thus combination between Forms is more than mere consistency, or agreement. At the same time, combination falls short of implication, since the participation of an object in a given Form does not require participation in all Forms compatible with that Form as well. The relation of entailment is present between some Forms, nonetheless, since some Forms fail to combine with the negation of other Forms. Thus Angler fails to combine with non-Artisan, and Angler accordingly entails Artisan.

say of things that they exist, that they have certain characteristics, or that they are identical to themselves.

Because Forms combine, moreover, it is possible to define
such things as the Angler and the Sophist. In general, a thing
X is definable as A B C only because the Forms A, B, and C
combine. The combination of A, B, and C, to be sure, is likely
to mark off a class less comprehensive than A or B or C itself.
Thus Sophist is less comprehensive than Artisan and less comprehensive than any other Kind going into its definition. But
this relation by which Sophist is less comprehensive than Artisan is not the relation of combination which Plato is illustrating in his discussion of the "very important Kinds." To be sure
Sophist and Artisan blend or combine with each other, otherwise the Sophist could not be defined as a type of artisan. But
the relation of combination is not the relation of predication.[69]

[69] There have been attempts in recent discussion of the "very important Kinds" to correlate different forms of predication with different grammatical constructions. Ackrill ("Plato and the Copula,"
Allen, *Studies in Plato's Metaphysics*, pp. 216–17), for example, purports to find that κοινωνία, κοινωνεῖν etc., when used with the genitive
mean 'share in', while with the dative they mean 'combine with' or
'communicate with'. The former construction, accordingly, is construed as expressing "the fact that one concept *falls under* another
(p. 217, author's emphasis)," while the latter "occurs in highly general remarks about the connectedness of εἴδη, where no definite fact
as to any particular pair of εἴδη is being stated (*ibid.*)." A similar
claim is made by K. Lorenz and J. Mittelstrass ("Theaitetos fliegt.
Zur Theorie wahrer und falscher Sätze bei Platon" [Soph. 251d–
263d], *Archiv für Geschichte der Philosophie*, 48 [1966], pp. 111–
52), based on the same instances in the text (following Ross: see
note 74 below). The verb with the genitive, they say, represents universal predication (or universal connectedness) as might be asserted
in an A proposition, while with the dative represents particular predication as in an I proposition. The textual instances cited, however,
support neither contention. Of the six instances (Lorenz and Mittelstrass, following Ross, list a nonexistent instance, i.e. 251E9) of use
with the genitive, only two (250B9, 256B2) clearly suggest a relationship of "falling under," or A-predication, and one of these Ackrill
disclaims from relevance (p. 216). The others either suggest no particular relationship beyond mere compatibility, or suggest *both* A-
and I-predication (concerning whether the "very important Kinds" are

Combination rather is the relation between Sophist and Artisan which makes it possible to define one in terms of the other.

Now how does this bear upon the question whether Plato in the *Sophist* distinguished predication from existence and identity? The most important result for our purposes is that the question does not interact with the claim above that the Forms going into a Platonic definition are not necessarily related in hierarchical order. What is essential is that the Forms involved in a definition of this sort combine with one another. If the relationship between two Forms combined in the definition turns out to be nonsymmetrical with respect to generality, as would be the case typically (but not necessarily) at some stage in the process, this is only incidental and in no way alters the fact that all Forms involved in the definition blend initially with all others. Thus Cornford [70] and Cherniss [71] are right in the claim that the relationships of blending or combination among the Forms is a symmetrical relationship.[72] Cornford, on the other

---

capable of combining with one another.) (254C5) Of the eight instances of use with the dative, on the other hand, one suggests both A- and I-predication (concerning whether Existence, Motion, and Rest are capable of association with one another) (251D9), one suggests A-predication (concerning whether some Kinds combine with all other Kinds) (254C1), and six suggest no particular relationship beyond compatibility. I see no reason in such grammatical considerations to conclude that Plato was attempting to distinguish particular forms of predication in these passages.

[70] *Plato's Theory of Knowledge*, p. 256.

[71] *Riddle of Early Academy*, p. 54.

[72] This means that Ackrill ("Plato and the Copula," Allen, *Studies in Plato's Metaphysics*, pp. 213–18) and Runciman (*Plato's Later Epistemology*, 88–89) are wrong in their attack upon this aspect of Cornford's analysis. It does not tell against Cornford, as both Ackrill and Runciman think, to point out that *some* relationships between Forms are nonsymmetrical. Indeed, who should ever have thought otherwise? Nor does the fact that Plato distinguishes attribution from other uses of εἶναι, if it is a fact, affect Cornford's claim. Of course Plato makes attributive statements (see above) even if he doesn't talk about them as such, but the relation of attribution is not the same as the relation of combination among the Kinds. Finally, the argument shared by both Ackrill and Runciman, that Plato's analogy of notes and letters suggests lack of symmetry in relation among the

hand, is wrong if he argues that the copula is not distinguished by Plato *because* the relation of combination among Forms is symmetrical.[73] One may maintain consistently both that the relation of combination is symmetrical and that Plato did distinguish the copulative from other uses of the verb 'to be'.

But the question remains: *did* Plato distinguish predication from statements of existence and identity? And I think the discussion above throws light upon this question as well. With respect to his discussion of the "very important Kinds," at least, I believe the answer is that he did not. It is not necessary to defend this answer in detail for purposes of the present discussion of Plato's methodology. My reasons for believing this, however, are as follows: Statements of predication, as we have seen, clearly are made elsewhere in the dialogue, so Plato certainly could handle the relationship in his own discourse. Thus it seems likely that Plato was aware of the distinction between predication and identity, and that he would not have considered himself enlightened to hear someone else point it out. But Plato did not *discuss* the relation of predication in *Sophist* 254–257. What he discussed there instead, among other things, is the relationships among Forms which make discourse possible, and in particular the relationships with Existence and Sameness which make it possible to formulate true statements saying of things that they *are*, and that they are *identical* to themselves. The reason he did not discuss predication is that

---

Forms, is simply a *non sequitur*. In reply, it is enough to point out that temporal and spatial relationships are essential among perceptual objects, but not present at all among the Forms. In this particular respect, consequently, relations among audible sounds and visible symbols simply are not analogous to relations among the Forms.

[73] It is not clear that Cornford *does* argue this way, as Ackrill (*ibid.*, p. 213) suggests. What he does say (correctly) is that the "Aristotelian terms 'subject', 'predicate', and 'copula' should not be used at all to describe what is in Plato's mind (p. 257)" in speaking of combination among the Forms. Cornford has *other* reasons for saying Plato doesn't distinguish the copula at all (*Plato's Theory of Knowledge*, p. 266).

such a discussion would not have been particularly appropriate at this stage in the dialogue.[74] It would have been more appro-

[74] I have indicated in footnote 32 why I think Ackrill was wrong in claiming that Plato needs the distinction between identity and predication to respond to the "late learners" of 251B–C. This is one phase of Ackrill's argument against the claim by Cornford that the relation of combination is symmetrical, and for the claim that Plato distinguishes the copula in his discussion of the combination of the Kinds. The other main phases of his detailed argument are as follows. (a) Cornford claims that 'Motion exists' means the same as 'Motion blends with Existence', and that because of symmetry this means the same as 'Existence blends with Motion'. But, Ackrill says, the latter by the same token must mean 'Existence moves', which certainly is not intended by Plato to mean the same as 'Motion exists'. Ackrill's analysis of the trouble is that the relation of blending is not symmetrical. His argument, however, shows an insensitivity to the difference between a grammatical relation and a relation among the Forms. Neither Plato nor Cornford say that whenever two Forms blend, this relation can be expressed in subject-predicate form. There is no justification for the claim that 'Existence blends with Motion' means for Plato 'Existence moves'. As we have seen above, the relation of blending is not the relation of predication. Ackrill is simply wrong in saying that the "rôle of 'partakes of' in Plato's terminology is clear: 'partakes of' followed by an abstract noun, the name of a concept, is equivalent to the ordinary language expression consisting of 'is' (copula) followed by the adjective corresponding to that abstract noun" (p. 218). (b) Although 'Motion is different from Rest' *is* equivalent to 'Rest is different from Motion', Ackrill continues, again it is not the case that the relation among the Forms involved is symmetrical. The argument here is as follows: Ackrill has suggested earlier that the negation of the 'is' of identity, when expressed in "the philosopher's terminology," is rendered by Plato (as at 256B) in the form '—communicates with Difference from ['with respect to' would be better]—' (p. 209). Hence 'Motion is different from Rest' becomes 'Motion communicates with Difference from Rest'; and if the relation here is symmetrical, then this would be equivalent to 'Difference from Rest communicates with Motion'. But this latter means 'Difference from Rest moves', which is not the same as 'Motion is different from Rest'. Against this queer interpretation, we may note (1), as above, that it is not the case in general that 'X communicates with Y' means 'X is Y' (or 'Xy's'); (2) that Plato does *not* use the '—communicate with Difference from—' formula when at 255E he *does* say Motion is different from Rest; and (3) that, regardless, the symmetrical opposite of 'Motion communicates with Difference from Rest' is 'Rest communicates with Difference from [with

priate in his subsequent discussion of falsehood in thought and
judgment. But what he talks about there is the "weaving together of the Forms," to which topic we turn in the following
section. The upshot would seem to be that the question
whether Plato explicitly distinguishes the copula in the *Sophist*
is less important than some commentators have thought, and
that it doesn't make much difference one way or the other for
his discussion of the relationship of combination among the
Forms.

Before proceeding to Plato's discussion of false judgment, we
should note one further consideration which in itself should be
sufficient to dissuade our thinking of Platonic definition in
terms of the Aristotelian model. It is a feature of definition by
genus and species, as we have seen, that the differentiae apply

---

respect to] Motion', and not 'Difference from Rest communicates with
Motion'. (c) The final phase of the argument is philological and at
best inconclusive. Ackrill claims (1) that Plato has a special construction of κοινωνέω to indicate the copula, namely use with the genitive,
and (2) that μετέχειν occurs five times from 255E to 257A in a way
indicating a copulative subordination of one concept to another. Regarding (1), the "predicate" in two of the examples (250B9 and
252A2—the examples follow W. D. Ross, *Plato's Theory of Ideas*,
[Oxford: Clarendon Press, 1951] p. 111 n) is existence (οὐσίας, for
which see Cornford, *Plato's Theory of Knowledge*, p. 252 n), which
indicates the 'is' of existence rather than predication. In two other
cases the "predicates" are 'difference' (θατέρου) (256B2) and 'not-
being' (μὴ ὄντος) (260E2), which again are scarcely copulative predicates. In another (252B9) *no* Form is mentioned specifically, so no
particular grammatical relation is indicated. And in the final (254C5),
the language actually *suggests* symmetry, for the Forms are considered with respect to how they combine with one another. Regarding
(2), three uses of μετέχειν (256A1, D9, E3) are with ὄντος, (Existence,
Being), and two (256A7, B1) are with ταὐτοῦ (the Same [regarding
256A7, see Cornford, *Plato's Theory of Knowledge*, p. 286 n]). All
uses are to indicate combination, which as we have seen is a symmetrical relation quite distinct from predication. Even if this were
not the case, to say that something is the same or that something
exists would be examples of the 'is' of identity and of the 'is' of
existence, not of the 'is' of predication. In short, Ackrill has no case
either for his contention against Cornford or for his claim that the
copula is distinguished in the present passage.

only within the genus which they specify. Only animals are risible, for example, so that to specify Animal with the differentia Risible is to mention a feature possessed only by things, but not by all things, falling under the higher class thereby divided. Being risible, that is to say, is a sufficient condition for being an animal. Being risible *entails* (in a sense presently defined) being an animal.

Now the thing to understand here is that any attribute entailed by another attribute within a Platonic definition can be eliminated without affecting the adequacy of the definition. In general, if A and B are features within a definition which gives both necessary and sufficient conditions of a thing or Kind X,[75] and if A entails B in the sense that all things conceived as A's are therefore conceived as B's as well, then B can be eliminated from the definition without altering either the necessity or the sufficiency of the remaining features.

An illustration can be taken from Plato's definition of the Angler, which includes both the features of capturing water animals and of capturing fish. All fish, let us agree, are water animals, while not all water animals are fish. Assuming that the definition shows all necessary conditions for being an Angler, we can see that the set of necessary conditions would be effectively the same if 'water animal' were simply eliminated, since being a water animal in turn is necessary for being a fish. In general, if A, B, and C are necessary conditions for being X, and if all things that are A are B also, then A and C impose the same requirements with regard to being X as does the set ABC.

We can see, similarly, that nothing is lost by way of sufficient conditions by effecting the same elimination. If the definition as it stands gives sufficient conditions for being an angler, then the conditions are no less sufficient when 'water animal' is dropped from mention, since being a fish in turn

---

[75] I have argued that a definition for Plato is a λόγος which gives necessary and sufficient conditions for being a thing of the type or Kind defined.

is sufficient for being a water animal. In general, if A, B, and C together are sufficient for being X, and if all things that are A are B also, then A and C together are sufficient for being X.[76]

The eliminability of a "more general" feature entailed by another within a definition does not in any sense invalidate a definition from which not all such features have been eliminated. But it does show conclusively that the relationship of genus to subordinate difference is entirely foreign to the Platonic definition in its purest and least cluttered form. Indeed the only attributes which are *not* eliminable from a proper definition are those which are not subordinated logically to other attributes within the definition.

A more felicitous model for conceiving the relationship among the Forms in a Platonic definition is that of class intersection.[77] Any given Form A marks off a class of Forms which combine with it. A few, like Existence, Sameness, and Difference, combine with all Forms. In most cases, however, A will combine only with some, B only with others, C only with others yet again, and so forth. This being so, A in general will combine with more Forms than will the pair A and B, which in turn will combine with more than A and B and C together.[78] Moreover, A and B together generally will combine with a different group of Forms than A and C, B

[76] Both of these claims, which as presented above rest upon informal understanding, are proven in the last chapter, where it is shown generally that if A entails B and if X = ABC, then X = AC.

[77] P. Kucharski assumes like Cornford that division for Plato is a matter of dividing genera into species. See *Les chemins du savoir dans les derniers dialogues de Platon* (Paris: Presses universitaires de France, 1949), pp. 264 ff. Although this in itself is wrong, Kucharski is right in his remark that this method involves "*la discrimination des espèces au point de vue de leur participation réciproque . . .*" (p. 265, author's emphasis).

[78] In this sense the Form defined (e.g., Angler) *is* less general than any one of the Forms going into the definition. But no one of these constituent Forms need in itself be any more or less general than any other.

and C, or any other grouping of Forms not exactly equivalent to the pair A and B itself.

According to this model, then, any grouping of Forms might be conceived as providing a "window" through which some but not all other Forms can be "viewed." The other Forms viewable through such a window are the Forms which combine with the original group. Perhaps the metaphor of a lens would be even more helpful, for then we could think of a given group of Forms as providing a unique focus under which only some other Forms come into view. The more Forms in general entering into the "lens," at least up to a certain point, the fewer other Forms stand sharply in view at its focal point. Metaphors aside, however, the function of a dialectical division is to bring together just those Forms and only those Forms which in combination articulate uniquely the nature of the thing or Form to be defined.

In working out his definition, there are three norms by which the dialectician must be guided if his result is to be worthy of his cause. First, he must assure that none of the various Forms A, B, C, and D, and so forth, which go into his definition, is such that it combines exclusively with the opposite of any other. Thus, for example, he must avoid any grouping of Forms A, B, and C, such that B combines only with not-C and not with C itself.[79] The dialectician, that is to say, must avoid inconsistency within his definition. Second, he must structure his definition so that the Forms entering into it collectively mark off only the Form of the thing to be defined. That is to say, his definition must display features which together are *sufficient* for being the thing in question. And finally, he must structure his definition so that the Form defined does not combine with the opposite of any of the Forms entering into it, which is to say that his definition must display only those features which are *necessary* for being the thing he

[79] Participating in the not-Beautiful is every Form different from Beauty, in the not-Tall every Form different from Tall, and so forth. In general, the not-A comprises all Forms other than A.

seeks to define. As we shall see presently, formal tests are available for determining whether these various conditions of the adequate definition are met in any particular case.[80]

Such are the requirements that prevent the free man's knowledge from being a cheap commodity in the marketplace of ideas. If any further incentive is needed for abandoning the unfortunately too common notion that Plato is not a precise thinker, or that one can understand Plato's methods and the most worthy of his results without careful attention to the logical structure of his arguments, it may be provided by the final speech in this section of the dialogue. Whereas there is nothing clever nor difficult in the discovery of apparent contradictions in discourse about the Forms, the Stranger remarks, "what is hard and at the same time worth the pains is something different" (259C). This is to leave quibbling alone as fruitless, and instead to follow the argument step by step and, "in criticising the assertion that a different thing is the same or the same thing is different in a certain sense, to take account of the precise sense and the precise respect in which they are said to be one or the other" (259C–D). Any other approach, with less respect for the utmost precision, "may be recognized as the callow offspring of a too recent contact with reality" (259D). Is there a more direct way of chiding those scholars, over-impressed by Plato's masterful use of metaphor and myth, who delude themselves and others with the thought that the proper approach to understanding what Plato said is through "intuition" and "sensitive insight," at the expense of a thorough logical analysis of the structure of the arguments themselves?

8 / False Judgment Explained

The remaining topic of general philosophic interest in the dialogue is Plato's account of truth and falsehood. Together

[80] Chapter IV, Section 1.

with the difficulties in finding a suitable sense of λόγος for an explication of knowledge, the problem of accounting for the possibility of false judgment has been a unifying theme not only of the *Sophist* but of the *Theaetetus* before it. It was under the assumption that some judgments *are* true and some false, first, that the Protagorean claim that man provides the measure of all things was refuted. And it was the attempt to explain how a judgment can be false that led, in the middle of the dialogue, to those complex and unsatisfactory considerations regarding the nature of the retentive powers which malfunction in false belief. The mind cannot be likened in this respect merely to a wax block in which perceptual and memorial images are confused, since this does not provide any analogy to the way we make mistakes in judgment about things which are never perceived. Nor is it satisfactory to liken the mind to an aviary, where images are not necessarily acquired through perception and are not stored as mechanical imprints, for in such an analogy there is no criterion to distinguish between correct and incorrect comparisons of contents. Whereas a judgment of correspondence between perceptual and memory images in the wax block model is reckoned true or false according to whether or not the two images derive from the same perceptible object, there is nothing in the model of the aviary to distinguish without circularity between correct and incorrect judgments of identification. The problem of false judgment then was shelved for the remainder of the dialogue, while Socrates turned to examine the third hypothesis that knowledge is true judgment accompanied by λόγος.

Nothing constructive can be salvaged from the latter two sections of the *Theaetetus*, however, if any serious doubt is allowed to remain about the possibility of false judgment. Given now an account of λόγος which will sustain the difference between true judgment and knowledge, moreover, the definition of knowledge as true judgment accompanied by λόγος can be counted secure if a coherent account can be provided of true and false judgment. To accomplish this is the purpose of *Sophist* 260A–264B.

Faced with a forceful explanation of the way in which "that which is not" nonetheless is, the Sophist might yet attempt to delay his capture in an adequate definition by the following ploy. He might claim that, although "not-being" (260D), in the sense of "that which is not," does after all exist, it does not have any part in discourse or judgment, so that the proper identification of the Sophist as a producer of false statements and false belief remains an impossibility. The Stranger's procedure in the face of this threat is first to explain his sense of 'discourse' or 'statement' (λόγος), next to show how a statement in this sense can be either true or false, and finally to reiterate from the *Theaetetus* (189E–190A) his notion of judgment as terminated inner discourse, which then can be said to be true or false in the same way as an explicit statement in public language.

The discourse or statement which is to be shown capable of sharing in "that which is not" is a combination of expressions referring to actions (verbs) and expressions referring to the agents which perform these actions (names) (262A). The only examples Plato gives of such statements are 'a (or 'the') man understands' (ἄνθρωπος μανθάνει [262C]), 'Theaetetus sits', and 'Theaetetus flies', each consisting of just one name and one verb. Given such modest materials to work with, it is not surprising that Plato does not cover the entire range of problems in contemporary semantics, such as those concerning the truth conditions of statements about nonexistent entities, or statements about the undetermined future or the unknowable past. His aim is merely to show what it is for certain statements of "the simplest and briefest kind" (262C) to be true, and what correspondingly to be false. The common feature of the statements with which he deals is that they give "information about facts or events in the present or past or future," and do so "by weaving together verbs with names" (262D).[81] A

---

[81] At 259E the Stranger points out that discourse (λόγος) depends upon the "weaving together of Forms" (εἰδῶν συμπλοκήν). Now it is claimed to depend upon the weaving together of names and verbs. The fact that 'Theaetetus sits' refers apparently to only one Form

further feature of such statements is that they "must be about something" (262E), although what a statement says about a thing in a particular case might be either true or false.[82] Although Plato's explication of truth and falsehood is exceedingly brief, I shall attempt to explain what I think he had in mind.

Both the statements 'Theaetetus sits' and 'Theaetetus flies' are about the same thing, the boy with whom the Stranger is conversing. In each case the expression 'Theaetetus' refers to this individual, so that the difference with respect to truth value of the two statements cannot lie in the referential function of the name. The difference lies rather with the difference in relationship of the two verbs 'sits' and 'flies' to the actions being performed by the referent of the name. The trouble with 'Theaetetus flies' obviously is that the verb does not correspond to any action being performed by Theaetetus at the moment. What is right about 'Theaetetus sits', on the other hand, is that its verb does correspond in its purported meaning to the behavior of Theaetetus at the moment of reference. Although these remarks in a commonsensical way are obvious, they contain expressions which a prudent philosopher would not accept immediately into his technical vocabulary. In particular, there are the expressions 'correspond' and 'purported meaning'. Plato's contribution to the theory of truth and falsehood in the *Sophist* is to provide explications, according to his own framework, of the relevant concepts associated with these English expressions. If we may consider the purported meaning of a term to be the conceptual content or Form [83] of which one is mindful in using the term, then we may say that for

leads to the problem whether 262D conflicts with 259E, where the weaving together of *Forms* (plural) was mentioned. This is discussed further in the text below.

[82] According to the discussion at 237C–E, a statement which is about nothing says nothing, and hence is no statement at all (263C).

[83] When one is mindful of a Form one conceives a Form, and the Form is the content of one's conception. This way of speaking may be admitted without raising the bottomless question whether Forms are identical with concepts for Plato.

Plato the meaning of a term is the Form indicated in its common (as against idiosyncratic) use. The meaning of the terms 'sits' and 'flies', thereby, are the Forms Sitting and Flying.

Now for Plato the sitting behavior of Theaetetus also relates to the Form Sitting, in a way never fully clarified but commonly discussed with the help of the concept of "participation." [84] While sitting, moreover, Theaetetus might also be smiling, nodding, and exhibiting wisdom, so that Theaetetus through his behavior at the same time participates in Smiling, Nodding, and Wisdom. He *might* conceivably, if transported into the seat of a modern airplane, be participating in Flying as well.[85] There are some Forms, however, in which Theaetetus *cannot* participate while sitting, among them Running, Standing, and Lying. If Theaetetus is sitting, then he is neither running, standing, nor lying down, nor is he engaged in any other activity the pursuit of which is incompatible with sitting. The mark of truth in the statement 'Theaetetus sits' is that all present activities of Theaetetus are compatible with the activity of sitting. To say this is to say, in the terminology of the Forms, that all Forms in which Theaetetus participates by virtue of his activity at the moment combine with the Form of Sitting.[86] The statement 'Theaetetus sits' is true because no Forms in which the referent of the name participates fail to

[84] Cornford argues convincingly (*Plato's Theory of Knowledge*, p. 297) that participation in this sense differs essentially from participation, or mingling, among the Forms themselves, since the latter but not the former is a symmetrical relationship. This is discussed in the preceding section.

[85] It does *not* go without saying, as Xenakis avows, "that 'sitting' means here 'sitting *on the ground*' not, say, 'in an airplane' . . ." (J. Xenakis, "*Plato's Sophist:* A Defense of Negative Expressions and a Doctrine of Sense and Truth," *Phronesis*, 4, no. 1 [1959]: 41 [author's emphasis]). Whatever the Kinds may be for Plato, they do not change with a changing technology. Sitting in an airplane is no less sitting, in the sense that one sits "on the ground" (or in a chair), than eating in an airplane is eating, or speaking is speaking.

[86] Sitting itself combines with Sitting, since each Form combines with Sameness. See note 68 for a discussion of combining and incompatibility.

combine with the Form which is the meaning of the verb. In
this sense the statement corresponds to the behavior of Theaetetus at the moment of reference.[87]

The statement 'Theaetetus flies', on the other hand, is false,
for although Theaetetus may be sitting or standing, and
speaking or laughing, none of his various activities is incompatible with his *not* flying. Now there are some things Theaetetus *might* conceivably be doing which are incompatible with
not flying, such as moving swiftly through the air, rising
vertically without support or, more directly (with the ill-fated
Icarus) flying itself. These acts, and such as these, are incompatible with not flying, since to fly is just to do one or another
of these things. The Forms of these activities, then, do not
combine with the Form not-Flying. Since Theaetetus is not
doing anything incompatible with not flying, however, the

---

[87] Lorenz and Mittelstrass (*"Theaitetos fleigt,"* Archiv für
Geschichte der Philosophie, 1966, p. 140) render 'Theaetetus sits' as a
dual proposition, asserting both that Theaetetus is a man and that
Theaetetus sits. In this they seek to avoid the problem of how Plato can
maintain that discourse "owes its existence" to the combination of
Forms (259E), while the statement 'Theaetetus sits' (as well as
'Theaetetus flies' and 'a man understands') seems to involve only a
single Form. The truth of 'Theaetetus sits', accordingly, is construed
as the inherence of the compatible Forms Man and Sitting in the
same individual. " 'Theaetetus flies' is false," on the other hand, means
(p. 142) that Theaetetus is a man and participates in a Form (e.g.
Sitting) which is contrary to Flying. Among the difficulties of this
account in general are: (1) although the individual named by the
proper noun in 'Theaetetus sits' may be a man, the statement does
not assert this; 'Theaetetus sits' is not contradicted by 'Theaetetus
is not a man': and (2) there is no apparent reason why a statement
about Theaetetus should be construed as asserting that he is a man
rather than, for example, an animal, a Greek, or a mathematician.
Surely 'Theaetetus sits' as Plato intends it does not assert *all* the
things that Theaetetus is besides sitting. But why, by the same token,
should it be construed as asserting any one of these other things?
This account of 'Theaetetus flies' as false, moreover, is unsatisfactory
in a more particular respect, since Sitting is *not* contrary to or incompatible with Flying. Theaetetus *might*, for example, be flying while
seated in an airplane. Possibilities such as this are discussed further
in the text.

statement that he is flying is false. To put it more formally, 'Theaetetus flies' is false because all of the Forms in which the referent of the name participates combine with the opposite (not-A) of the Form (A) which is the meaning of the verb.[88]

Although Plato does not deal explicitly with true and false negative statements, the account above can be seen to apply to these equally well. Consider that 'Theaetetus is not flying' is true and that 'Theaetetus is not sitting' is false. Now the first of these statements could be construed in the Platonic schematism as 'Theaetetus is not-flying'.[89] Adhering to the format of the extremely simple statements discussed in the dialogue, without regard for the inept English that results, let us render this simply as 'Theaetetus not-flies'. The second statement in the same fashion will be rendered, for purposes of illustration, 'Theaetetus not-sits'.

The statement 'Theaetetus not-flies' is true because all Forms in which Theaetetus through his various activities participates combine with the Form not-Flying. The statement 'Theaetetus not-sits', on the other hand, is false because all Forms in which he participates through his activity combine with the opposite of the Form not-Sitting. Every Form mani-

[88] Moravcsik, in "Being and Meaning in the *Sophist*," pp. 74–75, argues that an explanation of the falsehood of "Theaetetus flies" as involving the incompatibility of Flying with some of the predicates of Theaetetus cannot be correct, because (1) "one need not know any particular predicate of Theaetetus with which Flying is incompatible in order to ascertain that 'Theaetetus flies' is false," and (2) "Plato does not discuss incompatibility anywhere prior to 263b." It might appear that my explanation, involving the notion of compatibility (combining—see pp. 193–97 above), is subject to similar objections. However, (1) to know that "Theaetetus flies" is false *does* require ascertaining that Theaetetus is doing nothing incompatible (not combining) with not-Flying (such as moving swiftly through the air, rising vertically without support, and so on), and (2) Plato *does* discuss the relation of combining prior to 263B (see notes 66 and 68 and associated text above). Hence Moravcsik's objections cannot be adapted to oppose my account.

[89] Meaning: Theaetetus participates in not-Flying. Not-Flying, as we have seen, is the Form with which all Forms other than Flying, and those which entail Flying, combine.

fest in his various activities, that is, combines with Sitting, for there is nothing he is doing which is incompatible with sitting, as would be the case if the statement 'Theaetetus not-sits' were true.

This discussion goes considerably beyond any detail provided by Plato. It seems nonetheless to constitute a likely and reasonable interpretation of Plato's own distressingly brief discussion on the matter of false statement, the upshot of which is that such an expression "states *things that are-not* as being" (263B [translator's emphasis]). 'Theaetetus flies' states that "what is not" (a Form in which Theaetetus by his activity participates, i.e. the Form Flying) combines with all Forms in which Theaetetus by his activity participates. But this is not the case, since all such Form mingle with not-Flying. Similarly, 'Theaetetus not-sits' states that what is not (in the sense above, specifically not-Sitting) combines with all such Forms, which it does not since all combine with Sitting. Both therefore are false, being so formulated that "what is different is stated as the same or what is not as what is . . ." (263D).

With this background, we may formulate what is characteristic in general of true and false statements respectively. Speaking with Plato, we would say a statement (of the sort under consideration) is true if and only if all Forms in which the referent of the name participates by virtue of its activity combine with the Form which is the meaning of the verb. A statement is false, on the other hand, if and only if all Forms in which the referent of the name participates combine with the opposite ("negation") of the Form which is the meaning of the verb.[90]

---

[90] This explanation of Plato's account of false statements is evolved from that of Cornford (*Plato's Theory of Knowledge*, pp. 311–17), to whom (as so often throughout this essay) I am deeply indebted. But it has two advantages in comparison. One is that it provides an analysis of the truth and falsity of *negative* statements under the same general rubric as that of positive statements. Cornford's explanation of false statement is to the effect that a statement is false if the meaning of the verb is different from any Form in which an

Let us return to the problem of the aviary in the *Theae-tetus*. Although the model of the caged birds is tailored specifically to provide a place for thoughts which are not of empirical origin, there is no provision within the model for an account of the difference between true and false judgments

---

activity of the referent of the name participates. But in the statement 'Theaetetus is not-Flying' the meaning of the verb is different from any Form in which the referent of the name participates (as Sitting, for example, is part of not-Flying, but different from it), yet the statement is true. Another advantage is that it escapes the objection Ackrill brought against Cornford in "SYMPLOKE EIDON" (reprinted in R. E. Allen, *Studies in Plato's Metaphysics*, pp. 199–206). At 259E, Ackrill points out, the Stranger says "any discourse we can have owes its existence to the weaving together of Forms [with one another]." Yet on Cornford's account, only one Form is involved in the true statement 'Theaetetus sits' (p. 315), and there is no sense in speaking of one Form weaving together with itself. Surveys of attempts to meet Ackrill's difficulty may be found in J. M. E. Moravcsik's "ΣΥΜΠΛΟΚΗ ΕΙΔΩΝ and the Genesis of ΛΟΓΟΣ," *Archiv für Geschichte der Philosophie*, Band 42, Heft 2 (1960), pp. 117–29, and in Lorenz and Mittelstrass ("*Theaitetos fleigt*," *Archiv für Philosphie*, 1966), whose solution is discussed in note 87. Moravcsik's solution is to introduce a copula into the statement 'Theaetetus sits', rendering it 'Theaetetus is sitting', and then to posit a Form "relational Being" to which the copula might correspond. Thus in such a simple statement even as 'Theaetetus sits' we are to find two Forms represented, Sitting and relational Being. Now, although a Platonic Form might always be postulated to cover any form of Being a person for one reason or another happens to favor, I find nothing in the text to suggest that Plato himself had anything like Moravcsik's "relational Being" in mind when speaking of the blending of the Forms at 259E. The "relational Being" he does speak of there is combining, or "weaving together," and his claim surely is not that discourse owes its existence to the combining of Combining with other Forms. A less paradoxical solution to Ackrill's problem is preferable. In the analysis above, the interpretation of 259E is entirely straightforward. Discourse is possible in statements composed of names and verbs which are about something, and which are either true or false (262E). A true statement is one such that all Forms in which the referent of the name participates combine with the Form which is the meaning of the verb, while in a false statement all such Forms combine with the negation (not-A) of the Form (A) which is the meaning of the verb. In this way, all discourse owes its existence to the combination of the Forms.

involving these thoughts. Within the context of the aviary itself, that is, there is no basis for a distinction in kind between the judgment that $5 + 7 = 11$ and the judgment that $5 + 7 = 12$. This defeats the purpose of the image, for the very problem which led to its formulation was that of extending the account of the difference between true and false perceptual judgments, provided in terms of the waxen block, to judgments about objects like numbers which are not accessible to perception.

Within the expanded conceptual framework of *Sophist*, however, judgments about numbers pose no novel problem. Whereas in the context of the waxen block we could say that a judgment identifying a perceptual with a memory image is true if and only if the two images in fact derive from the same object, and is otherwise false, so now in the context of the mingling Forms we can say that a judgment identifying two numbers (say the complex $5 + 7$ and the single number 12) is true if and only if the Form which is the meaning of the expression for $5 + 7$ is the same as the Form which is the meaning of the expression for 12. Otherwise, if the two meanings partake in Difference relative to each other, the judgment is false.

The various parts of the definition of knowledge proposed in the final passages of the *Theaetetus* now are ready to fit into place. Judgment is the assertion or denial which terminates an inward dialogue of the mind with itself (*Theaetetus* 190A; *Sophist* 264A). True judgment is an assertion or denial of this sort which is such that the meaning of the verb involved in the judgment combines with all Forms in which the referent of the name or subject noun participates. And λόγος, finally, is the account concerning the object of judgment which exhibits necessary and sufficient conditions for its being what it is, thereby exhibiting the Forms which do and those which do not combine with its Form. With these explanations of the key expressions at hand, there is no remaining reason within either the *Theaetetus* or the *Sophist* why the equation of

knowledge with true judgment accompanied by λόγος should
not be accepted.

9 / The Authentic Sophist

There remains only the task of completing the definition interrupted at 237A, "[h]olding fast to the characters of which
the Sophist partakes until we have stripped off all that he has
in common with others and left only the nature that is peculiar
to him . . ." (264E). At the beginning of this definition, we
recall, Art was divided into Productive and Acquisitive, and
Sophist VII, unlike his phantom parts I through V, was pursued along the former branch. The distinction between human
and divine production (present but not clearly focused at the
previous stage in the definition) is now made explicit (265B–
E), and within each class the further distinction is made between production of images and production of originals
(266A–D). The originals of divine production are the various
living creatures and the elements depicted in the *Timaeus*, the
images of which are present in dreams and perception. The
originals of human production are the work of artisans and
craftsmen, imaged in the arts of painting, rhetoric and sophistry. Image-making of the human variety then is divided
again into the making of likenesses and the making of sem-
blances (266D–E), now granted to be possible after the long
"digression" which in fact has yielded the more important
philosophic results of the dialogue.

Semblance-making then is divided (267A) into production
by tool and production, by voice or person, called "mimicry."
Within the latter are further distinguished the productions of
those, such as professional mimes, who know the subject they
imitate, and those, like most public speakers on virtue, who
are ignorant of their subject (267B–D). These latter two
types cannot be given perspicuous names, "because the an-

cients, it would seem, suffered from a certain laziness and lack
of discrimination with regard to the division of Kinds by
forms, and not one of them even tried to make such divisions,
with the result that there is a serious shortage of names"
(267D).[91] The class of the ignorant mime is divided then into
those who are simplistically unaware of their ignorance and
those who are aware, but who through deceit are not thereby
deterred (268A). The latter class finally is subdivided into
the Demagogue who speaks at length in public and the Sophist who disputes in private (268B). Thus the quarry of this
unusually constructive dialogue is finally bagged, with the
magnificent dissimulation on the part of the Stranger that this
really is what he was concerned with doing all along.

[91] The reader of this passage may be reminded of John Austin's
call for a comprehensive science of language at the end of his paper
"Ifs and Cans," *Philosophical Papers*, edited by J. A. Urmson and
G. J. Warnock (Oxford: Clarendon Press, 1961), p. 180.

On Collection
and Division

1 / Criteria of an Adequate Definition

A definition of the sort which the *Sophist* exhibits is adequate
if it formulates both necessary and sufficient conditions for
being the kind of thing defined. The Angler has been adequately defined, for example, as (1) an artisan practising
(2) acquisition (3) by force (4) through stealth of (5) living
(6) water animals, specifically (7) fish, (8) by striking
(9) from below (10) during daylight. Each of these ten features is necessary, insofar as there are no anglers conceivable
to whom any of the ten fails to apply. Anything lacking one
of these features (let us agree for the illustration) would not
be conceived to be an angler. Thus, one who gets fish other
than by acquisition, for example by raising them from eggs,
is not an angler but a producer of fish. Nor is anyone an angler who coaxes fish into a bucket rather than securing them
by force, or who openly splashes about the water without any
attempt to be inconspicuous, and so on down the line. Even
the feature of capture by daylight comes to seem necessary,

under the conjecture that Plato had in mind fishermen who literally hook fish from beneath without benefit of bait by an opportune jerk on the line.

The combination of these ten features, moreover, is also sufficient for being an angler, for there is no conceivable thing possessing all these features which we would not conceive to be an angler as well. To conceive of something other than an angler would be to conceive of something which fails to possess at least one of these properties. If we disallow the relevance of the skin diver capable of striking his prey from below with a forcibly-ejected spear, along with other recent technical possibilities, Plato's definition seems adequate from this point of view as well. Let us at any rate assume for discussion that this definition makes explicit both necessary and sufficient conditions for being an angler.

The purpose of this section is to consider in more detail these conditions which together, in the context of the *Sophist*, mark off an adequate from an inadequate definition. To simplify matters, we will speak generally of a definition in which a sort of thing X is characterized in terms of the features A, B, and C. If the combination of features ABC is necessary for being X, there is a relationship between X and ABC which we shall designate 'conceptual entailment' and symbolize as follows:

(1) $X \rightarrow ABC$.

The reading of '$X \rightarrow ABC$' is 'X entails A and B and C', the meaning of which is that any thing conceived as being X is thereby conceived as being A, B, and C as well.[1]

---

[1] The arrow symbolizes a relationship among features or Kinds considered without reference to their manifestation in individual things. Thus (1) cannot be rendered in terms of the predicate calculus as '$(y)(X_y \supset A_y B_y C_y)$'. This latter expression is true only in a universe comprising only individuals which are either not X or are A, B, and C alike. Whether this latter expression is true therefore depends upon the properties of individuals rather than upon the relationship among X, A, B, and C themselves without reference to par-

If the combination of features ABC is sufficient for being X, then there is also the relation:

(2) ABC → X.

The reading of (2) is 'A, B, and C together entail X', meaning that anything conceived to be A, B, and C is conceived thereby to be X as well. If the combination of features ABC is both necessary and sufficient for being X, then the following relation holds:

(3) X ⟷ ABC.

This latter expression can also be written: [2]

(4) X = ABC,

which is an obviously appropriate way of symbolizing the claim that X is to be defined as ABC.

These relations make possible a precise specification of the conditions under which a definition is adequate, and of the conditions under which this is not so. If (1) is the case, then each of A, B, and C is a necessary condition of being X, and the following formulae also hold: [3]

---

ticular things. Nor can the arrow be replaced with Lewis' fishhook (C. I. Lewis and C. H. Langford, *Symbolic Logic* [New York: Dover Publications, 1959], pp. 122–78), for this latter connects statement variables and not expressions designating properties or features. Lewis' system however, provides the formality in which (1) is to be construed, if for 'X' we read 'a is X', and for 'A', 'B' and 'C', we read 'a is A', 'a is B' and 'a is C', for the same individual a in each sentence, and if we understand that the basis for this relationship among X, A, B, and C is conceptual rather than postulational. Whether someone considers (1) to be true for particular interpretations of the symbols depends upon whether his concepts are so structured, which is a matter for his own conceptual determination. Plato's method of division "according to Kinds" proceeds as if all those capable of such division would find their concepts structured in the same general fashion.

[2] *Ibid.*, 11.03.

[3] *Ibid.*, 19.62 and 12.43, et. al.

(1′) $-A \rightarrow -X$
$\qquad -B \rightarrow -X$
$\qquad -C \rightarrow -X$

Now whether any one of the formulae (1′) is true is a matter of conceptual determination for which there is no rule.[4] The conditions under which one would maintain any one of these formulae as true, however, can be put in a way which provides perhaps a more manageable, albeit still non-formal, criterion of necessity for definition (4). The formulae (1′) can be rewritten: [5]

(1″) $-(-A \circ X)$
$\qquad -(-B \circ X)$
$\qquad -(-C \circ X).$

That is, $-A \rightarrow -X$ is the case if and only if it is not the case that absence of the property A is conceptually compatible with being X, and so forth for $-B \rightarrow -X$ and $-C \rightarrow -X$. If a thing cannot be conceived as lacking A while being conceived as X, then A is a necessary condition of being X. In

[4] It should be emphasized that these (and any) formal criteria for necessity and sufficiency require informal application. Although recollection is explicitly associated with collection (and by implication with division) only in the *Phaedrus* (249B–C), something at least very much like recollection must be assumed to be involved in the dialectician's determination that a given set of conditions indeed *is* necessary and sufficient. In this connection, the reader may consult H. Cherniss, *The Riddle of the Early Academy*, (Los Angeles: University of California Press, 1945), pp. 54–55; and N. Gulley, *Plato's Theory of Knowledge*, (London: Methuen & Co., 1962), pp. 108–20. As Gulley remarks, "it is essential to have 'the additional power', at every state in the practice of the methods of collection and division, of recognising and selecting 'real' resemblances and differences, those which are resemblances and differences between Forms . . ." (p. 112). The superiority of collection and division over any method evident in the "Socratic" dialogues is primarily heuristic; with the relationships above Plato has a precise conception of what he is looking for in an adequate definition, and an effective procedure for conducting the search.

[5] Lewis and Langford, *Symbolic Logic*, 17.12, et. al.

other words, if the concept of being X cannot be conceived conjointly with the concept of the absence of A, then $-A \rightarrow -X$ is the case. And if in like fashion $-B \rightarrow -X$ and $-C \rightarrow -X$ are the case as well, then ABC is a conjunction of necessary conditions for X, and (1) is the case.

Parmenides had advised that the dialectician "make the supposition that such and such a thing *is* and then consider the consequences . . ." (135E–136A [translator's italics]). The procedure by which this is accomplished is the procedure by which necessary conditions are established for incorporation within a given definition.

Parmenides had advised also that the analyst take the supposition that the same thing *is not* and consider the consequences (136A). This is the procedure of determining the sufficient conditions for being the thing in question, as specified in (2). If (2) is the case, then it is the case also that:

$$(2') \quad -X \rightarrow - (ABC).$$

If ABC is the set of sufficient conditions for being X, then the consequence of the supposition that X *is not* is that at least one of A, B, or C *is not* in the correspondingly relevant sense. This expression also may be put in a form more perspicuous for purposes of analysis.[6] If and only if (2') is the case, it is the case also that:

$$(2'') \quad -X \rightarrow . -A \text{ v} -B \text{ v} -C.$$

If the conception of a thing as not X precludes its conceivability as A, B, and C in combination, then (2) indicates sufficient conditions for being X. That is, according to (2''), if to conceive of a thing as not being X is thereby to conceive of it as lacking at least one of the features A, B, or C, then these features in combination constitute a sufficient condition for being X.

There is no limit theoretically to the number of combina-

---

[6] *Ibid.*, 14.21.

tions of features which might be sufficient for being a certain thing or Kind. It is compatible with (2) that some entirely different set DEF might also constitute a sufficient condition for X. If ABC is sufficient for X, moreover, so also is ABCD, ABCDE, and so forth. If, on the other hand, ABC turns out according to relevant criteria not to be sufficient for X then the analyst bent on defining X will need to determine another feature (other features) D such that ABCD in combination conceptually entails X whereas ABC alone does not. The mark of this would be the truth of '−X →. −A v −B v −C v −D', while (2″) alone is not the case.

In an actual application of this method, Plato's dialectician might have to alternate between criteria of necessity and criteria of sufficiency. This is the case when the collection takes the form of several inadequate definitions, as of Sophists I through V, each giving conditions which are sufficient but none which is necessary. Let us consider a general case in which the criteria for sufficiency and necessity are applied in alternation, each more than once. Assume that a preliminary collection has shown D necessary for X, in that −D conceptually entails −X, but that the criterion for sufficiency shows that D alone does not entail X. A division ensues in which both DE and DF turn out to be sufficient for X, but neither E nor F is found to meet the test of necessity. The combinations DE and DF then are found by collection to carry with them the common property A. Subsequent division shows that ABC in combination are sufficient for X, and application of the criterion in (1′) shows finally that each of ABC is necessary as well. When this stage has been reached, ABC may be presented as an adequate definition of X, and its adequacy is established by the truth of (4).

But the fact that the set of features ABC gives both necessary and sufficient conditions for being X does not preclude other adequate definitions of X in terms of other features. This is trivially true when the other features are singly or in combination equivalent to one or more of A, B, and C. Thus, if $D = A$ and $E = BC$, and $X = ABC$, it is the case also that $X = DE$.

A more interesting case of equivalence among definitions occurs when one of the several features in a set of necessary and sufficient conditions entails another feature in the same set. Thus, again, the fact that being a fish entails being a water animal permits dropping the latter feature from the definition of the Angler without loss either of necessity or of sufficiency in the shortened definition. In general, if $X = ABC$, and $A \to B$, then it is the case also that $X = AC$.[7]

[19.62]	$X \to ACB \,.\to.\, X \to AC \,.\, X \to B$	(1)
[11.2]	$X \to AC \,.\, X \to B \,.\to.\, X \to AC$	(2)
[11.6] (1)(2)	$X \to ACB \,.\to.\, X \to AC$	(3)
[12.15] (3)	$X \to ABC \,.\to.\, X \to AC$	(4)
[11.2]	$X \to ABC \,.\, ABC \to X \,.\to.\, X \to ABC$	(5)
[11.6] (4)(5)	$X \to ABC \,.\, ABC \to X \,.\to.\, X \to AC$	(6)
[11.03] (6)	$X = ABC \,.\to.\, X \to AC$	(7)
[12.17]	$A \to B \,.\, X = ABC \,.\to.\, X = ABC$	(8)
[11.6] (7)(8)	$A \to B \,.\, X = ABC \,.\to.\, X \to AC$	(9)
[12.77]	$A \to B \,.\, BC \to X \,.\to.\, AC \to X$	(10)
(CA/C)(10)	$A \to B \,.\, BCA \to X \,.\to.\, ACA \to X$	(11)
[12.15] (11)	$A \to B \,.\, ABC \to X \,.\to.\, AAC \to X$	(12)
[12.7] (12)	$A \to B \,.\, ABC \to X \,.\to.\, AC \to X$	(13)
[11.2]	$A \to B \,.\, ABC \to X \,.\, X \to ABC \,.\to.\, A \to B \,.$	
	$ABC \to X$	(14)
[11.6] (13)(14)	$A \to B \,.\, ABC \to X \,.\, X \to ABC \,.\to.\, AC \to X$	(15)
[11.03] (15)	$A \to B \,.\, X = ABC \,.\to.\, AC \to X$	(16)
[19.61] (9)(16)	$A \to B \,.\, X = ABC \,.\to.\, X \to AC \,.\, AC \to X$	(17)
[11.03] (17)	$A \to B \,.\, X = ABC \,.\to.\, X = AC$	Q.E.D.

It is interesting to note, accordingly, that any term implied by another term within the same definition can be dropped without affecting the definition's adequacy. Thus in the paradigmatic Aristotelian definition "man = rational animal," if being rational were to entail being an animal, then "man = rational thing" would be equally adequate from the Platonic point of view. These remarks reinforce the observation above,[8]

---

[7] Derivation of the following theorem is within the provisions of Lewis and Langford, *Symbolic Logic*, pp. 122–77.

[8] Chapter III, section 7.

that it is entirely improper to conceive Platonic definition under the Aristotelian format of genus, subordinate difference and *infimae species*.

2 / Comparisons

The method Plato sketched in the *Phaedo* and refined in the *Republic* unquestionably is different from the method exhibited in the *Sophist*. This in itself makes plausible a distinction between Plato's "old" and "new" methods of philosophic analysis. Commentators who make the distinction, however, seem generally to be far more impressed by the differences than by the similarities.[9] Not only are the methods alike in fundamental respects, but moreover they are connected by a line of transition which suggests that it is no less arbitrary to speak of *two* methods than to speak of *one* method in two states of development. The turning point in this development is marked by the *Theaetetus*, in which the "old" method is vigorously but unsuccessfully applied, and in which the "new" method almost inadvertently begins to emerge. Let us compare these methods in detail, and attempt to trace the line between them.

[9] R. Robinson, who felt that the method of hypothesis met its downfall in the *Parmenides*, remarks that afterwards we hear no more of this method, "and the renewed enthusiasm of the *Phaedrus* and the *Sophist* is based on the new method of 'division'" (*Plato's Earlier Dialectic* [Oxford: Clarendon Press, 1953], p. 280). Ryle, with his own reading of the passages in question, finds it clear "that the Method of Dialectic as this is described in outline in the *Republic* and in detail in the *Parmenides* . . . has almost nothing to do with the Method of Division" (Plato's *Parmenides*.II," *Mind*, 48, no. 191 [July, 1939]: 321). W. G. Runciman believes "the *Parmenides* marks the renunciation by Plato of the hypothetical method and paves the way for the method of diaeresis as the means of resolving difficulties within the world of Forms . . ." (*Plato's Later Epistemology* [Cambridge: Cambridge University Press, 1962], p. 3). And so it goes.

The undoubted distinction between the method described in the *Phaedo* [10] (hereafter "method P") and that employed in the *Sophist* ("method S") is reflected in the key terminology of the two contexts. Given the absence of expressions equivalent to διαίρεσις and συναγωγή in *Phaedo* 100A–101D, it follows that division and collection are not explicit parts of the method described in that passage. And given that ὑπόθεσις does not occur in the methodological discussions of the *Sophist*, we may conclude that this dialogue, unlike the *Phaedo*, is not explicitly concerned with the method of hypothesis. Equally apparent is that method P involves the procedures of testing consequences for consistency and of seeking less assailable hypotheses from which a given hypothesis can be derived, while method S involves the distinct procedures of discerning common elements in diverse forms of the thing to be defined and of articulating a formula specific enough to mark this off from all other things. Method P, moreover, *begins with* a λόγος or ὑπόθεσις and works towards its vindication, while method S begins with a concept to be analyzed and *works towards* a λόγος or definition of the thing or kind in question. Leaving such obvious differences to speak for themselves, let us move on to compare these two methods as procedures for philosophic analysis.

One important similarity is that the application of each method proceeds stepwise through four more or less distinct stages. The dialectician's first step in applying method P is (a) to posit a λόγος which he judges "soundest," after which he proceeds (b) to test its consequences for consistency, both among themselves and with other theses which in the context cannot be disputed. If found inconsistent, it is necessary to re-

[10] The method described in *Phaedo* 100A–101D is mathematical, possessing just the features which in *Republic* 510C–511D distinguish mathematics from dialectic. The *Phaedo* passage, however, provides the methodological structure of which the *Republic's* method of dialectic is a refinement. This is discussed extensively in Chapter I. For this reason, and for convenience, *Phaedo* 100A–101D will be considered the primary source of Plato's "early" method.

place the initial λόγος with another, which is tested for consistency in turn. When after perhaps several applications of (a) and (b) a λόγος is found which is consistent within the context, the dialectician seeks (c) to posit a "more ultimate" hypothesis from which that λόγος can be deduced as a consequence. This hypothesis then is examined "by the same method," involving reapplication of (b) and if necessary (c). When the "more ultimate" hypothesis is established as consistent, the dialectician turns (d) to consider whether it is sufficient as it stands or requires further accounting within the context of the discussion. If the latter is the case, he returns to (c) in search of a "yet more ultimate" hypothesis, and continues until one is found which is "satisfactory." When the criterion of (d) is finally met, the result is a justification of the λόγος posited at (a) under a consistent and more general hypothesis which in the context requires no further justification.

Method P thus is a means of establishing necessary and sufficient conditions for an hypothesis under dialectical discussion. When this hypothesis regards the existence of a specific type of thing, the method accordingly aids in the discovery of the "causes" of that thing, in the sense of 'cause' (αἰτία) examined in Chapter I. Thus, in retrospect, the discussion of Forms as "causes" between *Phaedo* 100A and 101D appears related to the method adumbrated in these two passages in a way beyond those previously discussed.[11] Not only do Socrates' remarks following 100A purport (1) to *establish* his theory of causation by deducing it from the hypothesis of the existence of the Forms, and (2) to *illustrate* the method by so doing, but (3) the method itself is one which can be bent to the *discovery* of "causes" by establishing necessary and sufficient conditions for the truth of an hypothesis about the existence of a specific type of thing.

The application of method S can be conceived in a closely

---

[11] See the end of section 1, chapter I.

parallel fashion. The method begins, of course, with a collection to exhibit a common feature among instances of the Kind to be defined, and proceeds with a division of this feature in terms of others which collectively distinguish things of that Kind from all other things. Each of these two procedures, however, itself involves two stages. At some point in the collection the philosopher must formulate a conjecture regarding what features are necessary for being a thing of the Kind in question, after which that conjecture is tested by examination of further instances of the Kind. Similarly, at some point in the division the philosopher must formulate a conjecture regarding what features should be added to mark off things of that Kind from all other things, after which this conjecture is tested by considering whether things can be found outside the Kind in question which also possess this combination of features.

Method S, accordingly, leads the philosopher through the process of collection (a) to formulate an hypothesis attributing a certain feature to all things of the Kind to be defined. A consequence of this hypothesis is that each recognizable instance of that Kind possesses that particular feature. The philosopher's next concern is (b) to test this consequence in each case for consistency with the undisputed fact that each is an instance of this Kind. If an instance is found which does not possess that feature, the hypothesis is inconsistent in its consequences with a fact which in the context is not open to dispute, and the philosopher must return to (a) in the search for common features. If the results of (b) are satisfactory, however, he turns to the process of division in the attempt (c) to specify additional features which when combined with those already found necessary will mark off things of that Kind from various similar things. These features in turn must be tested for common inherence in all things of the Kind in question, calling for reapplication of (b) and if necessary (c) as well. The final stage is (d) to determine whether the combination of features at hand, each of which has been found necessary, is sufficient to distinguish things of that Kind from *all* other things. If this is not the case, the philosopher returns to (c) in search for additional necessary features. If the test at (d) yields satisfactory results, however, the philosopher has produced a proper definition of the Kind in question.

Each of these stages is illustrated in the definition of the authentic Sophist. The first collection, performed over an entirely inadequate range of instances, consisted (a) in positing (θετέον [221D]) that what is essential for the Angler is essential for the Sophist as well, namely the art of forcible acquisition of living animals.[12] At this stage, the Stranger should have (b) tested these features for adequacy as necessary conditions, whereupon he would have abandoned them and avoided the several faulty definitions which follow. Plato's purpose here, however, surely is not merely to define the Sophist, but rather to teach us some important things about definition which are brought out in the course of dividing Sophists I through V. So the Stranger moves next to the stages (c) and (d) of division, producing several sets of features any one of which is adequate to mark off its possessor from all non-Sophists. But the very fact that there are several irreducible sets of sufficient conditions in this series of divisions shows (b) that no one set is necessary as well. Thus the Stranger returns to the stage (a) of collection, using Sophists I through V as a more comprehensive field of instances out of which to discern the common and thereby necessary features of sophistry, namely production. With this common feature in view, he continues stepwise through (c) and (d) to isolate the authentic Sophist from other Forms of production with reference to fur-

[12] The collection over forms of acquisition which served in the successful definition of the Angler thus serves indirectly in the abortive definition of Sophist I. As remarked above, however, only the three successful definitions in the dialogue are directly preceded by an appropriate collection. The collection for the successful definition of Sophist VII is provided by the faulty definitions of Sophists I through V. This relationship among the several Sophists is discussed in chapter III, section 3.

ther necessary characteristics. The final result is a definition including only necessary characteristics, but characteristics which in combination are sufficient for being a sophist as well.

In this fashion, method S as well as method P can naturally be divided into four distinct stages. The fundamental point of similarity between the two methods, however, is not that each can be conceived in terms of a particular number of stages, but rather that each is directed towards formulating both necessary and sufficient conditions for the hypothesis or Kind to be analyzed. The role of stages (a) and (b) in method P is to disclose necessary conditions for the truth of a particular λόγος, while the corresponding stages in method S are directed towards displaying Forms which are essentially part of the type of thing to be defined. Stages (c) and (d) of method P, on the other hand, are to establish sufficient conditions for the λόγος in question, while the corresponding stages in method S are to display a combination of Forms which distinguishes the thing to be defined from all other things. Successful application of method P results in a "satisfactory" hypothesis which itself requires no further justification, and which is both *sufficient* for the truth of the initial λόγος and such that all its *necessary* conditions, including those of the initial λόγος, can be simultaneously realized. The successful result of method S, in like fashion, is a combination of Forms each of which is *necessary* for the type of thing defined, and which together are *sufficient* to mark off exclusively all things of that specific type. The fact that these logical characteristics have been generally overlooked by commentators on both methods explains by itself why so much attention has been paid to their differences and so little to their common features.

The main departure of method S from method P in this regard is that the latter is concerned with necessary and sufficient conditions for the truth of particular propositions, while the former is concerned with necessary and sufficient conditions for being a thing of a given Kind. But this difference is little more than superficial, since method S also is directed towards establishing the truth of propositions. If a set of features ABC is sufficient to mark off a certain Form X, and if A, B, and C separately are necessary parts of that Form, then it is the case both that X entails ABC and that ABC entails X.[13] But each of these two entailments in turn is necessary for the truth of the assertion of identity between X and the combined features ABC, while the two entailments together are sufficient for the truth of that assertion. And this assertion of identity is nothing other than the definition of the Form in question. In an entirely straightforward sense, therefore, method S is directed towards establishing definitions of specific Forms, and hence like method P is concerned with the necessary and sufficient conditions for the truth of particular propositions.

One further difference between the two methods should be noted. The effect of this difference, however, is to draw these two methods even more closely together in our conception of the Platonic goal of achieving knowledge in the form of proper definitions. This difference lies in the superior effectiveness and precision of method S in comparison with the earlier hypothetical method. The first criterion involved in either method is to test the necessary conditions of the λόγος (hypothesis [14] or definition) in question. In method P, however, it is never clear what the philosopher is to look for in applying the test. He is, of course, to determine whether the consequences of the hypothesis in question are consistent, both among themselves and presumably with other accepted theses. But there is no device or method available by which this could be established, or in terms of which consistency in this sense even

---

[13] The nature of entailment among Forms is discussed in note 1.

[14] In introducing the method of hypothesis at *Phaedo* 99E, Socrates announced his decision "to take refuge" in λόγοι, and goes on to explain how on each occasion he would hypothesize the λόγος which he judged to be soundest, and so forth. In retrospect, this use of the term λόγος appears closely associated with the use signifying "definition," as at *Sophist* 218C.

could be precisely explained. The criterion at stage (b) of method S, on the other hand, is straightforward and entirely general, and moreover can be precisely formulated. A definition of Kind X asserting the identity X = ABC gives only necessary conditions for X if and only if it is the case that each of −A, −B, and −C entails −X.[15]

The second criterion to be invoked in either method is one of sufficiency. Yet there is no hint in the *Phaedo*, nor (outside of metaphorical references to the Good in the *Republic*) in any other dialogue, how the philosopher could be expected to tell, in his search for more and more comprehensive hypotheses, when he had "reached something satisfactory" (101E). The criterion invoked at this stage of method S, however, is again entirely perspicuous. A definition of Kind X asserting X = ABC gives sufficient conditions for X if and only if −X entails either −A or −B or −C.[16]

With regard to procedures for *arriving* at λόγοι which are adequate in these two senses, method P is even more inscrutable. As far as I can determine, the clearest example in the entire corpus of an attempt to replace a hypothesis found inconsistent in its consequences with a more promising λόγος is in the transition from the first to the second hypothesis in the *Theaetetus*. And about all that can be said here about the nature of the procedure in question is that the second hypothesis was suggested by the difficulties which finally brought about the downfall of the first. There is also at least one clear instance in which a constructive dialectical argument advances to the point of seeking a more comprehensive hypothesis which will entail a λόγος previously under examination. This occurs at *Meno* 87B where Socrates is depicted as hypothesizing that virtue is knowledge, in order further to investigate the proposition that virtue is teachable. But the relationship between

---

[15] This criterion has been discussed in the previous section.

[16] This also has been discussed more fully in the previous section. This precision of criteria in itself indicates a considerable methodological advance between the *Phaedo* and the *Sophist*.

knowledge and teachability, in this context at least, is so immediate and intuitive that there is no help here towards formulating a general procedure to follow at stage (c) of method P. It might be said, indeed, that the only procedure Plato could propose for the philosopher to follow at stages (a) and (c) of this method is the careful exercise of intuition.[17] But if this is the only thing to say, then it is to say practically nothing at all. And coupled with the lack of clear criteria either of consistency or of self-sufficiency at stages (b) and (d), the lack of any procedure besides intuition at (a) and (c) leaves this method in a very amorphous state indeed. Perhaps it is more than fortuitous that Plato never gives an example of an hypothesis produced as necessary and self-sufficient by a successful application of method P.

Method S, on the other hand, admits well-understood procedures at stages (a) and (c). The procedure for producing necessary conditions for being a thing of the Kind subject to definition is the method of collection, while division produces sets of features which are sufficient in the same respect. Perhaps also it is not accidental that the *Sophist*, which employs collection and division throughout, is among the most constructive and least metaphorical of all the dialogues in the Platonic corpus.

Be this at it may, however, collection and division may aptly be conceived as means of achieving the same goals as those of the earlier hypothetical method, with the difference primarily that these procedures are considerably more specific and effective than any analytic procedures emerging from the *Meno*, the *Phaedo*, and the *Republic*. This may be illustrated in detail with reference to the dialectical structure of the *Theaetetus*. With this in mind, let us turn in the final section to a brief review of this important transitional dialogue.

---

[17] The intuition in question would not be "direct apprehension" of the Forms, which by some accounts constitutes knowledge in Plato's early epistemology, for the method which the intuition would serve is one *leading to* a state of knowledge.

3 / Convergence

The *Theaetetus* unquestionably is Plato's most ambitious and sustained attempt to apply the method of hypothesis in matters of philosophic argumentation. The suggestion that ἐπιστήμη is αἴσθησις is introduced quite explicitly (151E) as merely an hypothesis to be tested. After a clarification of the concept of αἴσθησις through the elaborate theory fo "fast and slow motions," it is shown that perception can be conceived as infallible only if its objects are conceived as somehow defective in existence. Since both infallibility and the existence of its objects are presumed to be necessary features of knowledge, the hypothesis identifying knowledge and perception is thereby deemed inconsistent. The argument of the dialogue through 186E thus falls within stages (a) and (b) of method P as outlined in the section above.

The second hypothesis, that knowledge is true judgment, is introduced as being consistent with the facts contributing to the downfall of its predecessor. The considerations under which the initial hypothesis was judged inconsistent show also that knowledge lies with the operations of the "mind . . . occupied with things by itself" (187A) rather than with sense perception alone. The second hypothesis is to provide an account of how this could be so. The transition into the second major section of the dialogue thus involves a reapplication of procedure (a) of the hypothetical method. Before this second hypothesis can be tested for consistency, however, Plato is obliged as before to clarify the concepts on which it relies. After a perfunctory definition of judgment (δόξα) as the termination of the mind's silent discourse with itself (190A), he turns seriously to the problem of showing how falsehood (hence truth) in judgment is possible. This leads to the compelling images of the wax block and the aviary. The first of these provides an account of truth and falsehood in a very limited class of judgments concerned with the identification of perceptual objects, but neither image leads to an account of false judgment in general. This problem is never solved in the *Theaetetus*, and Plato accordingly never comes to the point of being able to subject the second hypothesis to a test of consistency in an adequately clarified form. Instead he remains content to discredit the hypothesis with the simple counter-example of the true but unknowledgeable judgment of the juror. This shows that the second hypothesis is inadequate, but not that it is inconsistent in itself. Being inadequate, however, it requires further accounting on a "high level," and the attempt to provide this leads to the third and final hypothesis that knowledge is the same as true judgment accompanied by λόγος. If this could be shown true, then the proposition that knowledge is (at least but not exclusively) true judgment will itself have been established.[18] In this fashion, Plato's analysis moves into stage (c) of the hypothetical method, and he turns to the task of submitting the third hypothesis to a test for consistency. This task is never completed within the *Theaetetus*, however, for no sense of λόγος is allowed which would render the hypothesis immune from carefully contrived counterexamples. Thus the third hypothesis, like the second which (as construed above) it entails, is shown inadequate as it stands,

---

[18] Interpreted as a statement of *identity* between knowledge (in the sense of εἰδέναι [201B]) and true judgment, the second hypothesis has been shown false. (See note 51, Chapter II, for a discussion of the significance of the term εἰδέναι.) As the statement that knowledge (in the sense of ἐπιστήμη) includes true judgment, however, the second hypothesis would be shown true if it were shown that knowledge is true judgment plus an account. Thus the proposition that knowledge is (in part) true judgment which is accounted for by the third hypothesis is not the same in sense as the proposition that knowledge is (identical with) true judgment shown false by the counterexample. I am indebted to Professor Amelie Rorty for pointing out that the hypothetical method also finds use in the dialogues as a means of distinguishing several possible senses of a given hypothesis, which feature of the method I have not emphasized in this discussion. What we have here, however, would seem to be a case in point.

but not internally inconsistent. When Plato returns to these problems in the *Sophist*, an entirely different conceptual framework is at his disposal. Thus the approach to the problems of knowledge through the hypothetical method seems to be terminated with the final speeches in the *Theaetetus*.

A remarkable thing about the *Theaetetus*, however, is that it can be read equally well in conformity with the method of collection and division. The first attempt to construe perception as a necessary and sufficient condition of knowledge commits the dialectician to admitting that knowledge entails perception. It cannot be the case that all acts of knowledge are acts of perception, however, for knowledge possesses attributes in combinations which perception cannot admit. The proposition that knowledge entails perception thus is inconsistent with certain theses about the nature of knowledge which are not open to question within the context of the dialogue. In this respect, the movement of the dialogue through 186E falls within stages (a) and (b) of method S as schematized above.

The second definition of knowledge then is formulated to accommodate features of knowledge which could not appear under the first. The proposition that an act of knowledge is an act of true judgment, that is, at least is compatible with the proposition that knowledge is infallible and of what exists, and with the proposition that an act of knowledge is not an exercise of the senses alone. This second definition is accomplished through a reapplication of procedure (a), which follows the collection over instances of knowledge occurring from 184B through 186E. One necessary feature of knowledge discovered in the collection is that it involves the operation of the "mind . . . occupied with things by itself" (187A), an operation of the sort later (190A) defined as judgment. Another necessary feature is that the judgment must be true. In the second definition, accordingly, knowledge is equated with true as against false judgment. The division between true and false judgment, however, is not clear in itself, and Plato attempts various accounts of the distinction to make the definition viable. Failing in these attempts, Plato returns to the insufficiently analyzed concept of true judgment, and shows that the proposition that all acts of knowledge are *nothing more* than acts of true judgment cannot be maintained in the face of cases like that of the juror who reaches true but uninformed verdicts. The second definition, like the first, thus fails at stage (b), and a third definition is formulated in an attempt to accommodate the facts which are incompatible with the second.

The third definition continues the division of judgment into true and false, and divides the former again into that accompanied by and that lacking an account. This definition is explicitly accepted as consistent for, as Socrates rhetorically inquires, "how can there ever be knowledge without an account and right belief?" (202D) Thus with the third definition we move directly from (a) to (c), in the context of method S as outlined above, presupposing success in the application of criterion (b). After repeated attempts to find a sense in which an act of true judgment accompanied by λόγος is an act of knowledge, however, Plato prematurely gives up the third definition at stage (c) and terminates the dialogue. The next step would have been to provide a sense of λόγος in which true judgment accompanied by λόγος is knowledge, but this step can be taken only in the expanded conceptual framework of the *Sophist*. The details of these various stages have been discussed in chapters II and III.

It can be shown, in terms of a general formulation of the method of collection and division, that the fact that this dialogue can be conceived according either to method P or to method S is not accidental. Consider the attempt to define a thing or Kind X in terms of features A, B, and C, either singly or in combination. An initial definition of X as A, let us say, fails in itself to display necessary conditions for X which are mutually consistent, but provides a collection of cases which leads to the realization that B is necessary. The analysis thus proceeds through stages (a) and (b) to stage (c) and (d), where it is realized that B is not sufficient for X, and hence that B and X are not identical. Suppose, however, that it were found through a reapplication of (c) and (d) that B and C *together* are sufficient. Suppose further that C turns out to be necessary also, through another test at stage (b). Then it will have been determined that both B and C are necessary for X, and that B and C together are sufficient, whereupon the equation of X with BC will issue as the result of the completed analytic procedure.

But exactly the same steps of analysis can be viewed also as stages in the method taken from the *Phaedo* and the *Republic*. The hypothesis that X is identical with A, at stage (a) in method P, is found to be incompatible with undoubted facts, such as that there are instances of X which are not instances of A as well. (This corresponds to the disclosure in the *Sophist* that the thesis (with Sophist I) that all sophists are captors is incompatible with the fact that some sophists (II through IV) are instead merchants of ideas.) In view of these undoubted facts, it is determined subsequently that the statement that all X are B at least is consistent, and the hypothesis that X is identical with B comes to replace the previous hypothesis. Since, as determined at stage (d), B turns out not to entail X, the second hypothesis requires further grounds upon which the involvement of B in X can be accounted for. These grounds are sought at stage (c) in the more highly articulated hypothesis that all X are BC, which of course has among its consequences that all X are B. Suppose, contrary to what happened at the corresponding stage in the *Theaetetus*, that it is found to be the case that all BC are X as well. Under these circumstances the fact that all X are BC will be found, at stage (d), not to require further accounting, since it will have been shown that X and BC are identical in kind. The conclusion of this exercise in method P is the no longer hypothetical statement of identity between X and BC.

The startling lesson of this comparison is that Plato, in writing not only the *Theaetetus* but the *Sophist* as well, is applying a method which in basic logical structure is the same as that described, crudely and without refinement, in *Phaedo* 100A–101D. The appearance of a "brand new" method in *Phaedrus* 265E–266B, and in the *Sophist* and the *Statesman* generally, is in large part illusory. We can say only "in large part illusory," for there are noteworthy differences remaining between method P and method S. These differences, however, are differences of technique rather than differences of analytic purpose.

Both methods are directed towards an examination of the necessary and sufficient conditions for a thing's being what it is. And both, if successful, will culminate in a λόγος in which the thing to be analyzed is related definitively to other things on the level of the Forms, without reference to particular objects in which the Forms might happen to be manifest. Both therefore are methods of formal or, as I would prefer to say, conceptual analysis. The difference between the two methods comes with the evolving techniques by which these purposes are achieved. Plato's transition in the *Theaetetus* was not a breakthrough from an "old" method of hypothesis to a "new" method of collection and division, but rather the discovery of a more effective procedure for analyzing the formal structure of what it is to be a certain thing or Kind. This, after all, is what Socrates, as pictured in the *Phaedo* and elsewhere, had been trying to do all along.[19] Plato's contribution, through the Stranger of the *Sophist*, was to produce a practical technique by which this Socratic goal could be accomplished. This is no mean contribution on Plato's part to the cause of his master in the earlier dialogues.

This study has traced the development of an analytic

---

[19] Robinson points out, in *Plato's Earlier Dialectic*, that the "What is X?" question behind the Socratic quest for definitions is one dealing with equivalence. In asking such a question, the inquirer "wants an answer, say 'X is AB', such that every X is AB and nothing else is AB" (p. 53). The Socratic quest for definitions is an attempt, without benefit of a precise method, to discover the necessary and sufficient conditions for being a thing of a given Kind.

method from a crude form, expressed in the *Phaedo* under the apparent inspiration of the geometrical method of analysis, to a form exhibited in the *Sophist* with such appeal and power as to become notorious in its (perhaps undisciplined) application by members of the Academy.[20] Plato emerges from this study as the author of the first explicit and practicable method of philosophic analysis. It cannot be denied that Plato was powerful in his use of myth as a rhetorical and mnemonic device. And it is undeniable as well that Plato has had few peers as dramatist and as stylist of language. Those commentators who dwell upon these features of his dialogues to the exclusion of their logical structure, however, see only a minor part of Plato's philosophic genius. The time has arrived in the course of Platonic scholarship at which we can no longer afford to overlook Plato's own instructions for philosophic training. The dialectician competent to move among the Forms is first and foremost a student competent in the discipline of formal reasoning.

[20] See, for example, Cherniss, *The Riddle of the Early Academy*, p. 63.

Bibliography of Works Cited

Ackrill, J. L. "Plato and the Copula: *Sophist* 251–59." *Journal of Hellenic Studies* 67 (1957): 1–6. Reprinted in R. E. Allen, *Studies in Plato's Metaphysics*.

———. "ΣΥΜΠΛΟΚΗ ΕΙΔΩΝ." *Bulletin of the Institute of Classical Studies in the University of London*, no. 2 (1955): 31–35. Reprinted in R. E. Allen, *Studies in Plato's Metaphysics*.

Allen, R. E. *Studies in Plato's Metaphysics*. New York: Humanities Press, 1965.

Aristotle. *Categories* and *De Interpretatione*. Translated by J. L. Ackrill under the editorship of Sir David Ross. Oxford: Clarendon Press, 1963.

Aristotle. *Posterior Analytics*. Translated by E. S. Bouchier under the editorship of Sir David Ross. Oxford: Blackwell, 1901.

Austin, J. "Ifs and Cans." *Philosophical Papers*. Edited by J. A. Urmson and G. J. Warnock. Oxford: Clarendon Press, 1961.

Bluck, R. S. "Logos and Forms in Plato: A Reply to Professor Cross." *Mind*, n.s. 65 (1956): 522–29. Reprinted in R. E. Allen, *Studies in Plato's Metaphysics*.

———. *Plato's Meno*. London: Cambridge University Press, 1961.

———. *Plato's Phaedo*. London: Routledge & Kegan Paul, 1955.

Burnet, J. *Plato's Phaedo*. Oxford: Clarendon Press, 1911.

Cherniss, H. "Plato as Mathematician." *Review of Metaphysics* 4 (1950–51): 395–425.

———. "The Philosophical Economy of the Theory of Ideas." *The American Journal of Philology* 57 (1936): 445–47. Reprinted in R. E. Allen, *Studies in Plato's Metaphysics*.

———. *The Riddle of the Early Academy*. Los Angeles: University of California Press, 1945.

Cornford, F. M. "Mathematics and Dialectic in the *Republic* VI–VII." *Mind*, n.s. 41, no. 161 (1932): 37–52; and no. 162 (1932): 173–90. Reprinted in R. E. Allen, *Studies in Plato's Metaphysics*.

———. *Plato's Theory of Knowledge*. London: Routledge & Kegan Paul, 1935.

Cross, R. C. "Logos and Forms in Plato." *Mind*, n.s. 62 (1954): 433–50. Reprinted in R. E. Allen, *Studies in Plato's Metaphysics*.

Gulley, N. "Greek Geometrical Analysis." *Phronesis* 3, no. 1 (1958): 1–14.

———. *Plato's Theory of Knowledge*. London: Methuen & Co., 1962.

Hackforth, R. *Plato's Phaedo.* Cambridge: Cambridge University Press, 1955.

Hare, R. M. "Plato and the Mathematicians." *New Essays on Plato and Aristotle.* Edited by R. Bambrough. New York: Humanities Press, 1965.

Heath, Sir Thomas. *A History of Greek Mathematics.* Vol. 1. Oxford: Clarendon Press, 1921.

Hicken, W. "Knowledge and Forms in Plato's *Theaetetus.*" *Journal of Hellenic Studies* 77 (1957): 48–53. Reprinted in R. E. Allen, *Studies in Plato's Metaphysics.*

Kirk, G. S., and Raven, J. E. *The Presocratic Philosophers.* Cambridge: Cambridge University Press, 1957.

Kucharski, P. *Les chemins du savoir dans les derniers dialogues de Platon.* Paris: Presses universitaires de France, 1949.

Lewis, C. I., and Langford, C. H. *Symbolic Logic.* New York: Dover Publications, 1959.

Liddell, H. G., and Scott, R. *Greek–English Lexicon.* Rev. ed. Oxford: Clarendon Press, 1925.

Lloyd, A. C. "Plato's Description of Division." *The Classical Quarterly,* n.s. 2 (1954): 105–12. Reprinted in R. E. Allen, *Studies in Plato's Metaphysics.*

Lorenz, K., and Mittelstrass, J. "Theaitetos fliegt. Zur Theorie wahrer und falscher Sätze bei Platon (*Soph.* 251d–263d)." *Archiv für Geschichte der Philosophie* Band 48 (1966): 111–52.

Meyerhoff, H. "Socrates 'Dream' in the *Theaetetus.*" *Classical Quarterly,* n.s. 8, no. 3 (1958): 131–38.

Moravcsik, J. M. E. "ΣΥΜΠΛΟΚΗ ΕΙΔΩΝ and the Genesis of ΛΟΓΟΣ." *Archiv für Geschichte der Philosophie.* Band 42, Heft 2 (1960): 117–29.

———. "Being and Meaning in the *Sophist.*" *Acta Philosophica Fennica,* 14 (1962), 23–78.

Robinson, R. *Plato's Earlier Dialectic.* Oxford: Clarendon Press, 1953.

———. "Plato's *Parmenides* II." *Classical Philology.* 37, no. 2 (1942): 159–86.

Rose, L. "The Deuteros Plous in Plato's *Meno.*" *The Monist.* 50, no. 3 (1966): 464–73.

Ross, W. D. *Plato's Theory of Ideas.* Oxford: Clarendon Press, 1951.

Runciman, W. G. *Plato's Later Epistemology.* Cambridge: Cambridge University Press, 1962.

Ryle, G. "Plato's *Parmenides.*" *Mind* 48, no. 191 (1939): 129–51, 302–25.

———. "Letters and Syllables in Plato." *Philosophical Review* 69, no. 4 (1960): 431–51.

Schipper, E. W. "The Meaning of Existence in Plato's *Sophist.*" *Phronesis* 9, no. 1 (1964): 38–44.

Taylor, A. E. *Plato: The Man and His Work.* London: Methuen & Co., 1926.

Taylor, C. C. W. "Plato and the Mathematicians: An Examination of Professor Hare's Views." *Philosophical Quarterly* 17, no. 68 (1967): 193–203.

Thomas, I. *A History of Greek Mathematics.* Vol. 1. Oxford: Clarendon Press, 1921.

———. *Greek Mathematical Works.* Vols. 1, 2. Cambridge: Harvard University Press: Loeb Classical Library, 1941.

Wittgenstein, L. *Philosophical Investigations.* New York: The Macmillan Company, 1953.

Xenakis, J. "Plato's *Sophist:* A Defense of Negative Expressions and a Doctrine of Sense and of Truth." *Phronesis* 4 (1959): 29–43.

Index of Passages

Index of Names and Topics